A HOUSE DIVIDED

A HOUSE DIVIDED

Protestantism, schism, and
secularization

STEVE BRUCE

ROUTLEDGE
London and New York

First published 1990
by Routledge
11 New Fetter Lane, London EC4P 4EE

Simultaneously published in the USA and Canada
by Routledge a division of Routledge, Chapman and Hall, Inc.
29 West 35th Street, New York, NY 10001

Laserprinted by LaserScript Ltd, Mitcham, Surrey
Printed and bound in Great Britain by Mackays of Chatham PLC, Kent

British Library Cataloguing in Publication Data

Bruce, Steve
A house divided : Protestantism, Schism, and Secularization
1. Protestantism
I. Title
280'.4

Library of Congress Cataloging in Publication Data

Bruce, Steve, 1954–
A house divided : protestantism, schism, and secularization / Steve
Bruce
p. cm.
Bibliography: p.
Includes index.
1. Protestantism. 2. Protestant churches. 3. Sociology, Christian
4. Schism. 5. Religious tolerance – Christianity. 6. Secularization
(Theology) I. Title.
BX4817.B78 1989
280'.4 – dc20
89 – 32960 CIP

ISBN 0-415-04238-0

CONTENTS

ACKNOWLEDGEMENTS

This book draws on a number of studies pursued over the last decade and in that time I have become indebted to a number of organizations and individuals. My research on militant Protestantism in modern Scotland was funded by the Economic and Social Research Council, my work on Ulster Protestantism was funded by the British Academy, and the Nuffield Foundation has generously allowed me to make two extended visits to the United States. I am grateful to these bodies for their assistance and I am also in the debt of The Queen's University of Belfast, which has allowed me leave to pursue my research interests. I would also like to thank the Visitors of the University of Virginia for inviting me to be Scholar in Residence in the spring of 1986 and Donald J. Black and all the staff of UVA's Sociology Department for making my stay a pleasant one. Without such assistance I would not have been able to engage in the primary research which, despite the appearance of reliance on historical sources, has been a vital part of my developing understanding of conservative Protestantism.

Since he examined my doctoral thesis in 1980, Professor David Martin, recently retired from the London School of Economics, has been a helpful critic, as has Dr Bryan Wilson of All Souls College, Oxford. However, my greatest debt, as always, is to Professor Roy Wallis of The Queen's University, Belfast, who has now been a friend, colleague and critic for longer than I care to remember. I would also like to thank my badminton opponent, Dr Steven Yearley, also of The Queen's University, for his patience in listening to me talking endlessly about conservative Protestants.

The overall argument of this book has developed slowly and earlier 'working' versions of some of the elements have been

presented in various journals. Parts of Chapter 2 were published as
'Identifying conservative Protestantism', in *Sociological Analysis*, 44,
pp. 65–70, and 'Authority and fission: the Protestants' divisions', in
the *British Journal of Sociology*, 36, pp. 592–603. Chapter 3 draws on
an argument first presented as 'A house divided: Protestant
schisms and the rise of religious tolerance', *Sociological Analysis*, 47,
pp. 21–8. Part of Chapter 9 draws on 'Social change and collective
behaviour: the revival in eighteenth-century Ross-shire', *British
Journal of Sociology*, 34, pp. 554–72. I would like to thank the
anonymous reviewers of these journals for their helpful comments
on the drafts, and the journals' editors and publishers for permission to draw on my earlier publications. Furthermore, parts of the
overall argument were clumsily presented in *Firm in the Faith: the
Survival and Revival of Conservative Protestantism* (1984). My
justification for returning to these issues is that their presentation
in the broader framework of the arguments deployed here makes
their treatment far more successful, or 'I didn't do it very well last
time'.

Although most of the evidence used in this book is historical or
statistical, my claim to understand Protestantism rests firmly on a
decade of close involvement with the modern representatives of
the beliefs here described. Although few of them would endorse
the result, any merits of this work owe a lot to the patience and
indulgence of large numbers of British and American liberal and
conservative Protestants.

INTRODUCTION

> The logic of Protestantism is clearly in favour of voluntary
> principle, to a degree that eventually makes its sociologically
> unrealistic.

In the introductory description of the collection of his essays from
which this quotation is taken, David Martin says: 'This short book
contains several long books which I will never write' (Martin
1978b: 1). It is my belief that the single *sentence* quoted contains
one of those books that Martin will never write, and so I have
presumed to write it for him.

The main concern of this study is the part played by Protestantism in the complex of social processes which, for brevity, we call
'secularization'. Martin's claim that Protestantism is, eventually,
sociologically unrealistic, will be examined at a variety of levels and
will, I hope, be sustained by a detailed presentation of the
evidence. The two main themes of the book relate to the
precariousness of Protestantism. The first half deals with the way
in which Protestant schism and dissent paved the way for the rise
of religious pluralism and toleration. The second is concerned
with the fragility of the two major responses to religious pluralism:
the accommodation of liberal Protestantism and the sectarian
rejection of the conservative alternative.

The underlying argument of both parts is similar. I take for
granted much of the conventional wisdom about the part which
social, economic, and political changes played in undermining the
plausibility of religion in western Europe. What has rarely been
given sufficient weight, however, is the role which Protestantism
inadvertently played in its own collapse. Particularly overlooked
are the organizational consequences of core Reformation ideas. I

1

do not mean the specific teachings of Protestant leaders on the proper form for the Church, although those are not without importance. I am concerned to establish the repercussions of different beliefs about authority in competing Christian traditions.

As is the case in Max Weber's famous 'Protestant ethic and the spirit of capitalism' thesis, this argument, although it concerns ideas and beliefs, operates at the level of unintended and unanticipated consequences. It is thus not an 'idealist' explanation, although those social scientists who believe that only social structures can be causative will regard it as such.

In a review of Werner Stark's enormous and strange *The Sociology of Religion*, Bryan Wilson remarked: 'There is much to be said against ritualistic genuflection, which is too established a custom in sociology' (Wilson 1967: 214), before going on to chide Stark for almost completely ignoring the main body of sociology of religion literature. This book may be open to similar criticism, not because it is not permeated by mainstream sociological thinking on religion, but because it is constructed on the assumption that it is more important to do sociology than to discuss other sociologists. We all have our own pet theories of what it is that explains the present unpopularity of sociology. Mine is that nothing has recently damaged the reputation of sociology so much as its obsessive introversion; theorists writing critical commentaries on other theorists who built their careers on commentaries on the work of the founding fathers. The concern of sociology should be the explanation of social action, not the discussion of sociology. However, what the reader may expect from this book may be clarified by a brief word to locate its author's theoretical perspectives. The concern with the consequences of beliefs about authority and sources of knowledge is classically Weberian. Although there will be few specific references to it, Mead and Blumer's symbolic interactionism has also been a considerable influence, as have the sociology of knowledge and social psychology perspectives popularized by Peter L. Berger.

The major thesis of this book is not novel. It has long been recognized that Protestantism pioneered *laissez-faire* religion. As Martin notes:

It was partly adopted on principle and partly accepted out of necessity. Necessity is often the mother of a new principle. If a new faith fails to capture the state it may withdraw into the sullen superiority of the elect, or half-recognize that there is a variety of paths to the truth. Once you recognize the variety of ways of truth you are part of the way to accepting the right to be wrong and the idea of one inclusive church is undermined. Religion splits into various voluntary associations.

(Martin 1978a: 3)

Martin and others have sketched some of the consequences of this fragmentation. If the present book has value, it lies not so much in its novelty as in its detailed teasing out of connections and in the presentation of historical material to support the propositions advanced by sociologists of religion. Most scholars seem agreed about the inputs and outputs described here, but there remains considerable confusion about what is going on inside the black box of secularization.

THE LIMITS OF THE EVIDENCE

It is useful to offer some preliminary observations about the nature of the evidence on which the various arguments of this book are based. Although in some sections illustrations are drawn from a large variety of settings, a great many, especially in Chapter 3, come from the history of one form of Protestantism in one small country: Calvinist Presbyterianism in Scotland. A few words of justification are required. Taking the stress on Calvinism first, it seems reasonable to regard Calvinist Presbyterianism as being closer to the epitome of reformed Protestantism than its major sixteenth- and seventeenth-century rivals. There are some dangers of tautology; the way in which Protestantism is defined may unfairly ensure the validity of the subsequent explanations of some of its features and consequences. But such dangers are offset by the value of isolating something approaching a Weberian 'ideal-type'. The Episcopalianism of the Henrican and Elizabethan Anglican Church was a compromise between pre- and post-Reformation structures. The papacy was rejected but the democracy inherent in the notion that all men are able to discern the will of God was muted, as was the process of simplification of religious activity which the reformers set in train. Lutheranism similarly stopped short, the subordination of the Church to the

Prince tempering the Reformation stress on the believing individual. Calvinism pressed on to the logical conclusion. However, this argument will not be carried to extremes and is relevant only to the first post-Reformation period. Generally, themes will be illustrated initially with the Presbyterian material and then expanded with examples drawn from other and later forms of Protestantism. The second part of the book draws eclectically on a wide variety of examples.

There are three good reasons for beginning the discussion of the rise of religious toleration with Scotland. In the first place, it is sensible to focus on one religious culture, irrespective of which one is chosen. If it is social action rather than social theory which is to be explained, sociologists need to know a lot about the action in question. Sociology is not history or biography but it deploys both. There is heuristic benefit in grand theorizing but it can embarrass itself by being so removed from the data which it claims to explain that it can be readily dismissed by anyone with a working knowledge of the place or the people under consideration. Even if, like Martin's *General Theory of Secularization*, the design is so competent that it cannot be ridiculed by historians, it still leaves unanswered many questions about detailed causal connections.

A good reason for concentrating a consideration of the source and impact of religious pluralism on Scotland, rather than any other predominantly Protestant country, is that it simplifies the search for causes. Very few of the changes in the religious culture of Scotland were the result of external cultural influences. Or, more precisely, where there were external influences, they were mediated through the interests and actions of native Scots. Until the nineteenth century, when the Irish arrived in numbers, the main direction of Scottish population movement was outward. Religious fragmentation is thus easier to analyse because it occurred without the stimulus of the arrival of large numbers of immigrants with varied religious belief-systems and traditions.

Another reason for favouring Scotland is that, thanks to the excellent work of Martin, Wilson, and their students, English dissent is well known to sociologists of religion, and there are so many American sociologists that a great deal is known about that country. The Scottish material has the advantage of novelty.

A fourth, and perhaps less good reason for giving considerable space to examples drawn from the history of Scottish Protest-

But if unique in this way, is it a good case for study? [handwritten margin note]

4

antism, is national pride. I long ago got used to having my country either ignored (English newsreaders saying 'Britain' when they meant England) or caricatured (the shortbread tin tartanry of Bonnie Prince Charlie and Mary Queen of Scots) but I am a Scot and see no reason why I should be any more coy about generating general propositions from those parts of my country's history that are not unique than are American social scientists. Except where the Scottish case is so deviant that it will not bear generalization – and as Callum Brown (1987) has recently demonstrated, that is not often – the use of such examples will, I hope, add a certain freshness to the illustration of the general themes.

The first chapter 'makes straight the way' for the rest of the text by countering those scholars who have argued that secularization is a sociological myth. Having established that something which can sensibly be called 'secularization' has occurred, I briefly discuss various causes of the decline of religiosity. The unusual element in this presentation is the stress on the secularizing effects of pluralism. Chapter 2 proposes a general theory of propensity to schism in order to explain why Protestantism should be prone to factionalism and schism.

Chapters 3 and 4 detail the extent and consequences of Protestant dissent in order to establish that the rise of religious toleration was an unintended consequence of Protestant fissiparousness. To put the argument at its simplest, the case is made that pluralism and its acceptance in the doctrine of toleration were ironic results of attempts by conservative reformers to purify the religious establishment in order to justify, not to end, the enforcement of religious conformity. The failure of each movement to conquer the establishment forced, first the dissenters, and then the establishment, to accept the reality of pluralism and to develop attitudes which were consistent with that reality. Here I might stress that my concern is not with ideological innovation. It is not the invention of religious toleration but the circumstances under which such a notion became popular and widely accepted that interests me.

The second part of the book deals with Protestant responses to the culturally plural modern world. Chapters 5 and 6 consider the rise and fall of liberal Protestantism and its associated ecumenism. Chapter 7 examines the conservative Protestant alternative. Chapter 8 is concerned with Protestantism in America: a case which at

Part 1 of thesis

first sight offers scant support for the proposition that pluralism undermines religiosity. Finally, a discussion of religious revivals is used as the basis for a summary of the main themes of the study.

One final preliminary point: there is no doubt that historians of the particular periods and societies touched on in this book will find things to trouble them in my borrowings from their discipline. They may even find the odd howler. I think it reasonable to ask that they remember that they are themselves divided on the correct interpretation of some of the movements which are introduced in this narrative. Such errors as may be found should be judged in the context of the overall arguments. The question should always be, not have I correctly understood this or that movement but would an alternative reading seriously undermine the thesis.

Chapter One

SECULARIZATION

THE REALITY OF SECULARIZATION

This book is concerned with the part played by Protestantism in hastening secularization in most western European countries and with Protestant responses to a discouraging environment. Before embarking on an explanation of secularization, it is worth establishing that something which can sensibly be called by that name has actually occurred.

At first sight there would seem to be no problem in establishing the fact of 'secularization', if that term is taken to refer to (a) a decline in the economic, social, and political influence of the Protestant Churches, (b) a decline in the popularity of Christian beliefs, and (c) a decline in the proportion of the population who take any active part in the activities of the Protestant churches. The last three centuries have seen a considerable decline in the power and influence of the latter, which can now be said to have little authority over even their own members, let alone the population at large. The Christian Church in England has gone from being the civil service and judiciary to being a small and easily ignored opposition to the Tory government. Active membership of most Protestant churches has fallen drastically. There is considerable evidence, from sources as varied as diaries, novels, and attitude surveys, that there has been a decline in the plausibility of religious beliefs. One only has to read the literature of the seventeenth century, for example, to be struck by the constant references to the supernatural. As G. N. Clark has demonstrated, this cannot be dismissed 'merely as common form':

On the contrary, it is more often necessary to remind ourselves

that these words were then seldom used without their accom-
paniment of meaning, and that their use did generally imply a
heightened intensity of feeling. This sense of the closeness of
God and the Devil to every act and fact of daily life is an integral
part of the century.

(Quoted in Merton 1973: 233)

Even the most optimistic Christian would not assert that the
inhabitants of twentieth-century Britain live in a world where God
and the Devil are close to every act and fact of life.

However, it would be a mistake to suppose that changes in the
popularity and power of religious organizations and beliefs have
been so directly related that they can be treated as immediately
linked, or as having one cause. As Peter Berger put it: 'we would
regard it as axiomatic that a historical phenomenon of such scope
will not be amenable to any monocausal explanation' (Berger
1973: 116). Only the most mechanical and simplistic secularization
account would suppose anything else. Thus we may concede the
first point to those who have argued that many secularization
theories are naive and ahistorical. There is no single social process
which links the three elements which are normally mentioned in
discussion of the decline of religion. Although there is some heuristic value in constructing evolutionary models of social change,
such models invariably collapse in the face of the historical record.

We may also concede that the early sociological discussions of
secularization owed a great deal to a desire to promote a particular
philosophical position. Many of those who argued for the inevit-
ability of secularization were at least partly motivated to do so by a
desire to see humanity 'evolve' out of its need for superstitions.
Secular society would be society 'come of age'. Comte's model of
social development, with its replacement of religion by the science
of positivism, was obviously founded on the author's desire to see
the world move in that direction (Fletcher 1971: 165–96).
However, that early models of secularization were prompted by a
utopianism which we do not share, does not itself seem like
sufficient reason for following the 'young' David Martin when he
argued that 'secularization should be erased from the sociological
dictionary' (Martin 1969: 22). Despite what the more praxiological
Marxists seem to think, why someone believes something is not the
only criteria for judging the accuracy of such views. Anyway, a

belief that something which can be called secularization has occurred is not confined to those who like the results. Two of the most articulate documentors of secularization clearly regret the process. Both Berger and Wilson, one a Christian, the other not, hold to the Weberian view that the disappearance of a shared religious world-view has a delegitimating and hence destabilizing effect on modern societies. Neither could be described as an enthusiast for secularization and yet neither doubts the reality of the process.[1]

Importantly for my defence of the value of talking of secularization, Martin failed to follow his own advice and, a decade later, produced one of the most sophisticated and sensitive treatments of the topic (Martin 1978a). The moral of Martin's own scholarship is that we need better, not fewer, discussions of secularization. If we can abandon simplistic evolutionary perspectives and keep our minds focused on the complexity of the historical record, we need not, as Glasner would have us do, reject secularization as a social myth (Glasner 1977).

The logically initial objection to secularization is that it exaggerates the religiosity of whatever period is chosen for the starting point of the process. This is often a good point. It is tempting to follow Laslett when he says that 'All our ancestors were literal Christian believers, all of the time' and not notice the qualification that follows:

> Not everyone was equally devout, of course, and it would be simple-minded to suppose that none of these villagers ever had their doubts. Much of their devotion must have been formal, and some of it mere conformity. But their world was a Christian world and their religious activity was spontaneous, not forced on them from above.
>
> (Laslett 1971: 74)

It has to be said that there are considerable problems in assessing the religious lives of the common people in such societies as Elizabethan England or Jacobean Scotland. Much of what we know comes from the complaints of the godly about the poor church attendance, ignorance, and indifference of others, and from the records of ecclesiastical courts. We might expect that both sorts of source would give an unflattering picture of religious life. We would be wary of accepting as complete a view of undergraduate

9

student capacity and diligence based on the routine grousing of staff and on the records of student progress committees. But even allowing for that, Thomas presents considerable evidence to support the view that 'not all Tudor or Stuart Englishmen went to some kind of church, that many of those who did went with considerable reluctance, and that a certain proportion remained throughout their lives utterly ignorant of the elementary tenets of Christian dogma' (Thomas 1971: 189). Not surprisingly, people in those areas, where the provision of religious offices was poor, had little knowledge of, or interest in, Christian doctrine. Even when there was an active ministry, some clerics were hopelessly incompetent and could barely preach at all, while others preached far over the heads of their audience. But if we are to doubt the representativeness of the village of Goodnestone, where almost half the population took communion at Eastertide and most of the others promised to make amends at Whitsun (Laslett 1971: 74), we should be cautious of going to the other extreme. Peter Collinson (1982, 1983) argues that most inhabitants of Elizabethan and Jacobean England were active in support of the Church, even if they were sometimes poorly informed about their faith. It seems beyond doubt that the 'godly people', as Collinson calls them, then made up a greater proportion of the British population than they do now, that even among the ungodly a fundamental supernaturalism was considerably more widespread than it is now, and that 'Christian' beliefs, if one takes the notion broadly, were widespread then in a way that they are no longer.

The second objection to talk of secularization is located at this end of the process. It can be argued that secularization theorists have underestimated the religiosity of the present as much as they have exaggerated that of the past. Those scholars who are interested in 'implicit', 'common, or 'popular' religion would insist that the decline in church membership and attendance should not be taken as evidence of a decline in the popularity of religious beliefs. After all, it might be the case that the collapse of the Christian Church in Britain reflects only a lack of satisfaction with particular organizational expressions of Christianity and not with the belief system itself. Or, if evidence of a lack of faith in Christianity among those people who are not church members and attenders can be produced, their religion can be made even more 'implicit'. One could argue that interest in horoscopes, ouija boards, spiritualism, astrology, and other varieties of snake oil are evidence for a religiosity which endures despite a decline in interest in the Christianity which has been the dominant religion in the West.

There are two areas of difficulty with the implicit religion counter to the secularization thesis. The first concerns evidence for, and the significance of, implicit religion. One piece of evidence often deployed in these debates is the very small proportion of the population who are willing to describe themselves as atheists (Forster 1972: 153–68). But before we take this as proof of popular religion outside the churches, we should recall the general tendency of people to moderate their response to attitude surveys in order to appear decent or to avoid giving offence. People who do not describe themselves to survey researchers as atheists can no more be taken to be believers in a deity than most soldiers or hospital patients can be taken to be committed members of the denominations they name when asked their religion. We should also note that self-conscious atheism or agnosticism tends to be a particular feature of a religious culture! Only when there is a considerable interest in religion does one have people who feel moved to be irreligious. The highpoint for organized 'unbelief' in Britain coincides with the peak of Victorian evangelicalism (Budd 1967, 1977). In a secular culture, massive indifference is the dominant posture and committed atheists are as unusual as committed Christians.

What the implicit religion evidence shows is that a lot of people believe odd things and have strange experiences which they attribute to the supernatural. A lot of people suspect that there is 'something more to life than meets the eye'. One study of implicit religion which took the trouble to follow up those people who claimed some sort of religious experience produced a wide variety of stories, from reports of second sight, to a man who regarded surviving a serious car accident as evidence for the supernatural. By the 'normal' laws of mechanics, he should have been crushed. He wasn't. He concluded that he had had a religious experience (Hay and Morisey 1981).

Such experiences are important for the individuals involved. They are also interesting for social scientists because they show that many ordinary people are unwilling to confine themselves to the rational, law-governed universe of the natural scientist. But to deploy them as evidence against all versions of the secularization account is either careless or fanciful.

Those secularization approaches which suppose that religion declines as men become wiser might be undermined by evidence of implicit religion. The more enthusiastic Comtian and Huxleyite notions of religion as something which people abandon once they come to know better (and the related explanation: that religion is in decline because people are better educated) would be troubled by evidence that the beneficiaries of television, high technology, and eleven years of compulsory schooling could still believe that Granny spoke to them from beyond the grave. However, most reasonable secularization accounts would have no difficulty in accepting the limited evidence of widespread implicit religion and, indeed, would expect it. A decline in the popularity and influence of the dominant religious establishment allows people greater freedom to indulge their private fantasies and petty heresies. Only if one of these heresies became widely shared or if more than a handful of people took them seriously, would there be a challenge to a secularization thesis.

It is this final point which is often forgotten in the discussion of implicit religion. The important questions are not 'Do people read horoscopes?' but 'Do people who read horoscopes significantly alter their actions as a result?'; not 'How many people read horoscopes?' but 'To what extent does horoscope reading produce a shared world-view and common action?'. Does horoscope reading make any difference either to the lives of the readers or to the nature of their society? Let us just remind ourselves of the behaviour of people in religious cultures. In the early years of this century, a resident of the Isle of Lewis walked (because 'driving work be a form of work') twenty miles to church in Stornoway and back. On Monday morning he repeated the journey to collect his pension. He could have stayed overnight with friends in Stornoway and saved himself twenty miles. He refused to do so because that would mean that his Sunday walk to church had become an act of commerce and hence a violation of the Lord's Day.

The religious conversion of whole communities produced dramatic results in the closing of gin palaces and the return of stolen property.[2] Explicit religion mattered and it mattered at the level of the social system. It had social consequences. Implicit religion matters far less. Hence explicit and implicit religion are

12

different. Why a culture moves from one to the other thus calls for explanation, and the process might as well be called 'secularization' as anything else.

Another important refinement of secularization requires that we eschew any notion of a regular and uniform decline in religiosity. When Berger asserts that the irreversibility of secularization is one of the safest sociological predictions, he is not suggesting that an increase in religiosity has been impossible for all individuals, social classes, or societies since the seventeenth century. Religious revivals are a social reality: the first and second great awakenings in America, the Cambuslang revival in lowland Scotland in the late eighteenth century, the revival in the Scottish highlands in the early nineteenth century; these things happened. My treatment of secularization does not require steady decline. There is no problem in recognizing that the fragmentation of a dominant religious culture may produce an increase in religiosity. Such fracturing may be accompanied by an increase in commitment as social groups, previously alienated from the dominant culture, produce a religious variant better suited to their interests and concerns. Dissent has 'supply-side' consequences. Unable to rely on income from taxation, the founders of dissenting movements have to evangelize and convert in order not only to justify their schism but also to eat. The model supposed by this book, which will be presented in more detail in the closing chapter, is one of cycles of increasing and decreasing religiosity. The reason for describing this process as one of secularization is that each wave of revival has been smaller than the one which preceded it. The process is not circular; it is a decreasing spiral. The tide comes in and the tide goes out but our low tide-mark is further down the shore than that of pre-industrial society.

The functionalist alternative

Although they need not be, implicit religionists are sometimes also functionalists. If we suppose that religious belief-systems perform some vital social function, then secularization is impossible, unless it is accompanied by the collapse of the society which experiences it. The weaknesses of functionalist explanations generally, and functionalist views of religion in particular, have been well explored elsewhere (Cohen 1972) and need only brief revision here.

A lot of the strength of functional explanations of religion is derived from the starting assumption that religious beliefs are false. If dancing round in a circle actually caused the gods to make it rain, then the desire for rain would have been a sufficient explanation for the rain dance and anthropologists need not have troubled themselves further. If one supposes that rain dances do not work, then one has to find an alternative explanation for the persistence of them and similar religious ceremonies. If such ceremonies produce a sense of communal well-being and social solidarity, and especially if they are accompanied by rules such as 'You cannot take part in the rain dance until you have settled all your disputes', then one may suppose that it is the desire for these consequences (rather than a desire for rain) which led to the creation of the ceremony and which explains continued commitment to the religious belief-system which makes the dance a source of rain.

The problem with this approach, of course, is that there is very little evidence that 'social cohesion' was an *intended* consequence of the rain dance, and good reason to suppose the opposite: that the rain dance produces social cohesion precisely because it is not designed to do so. That is, activities generally only have 'latent' functions so long as they remain latent. Once they become 'manifest' one has a very different kind of activity. The rain dance is replaced by a 'secular' party. And if the latent function is not consciously intended, then how can the desire for it be a cause of the action or the belief? To put it simply, the functionalist account of the rain dance may explain social cohesion but it does not explain why the rain dance takes place.

Functionalists generally deal with the evidential problem by paying scant attention to the accounts which actors give for their own actions. The question of how 'system needs' might have been translated into individual motivations is rarely addressed.

Stark and Bainbridge (1985) have recently elaborated an interesting theory of religion which might be regarded as a 'functional for the individual' approach. In their view, religious belief systems perform the essential functions of explaining to people why they have problems and why they are not getting what they expect out of life. People who fail to secure 'rewards' will be in the market for 'compensators'. It is, after all, a great comfort to the meek to know that they shall inherit the earth. Mundane and this-worldly compensators are available but it is only by invoking the supernatural – rewards in the next life, for example – that one is able to offer compensators big enough to bridge the gap between many people's desires and actual circumstances. Thus religion is essential for personal well-being. And, if we suppose that the presence of lots of unfulfilled, frustrated, and deprived people whose pain has not been eased by satisfactory 'compensators' will disrupt a whole society, then religion is essential for the health of a culture.

Both the traditional social functionalism and the more modern Stark and Bainbridge version lead one to suppose that seculariz-ation is not possible without the end of civilization as we know it. Durkheim himself explained the Dreyfus affair as a consequence of France having to that date failed to find a substitute for a shared religious culture. If people are abandoning the major Christian churches and if the social order is not collapsing, then they must be doing something else which performs the functions previously performed by organized religion. The Stark and Bainbridge position is to see new religious movements as functional equivalents. Where membership in the established churches falls, there is an increase in the popularity of new religions. This argument is only spoiled by the evidence (Wallis and Bruce 1984). The number of people who become involved in new religious movements is considerably smaller than that lost to the old religions. The more traditional functionalists avoid this problem by finding 'functional equivalents' outside what we conventionally think of as religion, an option that is not really open to Stark and Bainbridge, given their insistence on the need for supernatural compensators.

But we need not spend much time on the social functionalism argument because, even if it is accepted, it does not prevent us talking of secularization. After all, even if one accepts that party politics or enthusiastic support for a football club may be 'functional equivalents' of participation in organized religion, one can still sensibly ask what led people to take up these alternatives. Why have more traditional ways of performing the necessary social functions been replaced by whatever one identifies as the modern alternative? Even for the functionalist the question remains worthy of answer.

As most scholars recognize, much of the argument hinges on the definition of secularization, which in turn is predicated on the definition of religion. Obviously, if one defines religion by its social functions, so long as the apostates have found functional equivalents, there can have been no secularization. Definitional arguments are of little value provided it is clear what one is talking about. This book is concerned with the changing fortunes of the Protestant variety of Christianity and the organizations which existed to maintain and promote it. For the reasons given in the introduction, the examples on which the various arguments are based are drawn primarily from Britain, America, and the Lutheran states, in that order of attention. There is no need to begin with a more detailed definition of the 'religion' which has been eroded because the detailed presentations throughout the text will make clear just what is at issue.[3]

To summarize this brief introductory discussion, the critics of secularization have made an important contribution in freeing us from the evolutionary models common in the nineteenth century and in suggesting important points which must be borne in mind in any examination of changes in religiosity. For example, that one can find similar changes in two generations – the scepticism of the intelligentsia in one generation and of the masses in the next – does not necessarily mean that the former caused the latter or that both shared a common cause. That the intellectual elite of a particular generation had problems sustaining its religious faith – and left considerable documentary evidence of their crisis – does not mean that we can assume a general crisis of faith. That there was a decline in the political power of religious organizations does not mean that we can assume a decline in 'religiosity'. These are all important cautions. They do not, however, rule out discussion of secularization. They simply remind sociology of its obvious, but often forgotten, reliance on history, ethnography, and biography. While sociological theorizing must always go beyond the particular, it should never become so blinkered by its own theoretical traditions that it replaces explanation with myth creation.

EXPLAINING SECULARIZATION

One of the main purposes of the first part of this book is to stress a major cause of secularization which has often been overlooked: the delegitimating effects of religious fragmentation. However, the claim made for the corrosive effects of schism in Protestantism is only that of contributing cause: other factors are involved and will be discussed briefly here.

Protestantism as rational religion ①

Many things have been suggested as causes of the decline of western religiosity. A summary may usefully begin with the *ideological* elements of secularization which are internal to Protestantism itself. In one sense, first Judaism and then Christianity can be seen as more secular than the religions which they replaced in that Judaeo-Christianity involved a considerable simplification of the religious: a pantheon was replaced by just one God. At the same time, a clear division between the sacred and the mundane, the religious and the secular, appears. The Reformation continued the process in that it further simplified Christianity by removing much of the magic and replacing it with an ethical and rational religion. There was, in Berger's terms, a 'radical truncation, a reduction to "essentials" at the expense of a vast wealth of religious contents' (Berger 1973: 117).

The relationship between the religious and secular worlds was also simplified as links between the two were narrowed down to one transcendent historically located miracle: the revelation of the Word of God in Jesus Christ.

> This is not to say that the English puritan or his European counterpart was less devoutly religious than his Catholic forebears. But his was a different kind of religious faith. The *post-mortem* alternatives of eternal bliss or eternal damnation retained a lively influence over his consciousness and behaviour. He detected the hand of God in all the exigencies of life. . . . But the puritan God worked through the natural order, not by miraculous disruptions of it. If He was accorded new majesty, He was also made more distant in a rational cosmos.
>
> (Gilbert 1980: 30)

In permitting the autonomy of man and his world from God, Protestantism considerably increased the possibility of men forgetting about the post-mortem world altogether, and this possibility was explored by the deists and other Enlightenment thinkers. Although they maintained a belief in a transcendent God, their God was hardly an important one.

Another important element of any comprehensive secularization account is Max Weber's 'Protestant ethic and the spirit of captialism' thesis (Marshall 1982). An unintended consequence of a combination of Reformation ideas was the creation of what Weber called 'this-worldly asceticism'. The thesis is so well known that it hardly needs expounding here beyond noting that when the notion of vocation was expanded to include secular occupations, when striving diligently in one's legitimate calling became a way of serving God, and when the fruits of that striving were not to be spent in ways which increased temptation for the sins of the flesh, the result was an increase in material prosperity which made it ever more difficult to maintain asceticism. The 'this-worldly asceticism' which replaced the previous medieval notion of monasticism gave way to simple worldliness.

2 Science, technology, and secularization

The above suggests ways in which the religious ideas of the Reformation divines themselves inadvertently contributed to the decline of Protestantism. In a less direct way, the breaking of the authority of the Catholic Church and the removal of God from the mundane world (coupled with a renewed interest in God's creation) contributed to the rise of alternatives to Christianity. Gilbert, Wilson and others have correctly noted that:

> Even in the most profoundly religious cultures . . . religion is a final resort, or an ancillary response, rather than a first option in human attempts to interpret and influence physical, social and psychological events and experiences. That is to say, where there has been a non-religious way of explaining or interpreting such events and experiences the human inclination has generally been to welcome it.
>
> (Gilbert 1980: 12)

18

If this is the case, then Robert Merton's thesis concerning the rise of experimental science becomes important. According to Merton, while Catholicism came to tolerate science, Puritanism positively demanded it. Science allowed the detailed exploration of God's handiwork and – a great motif with the Puritans – it was *useful* (Merton 1973: 228–53). However, one must beware of concentrating too much on the crisis of faith that is supposed to have afflicted Victorians when Darwin and others produced competing alternatives to Christian accounts of the world.[4] The Gilbert and Wilson point correctly stresses, not so much the abstract intellectual competition between Christianity and secular alternatives, as the more practical consequences of secular alternatives. Technology, rather than science, is the key. Religious beliefs were not abandoned because they were suddenly thought to be wrong. They simply became less and less important as alternative ways of dealing with mundane problems (and hence secular ways of viewing such problems), increased in number and efficacy. Prayer may save one's cattle from ringworm but chemicals are more reliable. The religious farmer may begin by combining prayer and chemicals and gradually reduce the range of things which he 'takes to the Lord in prayer' as chemical solutions are found to be successful. Technical advances gradually removed areas of uncertainty and unpredictability and by so doing, shrunk the regions of life for which religion was still thought to offer the best explanations and remedies.

Even if one rejects the claim that rationalization was in part an unintended consequence of the Reformation, one must still recognize the reality of rationalization and the impact which it has had on the plausibility of religious world-views. The extent to which the modern world is inhospitable to religion can be seen if one considers the notion of differentiation, used, not to describe the fragmentation of any population into classes (we will come to that later) but to characterize the fragmentation of life into a number of discrete spheres, each with its underlying values. The first such autonomous sphere was the economy. An important part of the process of industrialization was the separation of work from the home. The world of work became thoroughly secularized; production and exchange became governed by rational considerations of efficiency and productivity rather than religious, sentimental, or traditional attachments. No oil company could operate if it insisted on shutting down its wells on the sabbath. Even if it could, it would be put out of business by the first competitor which refused to temper rational calculations of costs and profits.

In terms of individual behaviour and attitudes, the drive to maximize efficiency requires that personal preferences and idiosyncracies be subordinated to role performance. Of course, some people rebel against the confines of their roles and attempt to rewrite the scripts for the drama of their lives; others simply distance themselves by going through the motions of acting out their public roles while investing as little as possible of their own emotions in the performance. None the less, the world of work is increasingly the world of 'mechanical' role performance.

The obviously superior efficiency of rational and mechanical methods of processing has led to their transfer from the production of goods to the processing of people. The bureaucracy is simply the factory system applied to people rather than inert matter. Civil servants, for example, are expected to treat all people as 'cases'. Only those properties (such as 'single mother' and 'with two children') which are deemed relevant to the task in hand by the rules of the organization are supposed to be considered. 'Nice-looking' and 'pleasant personality' are notions with which the Department of Health clerk may operate outside working hours or in mental fantasy, but to bring them into the job of 'clerk' is to act in a discriminatory way and, if discovered, might result in punishment. To move from these specific examples to the 'social system' as a whole is to gloss over a number of important consider-ations, but the consequences of the spread of rationality from the economic sphere can be summarized as the replacement of ethical by technical concerns, of moral constraints by practical problems:

A modern social system is increasingly conceived as operating without virtues; it becomes a neutral, detached, objective, rational co-ordination of role performances. The system induces those who actually man the roles – that is, human beings – to behave as if they had neither virtues nor vices. The pressure is towards the neutralization of human personality so that roles might be performed with ever greater calculability.

(Wilson 1982: 48)

The problem with rationality, of course, is that it is concerned only with method. If a car manufacturer wishes to increase his productivity, it is rational to replace one method of wheel fitting by a faster one, provided the faster method does not produce more sub-standard products. But rationality cannot tell us whether or not it is good to want to increase productivity. Wilson concludes that an important feature of modern industrial societies is the disappearance of 'ends'. The Shorter Catechism, the document constructed by the seventeenth-century Protestant divines as an aid to general religious instruction, begins: 'What is the chief end of man?'. The answer given: 'Man's chief end is to glorify God and to enjoy him for ever' is far less important than the fact that the question was asked at all. The obsession of modern societies with increased efficiency and procedural rationality has made it almost impossible for us to consider 'the end of man'.

This is the most abstract and comprehensive part of the explanation for secularization: the dominant values of the world of work – procedural rationalities – have permeated so much of our activity and thought processes that a fundamental element of religion – a concern with purpose – is far less common in our culture than it is in those of most pre-industrial societies. We can also offer more specific observations about the consequences of what Berger *et al.* (1974) call 'technological consciousness'. By this, they mean a cluster of fundamental assumptions about the nature of the world and our place in it which, even though we may often be unaware of them, are part-and-parcel of modern work. A good example of an element of technological consciousness is 'componentiality'. We assume that any radiator for a 1976 Vauxhall Viva will fit any 1976 Vauxhall Viva. We suppose that complex objects can be sub-divided into a range of components, all of which can be readily replaced by a substitute. Nothing is sacred. No particular bond between two components has any greater value or merit than that between one of those components and a replacement. Another element is 'reproducibility'. Modern technological work takes it for granted that any complex of creative acts can be subdivided into simple acts which can be repeated over and over. It also assumes that the same act will always produce the same results, and that the same act done by two quite different people will produce the same results. The fitting of the wheels to a Viva may be performed by a fascist one day and a communist the next but, provided they both perform the actions in the right way, the Viva will be the same.

Although it would take more space than is available here to trace all the links between technological consciousness and secularization, the basic point should be clear. Technology takes for granted certain assumptions about the world, time, and ourselves. These assumptions are basically antithetical to any kind of expressive activity and they gradually erode genuine belief in the supernatural. To offer a simple example, let us imagine a highly religious culture in which people genuinely expect miracles and where the intervention of the gods in the day-to-day affairs of men is taken to be common-place. Such people could not successfully operate a world which had train timetables. They would not be able confidently to expect that, human error and mechanical failure permitting, the 10.10 to Bangor would leave at 10.10 today, as it did yesterday and as it will tomorrow. The arrival of technology and its attendant rationality brings patterns of thought and action which gradually erode the expectation of miracles. The Victorians persisted in announcing their train times 'God willing', but by then 'DV' was little more than a pious token of a faith which was already disappearing. Few Victorians expected that God would be 'unwilling' to permit the 10.10 to leave. Industrialization thus creates a general consciousness which subtly undermines religion.

Two things make the Gilbert, Wilson, and Berger approaches to secularization more attractive than the more traditional stress on the explanatory superiority of secular ideologies: fit with the evidence and the logic of the argument. The weakness of secularization accounts which emphasize direct competition between religious and secular ideologies is that 'anti-Christian' ideas have been available for some considerably greater time than they have been popular. For example, in the early eighteenth century, conservative Protestants felt considerably threatened by the deists and by 'free thinkers'. Yet by the end of the same century, such ideas had become extremely unfashionable. The second reservation about accounts which stress ideological conflict is that they rather naively assume the obvious superiority of the secular alternatives. Because secular explanations of many of our problems and experiences have become taken for granted, they are supposed to be 'better' than the religious explanations which they have replaced. They might well be, but that, of itself, does not explain why anyone accepted them. There are enough instances of large numbers of people believing things which we now know to have been erroneous to make us wary of supposing that popular acceptance of an idea and the truth-value of that idea are consistently correlated. Or, to put it another way, that something is true does not explain why people believe it; that something is false does not explain why people do not believe it. Changes in belief, therefore, cannot be reduced to simple considerations of the relative internal merits of competing ideas.

Runciman plausibly argues that most attempts to find a clear demarcation line between 'religious' and 'secular' beliefs create more problems than they solve. Although he does not pursue the point he suggests that for social scientists the important difference is between matter-of-fact beliefs and more complex ambiguous systems of which ethical beliefs, political ideologies, and theologies would all be examples (Runciman 1970: 65–79). Provided one does not look for a clear boundary but thinks of them rather as polar ends of a continuum, this is sensible. Although there are other features which distinguish the two ends, there seems to be a clear difference in the extent to which and the way in which such beliefs can be tested. Whether chemical Zippo eradicates sheep-worm is a question which can be tested by most competent sheep farmers. Whether there is an after-life is beyond the testing competence of living humans. Clearly there is a middle ground: I am no more capable of testing for myself the explanatory value of the general theory of relativity than I am of investigating the nature of life after death. I have to accept propositions about both on faith. However, the existence of a large overlap does not detract from the general point. Road maps are excellent ways of conceptualizing and locating points in space. They tell us where things are relative to each other and they tell us how to get from one place to another. If two companies produce maps of southern Scotland which offer competing relative placings for Stranraer and Newtown Stewart, we can go and test for ourselves which of the two maps is more accurate. It is considerably more difficult to choose between competing versions of what Bob Dylan called 'road maps for the soul'.

Social support and plausibility

The value of the sociology of knowledge perspective is that it shifts
our attention from the intrinsic merits of ideas to the question of
their 'plausibility', which is seen as being, at least partly and often
largely, a matter of social construction. What makes one set of
ideas more plausible than another is, of course, a massively
complex question. One may begin to answer it by suggesting that
those ideas which 'work' are taken to be more plausible than those
which do not. This is the Gilbert and Wilson view. Secular
alternatives displace religious ideas because, while they may
illuminate smaller areas of the natural world and of social and
personal experience, and thus may be less satisfying in some
fundamental sense, they are more immediately efficacious. The
difficulty with this view is that, because it does not go far enough,
it leads us back in a circle. For well-known reasons, a position of
total relativism is untenable. While our perceptions of the world
are socially constructed, they are not made out of nothing, nor are
they completely free of the material world. None the less, there
remains an element of social construction in the decision to see a
secular belief or activity as being more immediately efficacious
than the religious belief or activity which it may replace. That is,
whether or not one thing 'works' better than another, is
something which people have to decide, either individually or
collectively. What will count as 'working better' is itself, to differing
degrees depending on the nature of the practice or belief, a matter
of social definition.

This raises the question of whether there is anything we can say
of a general nature about principles which govern such
'definitions of the situation'. One way forward is to recognize the
importance of authority. Most of what most people believe is taken
on trust: they believe one thing rather than another to be the case
because someone whom they trust has told them that this is indeed
the case. The authority of any belief-system may derive from the
social location and power of the advocate (young children tend to
believe their parents), from our relationship with the advocate, or
from the number of advocates. That 'almost everyone else'
believes X is a very good reason for oneself believing X.

Even if there were no difference in the testability of religious
and secular beliefs, the question of authoritative support would

still be relevant. Given that there is a difference between the two kinds of belief, in that 'Who says it works' is more important for religious beliefs and practices than it is for secular alternatives, the question of plausibility comes to hinge on the amount and nature of social support for religious beliefs.

What is at stake can be most clearly seen if two polar cases are considered. The most plausible belief-system is the one which is universally shared by all members of a society; where there is no alternative. In such a case, a world-view is not a system of 'beliefs' at all. It is just an accurate description of how things really are. Until one is presented with alternatives, the world-view into which one is socialized is not chosen. It is taken for granted. A universally shared belief-system is authoritative. It receives constant support from every act, every thought, and every instance of interaction with every like-minded believer. At the other extreme is the idiosyncratic world-view. One can imagine someone who believes that the world was created four days ago by a Martian and immediately appreciate the difficulties in sustaining such a view when it receives no support from the people with whom the believer interacts and no routine tacit confirmation. Newspapers will not report events in terms which can be assimilated to the belief that the world is only four days old. People in conversation will not assume (and hence tacitly confirm) the 'four-day-old-ness' of the world.

In practice, very few societies were ever so culturally homogeneous that one world-view went entirely unchallenged. One might suppose that even members of small simple societies such as the Zande occasionally disagreed. None the less, it seems correct to see most pre-modern societies as possessing overarching symbolic universes or, as Berger calls them, 'sacred canopies'. Although there may have been considerable variety in the degree of commitment to, and observance of, Christianity in, say, sixteenth-century Scotland, it still seems valid to see that world as having been informed by a shared world-view. Not everyone would have been a good Christian, but very, very few people were a 'good' anything else.[5]

There is always a certain element of artificiality in identifying any one historical point at which a major social change occurred but it seems sensible to identify the rise of the industrial cities as an historically significant choice-point. Although there was clearly considerable religious indifference in the pre-industrial country-side, a basic Christian world-view was established in the social relations of the rural community. The shift of population to the cities took many people outside the orbit of the church's social control. It also brought clearly into question the plausibility of a religion which was strongly linked to the existing social order. It may have been plausible to suppose that God had ordered the estates of the high and the lowly when they both lived on estates. The cities and the factories exposed the exploitative nature of social relations and in so doing called into question the plausibility of the faith. Of course, this did not prevent people from retaining some belief in the Christian faith but for many it broke the links between the established national parish church and that faith. Those who continued in their religion, or who found a new commitment, often did so through membership of dissenting denominations. Thus even where religion persisted, or was revived, it made no contribution to socio-religious cohesion. Halevy may have been right in seeing the Methodist movement as a conservative force which prevented England experiencing the revolutionary upheavals which tore Europe apart (Halevy 1938). It may be that evangelical revivalism inoculated the more affluent sections of the urban working class against radical politics but it did little to reverse the fragmentation of religion and society and hence nothing to reverse the trend from religious homogeneity to pluralism.

Pluralism places us in a world in which religion must be chosen. Even in rural Ireland, where almost everyone is a practising Roman Catholic, knowledge of alternatives is widespread. While the everyday life of a rural Irish Catholic may still give frequent affirmation to Roman Catholic beliefs and practices, the frequent interruptions of that world – those provided by television being the most obvious – bring the knowledge that there exist Hindus, Moslems, Protestants, Jews, Mormons, and unbelievers of fifty-seven varieties. For the inhabitant of a society like that of Great Britain, the need for conscious choice in religion is even more pressing. Choice, as Berger (1980) puts it, undermines religious belief by universalizing heresy. The essence of religious belief is its *necessity*. One believes in gods because one has to, because gods punish unbelief and reward belief. Gods are not chosen. Anything which can be a matter of preference is a poor substitute, an ersatz religion. Its gods no longer created us; we create them. They are in our power, not we in theirs.

At this point, the general outline of the relationship between religious fragmentation and secularization can be summarized. While there are other causes of secularization (such as social differentiation, the rise of a 'this-worldly asceticism', the subtle consequences of technological consciousness, the appearance of secular technical solutions and explanations, and the rise of the industrial city and the collapse of the previous rural social order which supported the Church and was in return legitimated by its teachings), the fragmentation produced by Protestantism was central in that a monolithic and hegemonic religious culture would have provided greater resistance to secularization. In many countries where the Catholic Church remained dominant, one sees quite a different pattern, with the society dividing into clerical and anti-clerical blocs (Martin 1978a). For reasons which will be explored later, such polarization may contribute to the survival of religion by making religious affiliation an important element of class, ethnic, or regional identity. The fragmentation of the religious culture which occurred in many Protestant countries was an important factor in secularization, in that it forced choice, while the other changes associated with modern industrialization made it less and less important for any social group to choose to believe. If people did choose to believe, then the resulting faith was of a quite different nature to that which one found in traditional societies.

AN ASIDE ON DISCONTINUITIES

Before leaving this general discussion of the causes of secularization, it is useful to add some subsidiary observations about discontinuties. In an interesting examination of various indicators of religious commitment (such as weekly church attendance and money invested in the construction of religious buildings) in America over a period from 1952 to 1972, Wuthnow concludes: 'The overall pattern in these indicators suggests that recent trends cannot be understood fully by established theories of secularization that link religious trends to relatively continuous modernizing processes, such as industrial expansion' (Wuthnow 1976: 853). The sorts of factor already mentioned in the explanation of secularization are all things which have been fairly uniformly increasing in importance. Yet the indicators of religious commitment show considerable discontinuity. This suggests that, if such things as increasing rationalization provide the background to the changes, there must be other elements which mediate such background features in a broken discontinuous fashion.

This seems sensible, not only at the level of major changes in the social environment but also at the level of the individual actor. It is safe to assume that most patterns of action take on a habitual nature. People do not normally stop to reassess their behaviour. Only when there is some radical change in their environment or in their own circumstances do they think about whether they wish to continue with what they were previously doing. Changing job, getting married, moving area; all invite reconsideration of commitment. For migrants to continue in church membership they must seek out a new church. Certain sorts of migrant – people moving to radically different societies and cultures, for example – show *increased* religious commitment. This is the case with West Indian migrants to Britain who joined Black Pentecostal churches in large numbers. However, one also finds considerable evidence that migrants drop out, especially where the degree of 'culture shock' is less (as in the case of people moving from rural to urban areas within the same society and culture). This is not to suggest that moving to a city causes the migrant to cease church membership. It is only to note that such a move breaks the habit and puts migrants in a position where they must go out of their way to find a new congregation. People whose religious commitment is not that high to begin with may well not bother. Thus the moment of discontinuity permits and forces a revaluation. The more people's lives are broken by such moments, the more frequent the test of their commitment and, if the various factors previously discussed are operating to reduce the plausibility of supernatural belief-systems, the more likely it is that such tests will result in disaffiliation.

Large-scale wars are a major source of dislocation. In the two world wars millions of men and women were recruited to the forces. Many women entered full-time employment for the first time and many of those men who were not called up, changed their jobs. In the Second World War, thousands of children were evacuated from their homes. In assessing various indices of church involvement before and after the Second World War, Currie, Gilbert, and Horsley conclude: 'despite the post-war rise in recruitment, war seems to have shaken certain loyalties permanently' (Currie, Gilbert, and Horsley 1977: 114).

The major social changes created by industrialization, urbanization, and wars were examples of dislocations which challenged the churches to respond and, in so far as they often failed to do so, they can be faulted for dereliction. Another sort of discontinuity with its attendant test of personal religious commitment results from the deliberate actions of churches. Although detailed discussion of this point will be postponed until Chapter 6, it is worth noting that ecumenical mergers, while partly intended to reduce costs, make churches more efficient, and stem decline, may be counter-productive. With their traditional and habitual attachments disrupted by schemes which are primarily designed to serve the interests of the professional activists, ordinary members may take the opportunity to reconsider their membership and disaffiliate.

To conclude this chapter, it is suggested that secularization is a complex process, the causes of which can be sorted into three types. First, one has a number of major social changes related to industrialization, urbanization, and rationalization. Second, one has the fragmentation of the religious culture and the creation of religious pluralism. Pluralism confronts modern man with the need to choose, while the nature of the modern industrial society makes it less likely that religion will be chosen. Finally, in the lives of individuals and communities there are a number of transition points, of discontinuities, which occasion choice, and when such choice takes place in a world informed by the first two types of change, the choice, more often than not, is to disaffiliate.

Chapter Two

THE FRAGMENTATION OF PROTESTANTISM

IDENTIFYING CONSERVATIVE PROTESTANTISM

As this book is concerned with the contrasting careers of conservative and liberal Protestantism, it seems sensible to begin with some definitions and identifications. The historical and biographical material in later chapters will make the nature of particular beliefs clear but some general clarification is required at this stage.

If one begins by assuming that the social actors whose behaviour is being explained know more about what they are doing than do outsiders, one also begins by accepting actors' definitions: conservative and liberal Protestantism are what conservative and liberal Protestants say they are. Unfortunately, material in this raw state is not generally amenable to sociological explanation. Some degree of processing is necessary to move away from the often arcane detail of every particular theological and ecclesiastical dispute. A further problem with definition in the raw is that people use labels such as 'conservative Protestant' to do more than merely identify the holders of certain beliefs. Such tags are also resources to be deployed in arguments. Consider for a moment the Calvinist–Arminian axis of beliefs about the degree of freedom man has to determine his salvational status. The outsider can readily identify two clear positions. The high Calvinist position is thoroughly predestinarian: whether we are saved or damned has already been determined by God before our birth. The Arminian position is that of 'free will': what we believe and how we act in this world determines our salvational fate. Unfortunately, most believers occupy positions somewhere in between the extremes and use the labels 'Calvinist' and 'Arminian' in different ways when describing their own position and that of others. For example, the members of the Free Presbyterian Church of Ulster call themselves 'Calvinists' and frequently claim to believe in predestination and effectual calling (the idea that once having been 'called', the born-again Christian will not fall sufficiently far from grace as to be damned). Yet two ministers defected from the Free Presbyterian Church, accusing it of Arminianism, and identified themselves as the true Calvinists. The Free Presbyterian Church called the defectors 'hyper-Calvinist', a term which is only ever used to describe someone else's position!

Apart from the need to be consistent in one's own work, clear definition and identification is essential for comparative and cumulative research. As Warner (1979) and Hunter (1982) have persuasively argued, sociological research is not helped by terms such as 'conservative Protestant', 'evangelical', and 'fundamentalist' being used by different researchers to mean different things.

In order both to be accurate and to lay the foundations for comparative research, the sociologist has on occasions to go beyond, and even to overrule, the actors' own definitions. The danger of going far beyond actors' self-definitions is that one courts tautology. It is all too easy for the social scientist to begin with a tentative explanation of some piece of social action and then arrange the definition of the material so that the explanation is assured of support. This is all too clear in the case of functionalist approaches to religion. It is sensible to argue that religious belief-systems have 'functions' in the sense of useful consequences. But if one defines religion as that which has these functions, the argument becomes circular. The aim of definition must be to identify in a systematic and consistent manner the phenomenon under investigation. The problem is to find some method of transcending the particular details of the various appearances of the phenomenon without going so far from the material, and without including so much of one's explanation in the initial definition, that one is guilty of tautology.

One solution is to find, in a number of belief-systems, a common central theme which seems to have considerable explanatory value. Although Weber's attempt to conceptualize all non-coercive relationships in a simple structure of three types has provoked considerable disagreement about particular aspects of traditional, charismatic, and rational–legal authority, the extent to which his work has stimulated and guided generations of scholars suggests that the area of authority and legitimation provides a useful place to start (Weber 1964).

Whether they consciously consider epistemology, all actors have to face the basic epistemological issue: how is the truth to be known? Or, to narrow it to the field of religion: how will we know what is necessary for salvation? It is obvious that different traditions within Christianity give quite different answers to that question. Although all believers assert that they know what is required for salvation because God told them, they quickly divide to adopt quite different views of how it is that God tells them.

The major division in Christianity between Catholic and Protestant concerns epistemology. The non-reformed section of the Christian Church believes that the knowledge of Christ exists in two locations. The record of his work and his teaching is available in the written texts of the Bible. But before his death he also passed some of his authority to the disciples, and particularly to Peter. Peter's authority was 'routinized' in the bureaucracy of the papacy. Although much of the day-to-day power of the Catholic Church comes from its ability to perform religious offices, its authority rests on its claim to be the source of valid interpretations of the Bible and the Christian doctrine.

The centre of the Reformation was its rejection of the Church's authority. Protestants believe that the Bible contains all that is necessary for salvation and that it can be comprehended by the common man. Certain passages may be obscure but what is essential to salvation is available to all who can read or listen to others reading. It seems no accident that the Shorter Catechism has, as early as the second question, the epistemological one: 'What rule hath God given to direct us how we may glorify and enjoy him?' It is answered: 'The word of God, which is contained in the scriptures of the Old and New Testaments, is the only rule to direct us how we may glorify and enjoy him.' Thomas Vincent, in his commentary on the Catechism (which was endorsed by John Owen and other leading seventeenth-century Protestant leaders), makes clear his rejection of the Catholic Church's epistemology. He elaborates the Catechism by adding a subsidiary series of questions and answers. On the epistemological issue, he adds: 'Are not the unwritten traditions of the Church of Rome to be made use of as a rule for our direction?' and argues that they are not, because their method of transmission could have permitted distortion, because the corruption of the Church will have corrupted the traditions, and because some of the traditions are contrary to the teaching of the scriptures (Vincent 1980: 17–23).

If we use the term 'conservative Protestant' to describe the position which accords primacy to the Bible, then liberal Protestants are those who accept the modern hermeneutic view of the scriptures. The liberal Protestant denies that the Bible can simply be 'read' in a naive fashion. Reading always involves interpretation. Knowledge is culturally relative. For the liberal, 'the Bible has presented a changing face to changing circumstances. It is not as permanent as might appear at first . . . . The Bible belongs to its world and we belong to our world and the gap between the two amounts to a great chasm' (Bowden 1970: 91–2). The symbols that were potent for the Hebrews are meaningless to modern man. The discovery of God's message for us requires that the Bible be demythologized and the core re-presented in terms which make sense to the inhabitants of a world which has electricity. One method of doing this is to separate 'events' from 'the significance of events'. We can thus cease to believe that some of the events reported in the Bible actually occurred in the manner described while maintaining that we accept the 'spirit' of the events. Thus the miracle stories can be rejected as the props which a simple and superstitious people needed to signify and sustain their faith in God's providence. 'God parted the waves for the Children of Israel' becomes 'God looks after his people'. The miracle is explained away as a rare but natural phenomenon, or as a metaphorical or mythical interpretation of some real but less dramatic phenomenon. The hermeneutic method permits any particular generation to develop a novel understanding of the faith without having to argue that earlier generations were wrong. They were right for their time and culture and we are right for ours.

Liberal Protestantism accepts the assumptions and agenda of the modern secular world. Although the Bible is still accorded pride of place in the rhetoric of liberal Protestants, it is interpreted in the light of modern reason and culture.

The classic conservative Protestant position is that the Bible can be read and taken at face-value. It means what it appears to mean.

There is no hermeneutic problem. Obviously, thoughtful conservatives are aware that they are involved in 'interpreting' a text but they do not share the liberal pessimism about the size of the task; after all, the Bible is the word of God and God will not have given us texts we cannot understand. The hard conservative position is that the Bible is entirely true in every word: it is inerrant.[1]

A fourth source of authoritative knowledge is the Holy Spirit. God may make his will known to us by spirit revelation. Pentecostalists and charismatics believe that the gifts of the Spirit listed in the Acts of the Apostles (in particular, prophecy, speaking in tongues, and healing) are still available to born-again believers.

To summarize, the various responses within Christianity to the epistemological question can be compressed and sorted into four main sources.[2] The priority given to each of the four sources defines the four main traditions within Christianity:

	Source	Tradition
1	Culture/Reason	Liberal Protestantism
2	Bible	Conservative Protestantism
3	Church	Roman Catholicism/Orthodoxy
4	Spirit	Pentecostalism

Qualifications

A number of qualifications should be entered. An important preliminary point is that this classification is primarily (although not exclusively) based on the claims which believers themselves make. Using such claims to identify groups of believers does not, of course, commit us to endorsing their claims. For example, to define conservative Protestantism as that position which claims the Bible as its sole source of legitimate authority does not commit me to accepting the implied claim that the Bible can be read 'naively' without one's culture colouring interpretations of the words. To know that conservative Protestants solve the hermeneutic problem to their own satisfaction by arguing (a) that the Bible is different to all other texts in that it is divinely inspired, and (b) that the indwelling of the Holy Spirit aids the reader to a correct interpretation, is not to endorse either of these claims. Similarly, identi-

34

fying pentecostalism as that tradition which places stress on the direct revelations of the Spirit does not commit me to being able to distinguish true Spirit teachings from the ramblings of the insane. The four sources are derived from the actors' accounts and are presented simply as the epistemological claims of those actors. My position here is very much that implied in Thomas's famous dictum about the 'definition of the situation'. The differing views which Christians have about legitimate sources of authority have the consequences they have because they are believed to be true and are acted upon, irrespective of whether they are true or not.

One simple example will suffice. In the later discussions of the organizational precariousness of liberal Protestantism much will be made of the cohesion and continuity given to conservative Protestantism by its claims to be rooted in the unchanging source of the Bible. Any outsider would have to conclude that conservative Protestant interpretations of the Bible have changed a great deal. None the less, the often repeated claim to an unchanging faith disguises the extent of change and mutes its disruptive effects. Even if the message is changing, denying that it changes creates greater stability than does asserting, as liberals do, that the message changes and ought to change.

A second qualification concerns the relationship between the four sources of authority. Most groups of Christians combine elements of more than one source. The sources are not treated as if they were exclusive. Total reliance on Culture/Reason amounts to complete subordination to the values and beliefs of the secular world and is advocated only by those liberal Protestants in the 'Death of God' school of thought; those who would abandon all trace of traditional Christianity. Although the Roman Catholic Church lays great stress on its traditions, it also makes use of the Bible and periodically there have been 'Protestant' movements within Catholicism. However, to put it like that is to show the usefulness of the system of classification in the degree to which the divisions of the four sources correspond to our common-sense understanding of developments within Christianity. Those within the Catholic Church who question the authority of the papacy by showing its lack of grounding in the scriptures are accused of 'Protestantism'.

The Church of England, other Episcopalian churches, and the

Lutheran churches draw on both Bible and Church for their authority and many of the disputes within such churches can be understood in terms of greater weight being given to one or the other source of authority. Even the most 'reformed' Protestant organizations make use of the Church source. Their understanding of the Bible is mediated by the traditions of the reformed churches and guided by the creeds, which, sociologically speaking, can be seen as a form of Church tradition. However, the crucial difference between Roman and reformed traditions is the degree to which they are legitimated by the core of their belief-systems. The traditions of the Catholic Church are at the centre of its identity and its claims to know the will of God. The traditions of the reformed churches are matters of human convenience which gain very little support from the ideology, as is demonstrated by the frequency with which they are rejected by sizeable numbers of schismatic Protestants.[3]

Furthermore, we sometimes find that broad claims to a variety of sources disguise a more narrow reliance. Many evangelical Protestants continue to use the language of direct Holy Spirit revelation, but when one looks at the practical use of the language of the Spirit, one finds a heavy dependence on the Bible. Ian Paisley believes that the Spirit leads him to this or that course of action but such revelations usually come through reading the Bible. He 'takes a problem to the Lord in prayer' and the Lord answers him by drawing his attention to a passage of scripture.

Far from being undermined by the lack of exclusive reliance, the division of authority into four main sources provides us with a useful means for characterizing both differences and tensions within denominations and movements and changes in the religious climate. Quite subtle differences can be identified. For example, those who have trouble distinguishing Protestant pentecostalists from Catholic charismatics should be helped by seeing that the primary source of authority for the former is a combination of Spirit and Bible, while for the latter it is Spirit and Church. Protestant pentecostalists often 'test' spirit leading by its accord with conservative Protestant interpretations of the Bible and insist that true leading does not contradict the Bible.

As an aside, it is interesting that an understanding of the nature of authority explains an observation about conversion which is otherwise a paradox. In a series of interviews with Protestant missionaries in the Irish Republic, I was frequently confronted with the view that secularization did little to make their task any easier. Although a number of those who had worked in the Republic for more than a decade reported a gradual reduction of overt hostility to their activities and a weakening of the power of the priest, none claimed that the more liberal climate had made their work any more successful. The missionaries argued that it was easier to convert a conservative than a liberal Catholic. The former had a strong notion of authority: the only problem was changing the belief about the source of that authority. Church could be replaced by Bible more easily than Culture/Reason could be. Why that should be the case is explored in detail in a consideration of liberal Protestantism but the basic principle can be mentioned here. The traditions of the Church or the teachings of the Bible can be kept concentrated, and promoted and reacted to in an authoritarian or totalitarian manner; the culture of the modern world cannot. In a pluralistic democracy, Culture/Reason has a strong relativizing tendency, which makes it difficult to organize as a 'totalitarian' faith, and makes it unlikely that its carriers will return to an authoritarian form of religion.

To summarize this definitional introduction, one can identify four major sources of authority in Christianity, reliance upon which defines broad Christian traditions. The rest of this book, and especially the rest of this chapter, is concerned with the different sociological consequences of the two of the four sources with the greatest relevance for Protestantism: Culture/Reason and Bible.

THE SOCIOLOGY OF SCHISM AND PROTESTANT FRAGMENTATION

The following chapters describe in some detail the fragmentation of Protestantism into competing organizations and discuss the consequences of such fission. Here I want to identify and explain the roots of this fissiparousness.

Every particular schism obviously has its own historical causes in particular sources of discontent and a specific occasion to demonstrate dissension by withdrawal. However, there is no merit in the description of schism after schism; the hoarding of data does not itself produce explanation. One way of trying to give some analytical shape to the mass of schismatic events is to concentrate on the ambitions of those who lead such movements. Factionalism and schism are then explained as a natural result of the presence within any movement of a number of individuals who feel themselves capable and worthy of leadership. The problem with an approach to schism which concentrates on the desires of leaders is that it fails to explain why the propensity to schism should differ markedly between different kinds of movements. It also forgets that leaders require followers. That any individual sees himself as a good candidate for leadership does not explain why anyone else accepts this self-image.

One sensible approach to the 'propensity to schism' problem is to augment the point about the existence of competing leadership figures with the observation that the actions of such leaders may be related to pre-existing divisions within a movement. Thus the attention is shifted from individuals to strata. A propensity to factionalism and schism may be related to the possibility of different interests arising within the organization. Conflicting class interests, for example, may be at the root of schism. Certainly many Protestant sects begin as movements of one social stratum defining itself against another. Movements of the dispossessed attract the support of those sections of the population who have least affinity with the dominant ideology. Hence many enthusiastic religious movements, 'religions of the oppressed', offer a re-writing of the religious orthodoxy in which the social system is turned upside down: the last shall be first and the first shall be last.

Another common source of the stress lines along which movements fracture is regional diversity. Schismatic groups may reformulate the dominant religious tradition in ways appropriate to their regional interests: the north and south division of American churches over slavery and the Civil War is a good example. If the centre has become relatively modernized and cosmopolitan, the periphery may maintain and enhance its traditional religiosity as a vehicle for criticizing the centre: the traditional Catholicism of regional groups in Spain would be an example.

Generalizing from these two types of example, we can arrive at Niebuhr's point that ideological divisions within a movement tend to follow existing lines of internal differentiation (Niebuhr 1962). Zald and Ash (1966) offer 'heterogeneity of social base' as one of the major preconditions for factionalism and schism. Smelser's theory of collective behaviour argues that increased internal differentiation encourages a propensity to schism (Smelser 1966).

However, pre-existing differentiation is not a sufficient explanation of fissiparousness. It fails in both directions. It neither illuminates the cohesion of the Roman Catholic Church nor the fissiparousness of those Protestant organizations with relatively homogeneous social bases.

Zald and Ash try to relate differentiation to movement ideology without falling back to simply listing the ideological disputes behind every particular split. In looking for some general quality of beliefs which might be related to schism, they settle on the way in which beliefs are held. For them, the 'seriousness' of any movement's ideology is an important element in fissiparousness: those movements which are strongly ideological are more prone to schism than pragmatic movements. Although there is something intuitively appealing about the notion that movements full of passionate ideologues break up more often than those populated by more pragmatic characters, it takes us little further. After all, conservative Catholics are no less serious about Catholicism than conservative Protestants are about their religion. In the context of broad traditions in the Christian Church, seriousness cannot be taken as a single variable with constant effects. Indeed, conservativism, traditionalism, and seriousness have opposite effects on Catholics and Protestants. In the former they produce cohesion; in the latter fissiparousness.

This paradox can be resolved if one moves away from the motives of the people involved in factionalism and schism to the 'structural' consequences of the epistemological elements of belief-systems. Although this might seem vague as a programme, what is intended is almost embarassingly simple, as the following will make clear.

The Wallis/Nyomarkay theory of schism

Nyomarkay's discussion of the different potential for schism of the Nazi Party and Marxist groups rests on a distinction between charismatic and ideological leadership. In the Nazi Party, authority and legitimation were derived from Hitler's charisma:

Hitler was the primary source of group cohesion, the focus of loyalty, and the personification of the utopian ideal – he was, in short, a charismatic leader. In contrast with the Marxist parties, where ideology provides the highest source of authority, the Nazi Party was based on charismatic legitimacy.

(Nyomarkay 1967: 4)

Hitler's charisma kept him above factional disputes. As he was the sole source of legitimate authority, each faction had to justify its actions by claiming to be his representative. Only when a faction challenged his own position, did Hitler intervene: 'Once Hitler disowned a faction, he deprived it of its legitimacy' (ibid.:146). Support disappeared, the faction lost influence, unity was restored, and Hitler's personal authority remained unimpaired.

In contrast, Marxist movements have no source of authority superior to the ideology from which legitimacy is derived. Hence any factional leader can claim to have the correct interpretation of the ideology. In the absence of any superior power to arbitrate such disputes, schism becomes common.

Wallis (1979) accepts that Nyomarkay's discussion is important because it raises the question of authority but offers the case of Stalin as evidence of the limited usefulness of Nyomarkay's treatment. As Nyomarkay himself recognizes, Stalin, although not a charismatic leader, achieved a position of autocracy similar to Hitler's and 'by the 1930s factionalism in the CPSU approached the character of Nazi factional conflict' (Nyomarkay 1967: 147). This suggests that a simple distinction between charismatic and ideological movements is not sufficient.

An important qualification must be introduced at this point. This discussion is concerned solely with 'monist', 'totalitarian', or 'uniquely legitimate' movements. Traditional Catholicism and conservative Protestantism are uniquely legitimate. They claim that they have a monopoly on salvational truth and that competing views are mistaken. Both believe that there is only one way to God and that they know what that way is. As will become clear in Chapters 5 and 6, liberal Protestantism is 'pluralistically legitimate', to use Wallis's ugly but accurate phrase.[4] It accepts that there are many ways to God. Liberal Protestants do not believe that they have sole possession of the saving truth. This is the important

40

point which Zald and Ash approach before losing sight of it in their concern with the 'seriousness' of a movement's ideology. It is not, in the first place, the zeal of the believers which is important. What is vital is the nature of the claim, explicit or implicit, which the movement makes about its grasp of the truth.

Clearly, those movements which make no great claims to special insight into the mind of God, or the working of history, will tolerate the existence of other similar movements. They will not demand exclusive loyalty of their members. Being tolerant of other movements, they will also be tolerant of diversity within their own membership. Factionalism will not be a problem for this sort of movement because there is no need for the supporters of diverse opinions to struggle for command of the movement. Diversity only leads to factionalism in totalitarian, uniquely legitimate, and monist movements. It is to this sort of belief-system and movement that the following applies.

A second qualification worth noting is that the Wallis theory, like Weber's typology of authority, is concerned solely with 'non-coercive' relationships. Unfortunately Wallis blurs this point by using the examples of Hitler and Stalin, both of whom frequently used violence or the threat of violence to attain compliance. This discussion is concerned with support for, and membership of, what are essentially voluntary associations.

Wallis begins, as does Nyomarkay, by insisting that 'successful schism depends upon the ability of a factional leader to secure legitimation for separation' (Wallis 1979: 183). This ability can be abstractly construed as varying 'directly with the availability of the means of legitimation'. Availability is a function of two factors: the number of sources of legitimation which are held to exist and the beliefs the movement has about access to these means. This latter point is the core of Wallis's addition to the Nyomarkay account. In Nyomarkay's account both the charismatic Nazi Party and the ideological Marxist party are similarly monist: there is only one source of legitimate authority. But, as Wallis notes, what distinguishes the two is that, while there is only one Marxist ideology, it is potentially 'accessible' to anyone who can master the canon. A charismatic movement has only one source of legitimation and it is available only to the charismatic leader. Anyone can be a Marxist but there was only one Hitler. Hence, although both sorts of movement are 'monist', ideological movements have a considerably greater tendency to factionalism and schism than do charismatic ones. The general principles of the Wallis theory are presented in the following diagram.

| | Means of legitimation | |
	Singular	Plural
Availability		
One	1	4
Few	2	5
(i.e. an elite)		
Many	3	6

The Nazi Party fits into cell 1. Marxist movements fit better into cell 2. There is only one means of legitimation but it is open to the fairly large number of people who are sufficiently literate to master the sacred texts. As an example of a movement which fits well into cell 3, where there is only one source of legitimation but it is accessible to a large number of people, Wallis offers spiritualism. Contact with transcendental power is believed to be available to all members. The possession of 'mediumship' powers is so widespread that challenges to established authority are readily made, which explains why 'it has rarely been possible to inhibit the disintegration of a following organized at a level of greater complexity than the characteristic professional–client relationship' (Wallis 1979: 185). Cell 4 is illustrated by the example of Stalin who could legitimate his decisions either by reference to (a) his role as the sole interpreter of the ideological canon, (b) his position as head of the party bureaucracy, or (c) his position as head of state: three different means of legitimation but all open only to one and the same man.

As an example of a cell 5, 'more than one way; more than one person' type, Wallis offers Theosophy.

> During Madame Blavatsky's lifetime, authority and legitimation within Theosophy were split between the charismatic claims of Madame Blavatsky based on her revelations from the Mahatmas, and the rational–legal authority wielded by Colonel Olcott as General Secretary . . . . Since contact with the Mahatmas was in principle available to an elite of committed

disciples ... on Madame Blavatsky's death the charisma conveyed by the claim to be in intimate communication with the Mahatmas was readily available to William Q. Judge, already *de facto* leader of the Theosophists in America, to legitimate his schism from the international body.

(Wallis 1979: 185)

Like the movements which would be placed in cell 3, those which fit cell 6 have a high propensity to schism because the means of legitimation are available to a large number of people. Wallis offers the example of pentecostalism where the principal basis of legitimation is being filled with the Holy Spirit. In theory this experience is open to all born-again believers.

It would be hard to disagree with Wallis's main conclusion: that propensity to schism increases with the availability of means of legitimation. But what is equally important is the logical level at which this argument works. Wallis begins by sensibly leaving aside the question of motivation to schism. After all, we can infer from any number of detailed accounts of schism that motives vary considerably from case to case; hence the concentration on opportunity rather than motive. This approach is 'structural' in the sense that a pattern of social action is being explained by regularities which are, to some extent, remote from what the actors think about the world. However, the structural properties are not thought to operate independently of the motives of the participants. Wallis suggests that:

one factor under consideration when a line of conduct likely to lead to a schism is undertaken, is the probability of successfully carrying some of the following or membership into separation. That probability will be seen to depend upon the degree to which a schismatic leader can successfully justify and legitimate his course of action, which will in turn depend upon whether he sees some means of legitimation as available.

(Ibid.: 191)

And – a point which Wallis does not make – even if a putative schismatic leader fails entirely to understand the nature and location of legitimate authority, there is no reason to suppose that his potential followers will make the same mistake. Members of a movement who are presented with a schismatic leader will be asking themselves whether this person deserves to be followed and on what authority he speaks.

An earlier statement of our programme for a non-reductionist sociology (Wallis and Bruce 1986: 11–46) was quite correctly described as supposing that social actors were usually rational decision-makers, people doing the best they could to consider their goals and achieve them (Yearley 1988). In part, this position is adopted because no other is viable. Of course, we did not mean that people are always explicitly aware of the logic of their actions. The propensity to schism model does not require that every Nazi should have been aware of the charismatic nature of Hitler's authority and hence of the problems of gaining legitimation for any move which Hitler did not endorse. None the less, when committed Nazis refused to support a particular path of action because 'Hitler wouldn't approve' they were acting in accordance with an implicit knowledge of the availability of legitimation. When one faction of a Marxist party challenges another by arguing that an important tenet of Marxist theory is being neglected, it is recognizing the nature of legitimation and acting accordingly.

That the Wallis theory is concerned with opportunity rather than motive means that it is perfectly compatible with those approaches which concern themselves with the possibility of differing interests and ambitions arising within any movement. The sort of combination I have in mind can be seen if we create an analytical distinction between the initial appearance of divergent interests and their evolution into all-out factionalism and schism. If we assume that all movements have a similar potential for producing the germs of disputes, then we can see the Wallis theory as an explanation for why, in certain kinds of movements, those initial germs grow into significant plants. Of course, this is an artificial way of posing the problem because, as Wallis sensibly argues, a feedback mechanism operates so that a movement, whose belief-system offers only restricted access to the means of legitimation, socializes members into an awareness of that reality so that the initial germs of divergent interests are usually repressed by the members themselves.

WHY PROTESTANTISM FRAGMENTS

If the two sections of this chapter are brought together, the explanation for the fissiparousness of Protestantism should be obvious. The Roman Catholic and Orthodox Christian traditions, by virtue of their belief in the legitimate authority of the Church's traditions, are relatively immune to schism. Provided one continues to believe in something like apostolic succession, there can be no salvation outside the Church. Potential schismatic movements will have a great deal of difficulty in convincing potential supporters to support them in their break from the Church. Although there was a period of the Church's history when it had more than one Pope, the contenders claimed to be *the* Pope and head of the one true Church, and the Church was reunited. It is also the case that the divisions in the 'church' type of christianity tend to be national, as is the case with the ethnic variants of Orthodoxy. Within any country, there is normally only one Church. An accurate assessment of the Catholic and Orthodox position would be to say that schism is not impossible but it is rare.

For Protestants, schism is easy. The Bible, the sole legitimate source of authority, is accessible to all believers and hence it is always open for one group to challenge the dominant orthodoxy by showing that its new revelation accords better with scripture than do the doctrines of the establishment. While committed Protestants believe that the Bible is in some sense self-interpreting, the history of conflict among those who claim no source of authority other than the Bible makes it clear that such a belief does not solve the problem of divergent interpretation.

In their early years, many Protestant movements are held together by loyalty to the personality of the founder or founders.[5] Those which have endured for any length of time beyond the demise of the founder have done so by finding alternative devices for muting the schismatic tendencies of democracy. The most common is the idea that learning and training create a special strata of skilled interpreters of the scriptures. Another technique, as in Presbyterianism, is to establish some form of collegiate authority. Recognizing the anarchy inherent in congregational autonomy, one stream of Protestantism advocated a system of democratic centralism, in which the church (that is, the various congregations of believers) elects representatives to act as the final arbiters of the propriety of the acts and beliefs of all the congregations. Even those who did not fully subscribe to a Presbyterian model held to some notion of an interpreting *community*. A good example is provided by the disputes between Roger Williams and John Cotton over Anne Hutchinson in the early New England colony. When Cotton withdrew his support for Hutchinson and joined her critics, he was accused of betraying his own conscience by accepting the view of the majority of the clergy. Although it may have seemed like an about-turn, Cotton's change of position was in harmony with his and the general Puritan notion of 'conscience rightly informed': 'informed, that is, by the Word of God rightly interpreted by the best gifts granted to a community of Saints rather than by the meteoric flash of an individual's own vagrant thoughts' (Howard, in Barbour and Quick 1986: 108).

The problem is that such a system is circular. The correctness of the judgements of a community of saints depends on the principles of selection which govern who is and is not a saint. This in turn must be decided by the Word of God, which raises the possibility of diverse interpretations. And so it goes.

Training and organization provide some sense of continuity and cohesion but they are relatively feeble defences against factionalism and schism because they receive very little legitimation from the core of the belief-system. They are matters of convenience and human construction and are often seen to be such.

To return to the four sources of authority, it should be obvious that only 'Church' is protection against schism. The other three share a similar propensity to fission. However, one of them – liberal Protestantism – does not suffer to the same extent as the others because it makes no claims to being uniquely legitimate. It permits and even rejoices in internal diversity. 'Fragmentation' thus remains internal rather than being evidenced in the creation of competing organizations. But the diffuseness of beliefs which results from the toleration of diversity brings its own variety of problems which will be discussed in detail in the second half of the book.

There is one final qualification to the Wallis typology which clarifies its application to conservative Protestantism. Its rather unusual concentration on opportunity rather than motive might create the possibility of confusion in that one can rightly point to a number of settings in which conservative Protestants do not act out their supposedly high propensity to schism. For example, Ian Paisley's Free Presbyterian Church of Ulster has survived for over thirty years without dividing over the persistently contentious issue of baptism (Bruce 1986). It permits both infant and adult baptism. While the majority of members have no strong feelings for either position, there are minorities which are strongly paedo-baptist and believer's baptist. The reason why they have not developed their differences on this issue into public controversy and schism is that both sides feel that they share a more important common cause: the maintenance of more basic conservative Protestant beliefs such as the inerrancy of the Bible, the need for conversion, and so on. In the circumstances in which they find themselves, they are prepared to subordinate particular beliefs in order to promote others. My point is this: the propensity to schism does not operate independently of the motive to schism which may arise from ideological or other forms of disagreement. Thus, while we can very usefully distinguish movements, and, in this study, religious traditions, in terms of their propensity to schism, this principle is not thought to operate in some sort of social vacuum. The movements and traditions in question exist in particular historical and social contexts. Whether or not the desire to disagree will arise in such a way as to turn the *propensity* to fragmentation into the reality of schism will depend on the extent to which circumstances (especially that of feeling threatened by some external enemy) allow people the luxury of making something of their dis-agreements.

Chapter Three

DISSENT AND TOLERATION

The previous chapter has explained why Protestantism is especially prone to fragmentation. This chapter and the next will argue the often overlooked point that the fragmentation of Protestantism was an important element in the rise of religious toleration. To introduce the argument before the evidence required to support it, I wish to demonstrate that the destination of religious toleration could be arrived at via three related routes – dissent, establishment, and modern democracy – and that the first serious steps on the journey were largely unintended.

The dissenting route, being the first and hence the most important, was profoundly ironic. There were, from the Reformation on, small and unpopular groups which argued for religious liberty but while the Anabaptists, for example, are of interest to the church historian or the chronicler of ideas, they are not central to my argument precisely because they remained small and unpopular. They did not succeed in creating the social conditions for the triumph of their ideas. The irony is that those conditions were inadvertently created by the more successful dissenters who were anything but advocates of religious toleration. They did not leave the establishment as spokesmen for denominationalism and the free choice of voluntarism. Only when their failure to win over the majority of the establishment had clearly condemned them to minority status did they begin to argue that their own nonconformity should be respected. Later they became advocates of toleration as a virtue in its own right. The second route to toleration – to be explored in the next chapter – concerns the reactions of religious establishments that failed to prevent dissent. Finally, the case of those cultures which remained religiously homogeneous into the late nineteenth century and adopted religious toleration as part of a general package of democratic reforms (exemplified by the Scandinavian Lutheran countries) will be examined.

It is no accident that the dissenters' advocacy of toleration preceded the religious establishment's acceptance of voluntarism and the state's increasing reluctance to use its power to enforce an establishment. It was only after significant dissenting movements had eroded its popular base that the establishment accepted a reduction of its power. So that they might not get lost in the damp mists of Scots church history, the main points of this account of Scottish dissent are advertised as follows. Although initially conservative, the unintended consequences of the actions of the dissenters created circumstances which gave them good reason to become liberal. Put bluntly, most dissent was not liberal until its conservatism failed. Second, it paved the way for an expansion of the secular state, not because an expansionist state took advantage of the weakness of a fragmented Presbyterianism but because the break-up of the Church led all but the most purblind partisan to realize the increasing incapacity of competing religious organizations to maintain the previous functions of the national Kirk.

Before proceeding further I should make clear the nature of what follows. This and the next chapter make no pretence to being a complete or comprehensive history of the Christian Church in Scotland, England, and Scandinavia. Excellent histories of dissent – Drummond and Bulloch (1973, 1975, 1978) on Scotland and Watts (1978) on England, for example – are available, and even if space permitted the task in hand does not require that such work be repeated. It is enough that the reader be introduced to the most basic elements of the changing relationships between the established churches, dissent, and the state. Furthermore, it is important to note that my treatment differs from the method of many historians in that I am not concerned with the genesis of ideas and practices but with the circumstances and conditions under which innovations become popularly accepted. Hence my focus is on the major, rather than the most innovative, elements of Protestantism.

THE DISSENTING ROUTE TO TOLERATION:
THE SCOTTISH CASE

Scottish Protestantism offers an excellent example of the fissi-parousness of Protestantism which has the added value that the high degree of fragmentation was almost entirely a result of internal dissent. Unlike American Protestantism, which acquired much of its variegated nature from the pattern of settlement in which various ethnic groups imported their own variant, almost all the competing organizations in Scottish Protestantism were the result of schism from the national Presbyterian Church. Although the details of Scottish church history are almost numbing in their complexity, it is essential that some detail be presented because the analytical observations depend for their force on the historical reality they claim to analyse.

The issues which produced the numerous divisions in Scottish Protestantism were much the same as those which excited Christians elsewhere; questions of authority and of church/state relations. Before looking closely at the schisms of the modern period, I will briefly introduce the post-Reformation Scottish Church. The Reformation had considerable impact on the accessible parts of Scotland: the lowlands. The highlands remained Catholic considerably longer and small individual pockets of Roman Catholicism remained in parts of the north-eastern lowlands of Banff and Buchan. However, it is the Reformed Church in Scotland which concerns us. Church government in those days was not regarded as a purely spiritual matter. James VI and Charles I wanted episcopal rule in the Kirk because, quite rightly, they saw the democracy of Presbyterianism as a threat to their authority. It was a similar desire to consolidate his rule which led Charles II, when the Stuarts were 'restored' after Cromwell's Protectorate, to renege on his commitment to Presbyterianism. Almost a third of the ministers in the Kirk refused to accept the reimposition of bishops. The King's Commissioners in Scotland decided to tighten the screws and, with penal acts and expulsions, began a conflict which gradually developed into civil war. Especially in the lowlands, where Presbyterianism had its strongest popular support, large numbers of people supported their deposed ministers. In 1663, the King's Council enacted that:

all and every ... person or persons who shall heirafter
ordinarily and wilfully withdraw and absent themselffs from the
ordinary meitings of divine worship in their oune paroche
church on the lord's day (witherupon the accompt of poperie
or other disaffection to the present govenment of the church
shall be fined.

(Cowan 1976: 58).

As the legal and military power of the state was mobilized to
enforce the act, the 'conventicles' of dissenters in the hills:

imperceptibly changed their character from that of groups of
worshippers gathered for prayer to armed convocations for
whom worship was still the prime object of their meeting but
who would certainly retaliate if attacked and might, under
certain circumstances spontaneously take to arms.

(Ibid.: 59–60)

The history of the (exaggeratedly named) 'killing times' need not
be rehearsed here. The dissenters were persecuted, not especially
harshly for the fashion of the day, and when they reacted with
outright war, they were routed.

Under James VII, the remaining supporters of radical Presbyterianism found their position improving as they ironically
benefited from the Catholic King's desire to indulge his
co-religionists. Then came the English Revolution, the replacement of the House of Stuart by the Protestant William of Orange
and his wife Mary – James's daughter – and the restoration of
Presbyterianism in Scotland.

A simple description of Scottish Christianity in 1690 would be
that of a national Presbyterian Church enjoying popular support
in the lowlands, a moderately large Catholic (in so far as it was
anything) remnant in the highlands, a small remnant of convinced
(rather than forced) Episcopalians, and the radical Presbyterian
Covenanters.

The Covenanters

Those Presbyterians who had been the most vigorous supporters
of the 'conventicles' and who had been most ideologically
committed to the Covenants, refused to accept the national Kirk of

the 1690 William and Mary settlement. The Covenanters (or, to give them their later title, the 'Reformed Presbyterians'), were the descendants of the victims of the 'killing times' who refused to join the Kirk because they believed that the terms of the old Scots Covenants, which bound the people to support the civil magistrate in return for the state enforcing 'the true religion', had not been met by the terms under which Presbyterianism had been restored (Vos 1980). The Covenanters were extremely conservative in their theology and in their attitude to religious diversity, which they regarded as sinful. They were not liberals or democrats. They were politically radical in that the Covenants had pioneered the notion of a constitutional and contractual monarchy before the English Revolution had successfully established the principle, but they were not advocates of religious toleration, let alone tolerance. They believed that it was both possible and necessary to identify the true religion, and that it was right and proper to use the power of the state to force the population to adhere to that faith. Prelacy, popery, blasphemies, and false worships were to be 'extirpated'. Alternatives were to be outlawed. Although it was the King's agents and the bishops who had begun the covenanting wars, the willingness of Richard Cameron and his followers to fight back was indicative of their similar refusal to see anything wrong with compulsion. The military defeat of the Cameronians robbed their heirs of some of their belligerence, but the Reformed Presbyterians remained committed Calvinists.

If 'church and state' was one issue, patronage was the other. Although the legal details are complex, the core of the dispute was simple. The Kirk, like the Church of England, was funded by what amounted to a local tax. The fundamental organizational principle of Presbyterianism was that authority lay with the people of God; in practice, that meant the local congregation. The Presbyterian system allowed no radical distinction between people and pastor. The minister was simply one of the elders and the elders were to be chosen by all members of the church. However, in 1712, Queen Anne's Patronage Act restored to the major landowners, who paid most of the tax, the right to select the local minister. This brought the Scottish Church into line with the Church of England system of local grandees having control of 'livings' to which they could appoint anyone who was minimally qualified (Burleigh 1973: 277–9).

In one sense, the Patronage Act was simply legal recognition of the reality of the local gentry's domination over parochial life. The system of low-profile government, at national level, was founded on a local system of concentrated authority, under different hats, by the landed class. The 'heritors' (as the Scottish patrons were known) effectively ran parish affairs. When they were not Episcopalian in allegiance, they were elders in the Kirk session. Almost always the 'ruling elder' representing the parish at high levels of the Church was landed. As payers of stipends, supporters of the material fabric of church, manse, and school, and the main source of the schoolmaster's salary as well as of poor relief, the landowners had wide opportunities for intervention in church and social matters (Mitchison 1983: 142).

Initially patronage caused less conflict than might have been expected. Many heritors consulted local people before nominating. Absentee landlords left such matters to their agents. There was also a shortage of candidates. None the less, the shift from *de facto* to *de jure* patronage laid the foundation for recurrent conflict in the Scottish Church. In part, it was the principle which offended, but there was also a practical concern. Few of the heritors were religious enthusiasts. As was often the case in this period, lords and lairds cut their religion to suit their political cloth. There were certainly few of the aristocracy or the gentry (except perhaps in Cromarty) who were committed evangelicals: their dominance of church affairs owed more to their interest in social discipline and order than to piety. Hence the principle of patronage prevented the evangelicals from achieving the presence which they felt would have been theirs if the choice of ministers was left to the common people.

The Seceders

The first split from the Kirk came in 1733, only forty years after the restoration of Presbyterian government. Ebenezer and Ralph Erskine and two other ministers 'seceded' from the Kirk because they regarded it as insufficiently evangelical and because they objected to patronage. Generally speaking, the Seceders recruited 'the responsible and the convinced while the parish churches drew the poor and dependent' (Drummond and Bulloch 1973: 118). This was true of much of nonconformity the world over. In addition to a special resonance between the interests of this social stratum and the theology of evangelical dissent, there was the mundane consideration of being able to support a dissenting minister. While the state church was paid for by taxation of the better-off, voluntaries had to volunteer their cash as well as their attendance. Hence dissent generally attracted those who possessed financial means and personal commitment in the right mixture. It recruited 'from a class which was growing in numbers and wealth: the small tradesmen, the farmers and the craftsmen' (Drummond and Bulloch 1973: 43)

In most things, the Seceders were similar to the Covenanters: conservative in theology, firm believers in the idea of a state-supported church, and enthusiasts for the vigorous suppression of religious deviation. The much-hated Patronage Act was accompanied by an act of toleration which permitted Episcopalians to meet for worship without penalty and, more significantly, limited the power of church courts so that they could really only discipline those people who wanted to be bound by them (Ferguson 1978: 110). Although they stood to benefit from it, the Seceders objected to the Act because it was not sufficiently selective in what it tolerated. They also objected to the repeal of penal statutes on witches; less of a self-defeating act but a mean-spirited and illuminating one none the less (McKerrow 1841: 105).

The Secession grew fairly rapidly as every imposition of an unpopular minister gave ever more people reason to leave the Kirk. By 1742 there were twenty Secession ministers and more demand than they could service. Four years later, there were forty-five congregations (ibid.: 148). As they became more numerous, they began to be reconsider their relationships with the state. In 1742 one minister was expelled for continuing to hold what were rapidly becoming unacceptably conservative views on the role of the civil magistrate. The arguments were, to say the least, obscure, but it seems that some Seceders were beginning to argue that civil rights were 'common grace', those good things which God gave to a sin-cursed world and which were independent of salvational status. They seemed to be moving in the direction of separating civil and political liberties from religious orthodoxy. Three years later, only twelve years after the Erskines' original protest, came the debate over the burgess oath. As part of the then common practice of attempting to maintain social and political order by administering oaths, all inhabitants of burghs were required to acknowledge publicly their support for 'the true religion professed within this realm'. Some Seceders refused to take the oath, claiming that to swear it was to accept the validity of the national Kirk. Others, including the Erskine brothers, felt that, with a little mental reservation, the 'true religion' could be taken to mean whatever the swearer wished it to mean. The Antiburghers, as they were rather charmingly known, brought the Burghers to the bar of the Synod to answer charges. When the revisionists failed to appear, they were deposed and excommunicated. Thus, in 1747, the Seceders split into Burgher and Antiburgher Synods.

The Relief Presbytery

The second secession was also the result of a protest against patronage. The 'moderates' who led the Kirk determined to stamp out dissent. In 1751 one Andrew Richardson was presented to (or, in Anglican terms, 'given the living of') the parish of Inverleithing. As his settlement was opposed by the town council, the Kirk session, and most of the parish, the Presbytery of Dunfermline refused to induct him, even after an order from the Commission of the General Assembly to do so. The Assembly instructed the Presbytery

> to meet at Inverleithing while the assembly was still in session, five members instead of the normal three to be a *quorum*, to induct Mr Richardson to the charge, and to appear at the bar of the assembly on the following day to report what they had done. Three of them reported that they had duly turned up at the appointed hour, and had waited in vain for two hours for others to come to complete the *quorum*. Two said they had gone to Inverleithing in the morning and endeavoured to persuade the people to abandon their opposition, but failing to do so they had gone home. Six members gave in a 'Humble Representation' in vindication of their abstention, quoting the Act of 1736 against intrusion of ministers contrary to the wishes of congregations. The assembly then decided by 93 votes to 65 to make an example by deposing one of these six. They were recalled one by one the next day, and given an opportunity to

defend themselves. Five of them added nothing, but Thomas Gillespie, minister of Garnock, made a further statement and he was accordingly selected to be the victim.

(Burleigh 1973: 283–4)

Gillespie was a suitable candidate for exemplary punishment. He had been less than consistent in his adherence to the Kirk. While studying divinity in Edinburgh he had followed his mother into the Secession Church. After ten days of their instruction, he left for England where he was educated at Dr Philip Doddridge's famous nonconformist college in Northampton, and later ordained by the English Independents. Curiously, when he returned to Scotland he was accepted into the ministry of the Kirk without comment about his lack of constancy.

Although Gillespie was an evangelical, he did not return to the Seceders, presumably because he had absorbed enough of the more liberal spirit of the English Independents to do what the Seceders had not yet done and generalized his opposition to patronage into an opposition to the imposition of conformity (Ferguson 1978: 126). He was a voluntary who rejected the Covenants and the small 'Relief Presbytery', which grew from his secession, was the first of the Scottish dissenting groups to advocate religious toleration. Like the Seceders, the Relief recruited mainly from the better-off in the lowlands. Unlike them, the Relief tried to remain on good terms with the national Kirk. Just before his death, Gillespie recommended to his congregation that they rejoin the Kirk, which they did. However, the Presbytery continued and would have remained in 'fellowship' with the national Church but, like the Methodists, the Relief was expelled by an establishment which cared little for doctrine but a lot for proper order and organization. The ministers who dominated the Kirk, like many of the bishops in the Church of England, were prepared to tolerate considerable diversity within the establishment but they would not tolerate any challenges to their authority. The Relief Presbytery grew but less quickly than the two Secession Synods.

Auld Licht and New Licht

Both Burgher and Antiburgher Seceder Synods grew and, at the end of the century, both split. The issue this time was theological.

It would be difficult to argue that the majority of Scottish Presbyterians of this period were convinced Calvinists. True, they all learnt the Shorter Catechism and the Westminster Confession was the subordinate standard of all the Presbyterian Churches, but the Kirk was largely moderate and many – perhaps most – lay people knew little of the theology of predestination and cared even less. But the Seceders knew that God died only for the elect, among whom they numbered themselves. One minister who was a little ahead of his times had the temerity to suggest that 'Christ died for all and every one of mankind sinners' and was excommunicated for his heresy (Drummond and Bulloch 1973: 62). But in the last quarter of the eighteenth century, a number of Seceder ministers began to question fundamental parts of the Confession. The generally more liberal Burgher Synod divided first, in 1799; the Antiburghers divided seven years later.

It was not long before the various Presbyterian groupings reorganized. The 'New Licht' or liberal wings of the two Seceder Synods united in 1820. As the United Associate Synod, they were forced by the increasingly aggressive policy of the established Kirk to enter more and more into public defence of dissenting rights. They fought the plans of Thomas Chalmers and other evangelicals in the Kirk to extend its ministry, especially in the growing urban areas, with new state funding. In this agitation they were successful, as they were in opposing a bill to 'improve the Scottish Universities' which, among many practical suggestions for reform, repeated the Kirk's claims to its 'rights, privileges, controls and superintendance' over the universities. As the drafters of the Seceders' complaint observed, such rights and privileges were, 'in consequence of the advanced state of society' (note the Enlightenment language), a dead letter, but to refresh their legal standing would have meant the expulsion of many dissenting professors and the withdrawal of dissenting students. The increasing liberalism of the United Associate Synod members was pointedly signalled a number of times in the 1830s. They responded positively to a request from the Congregational Union of England and Wales for fraternal correspondence and they engaged in discussions with the Relief Presbytery about merger, which was achieved in 1847, under the parsimoniously accurate title 'United Presbyterians'. As McKerrow had put it six years earlier:

the eventful nature of the times in which we live, and the extraordinary struggle at present carrying on betwixt state-endowed and unendowed churches, render it an imperative duty on those, who hold the same general views of ecclesiastical polity to merge smaller differences, and to unite together for the purpose of giving more complete effect to the grand principle involved in the struggle, viz. entire religious freedom.

(McKerrow 1841: 704)

Acting on the same logic, the conservatives also regrouped. The 'covenanting' wing of the Secession moved to reunite with those who still endorsed the idea of establishment. The 'Auld Licht' Burghers rejoined the Kirk just in time to leave again in the largest schism to disrupt the Kirk.

The Free Church of Scotland

The creation of the 'Church of Scotland Free' in 1843, when about one-third of the ministers of the Kirk walked out of the General Assembly, was the largest of the Scottish schisms. As in the Secession, the issues were patronage and theology. From the 1820s, the evangelical wing of the Kirk had been gaining ground over the moderates. A series of bitter disputes in the 1830s convinced the evangelicals that the institution of patronage and the general legal status of the establishment Church, which made it subject to a parliament, the majority of whose members were not even Presbyterian, prevented the organizational reforms which were necessary for spiritual revival.

As Thomas Chalmers was keen to point out in his address to the opening of their first assembly, the Free Churchmen were not voluntaries. As they stated in their departing declaration, they went out on 'the establishment principle'. They only objected to the particular terms of an establishment which, they felt, gave too much power to the state. This would not have been a problem if the state had been run by committed evangelical Presbyterians. Instead, it was run by the Westminster parliament which was made up of people drawn from a wide variety of denominations and which had little interest in Scottish affairs, let alone Scottish church affairs. Furthermore, the Free Church's commitment to the belief that the 'civil magistrate' had an obligation to sponsor the true religion was twice reinforced by injections of older conservative dissent. The Auld Licht Burghers were already in the Free Church, having rejoined the Kirk just in time to side with the evangelicals and leave it again. In 1852, the majority of the other conservative Seceder movement – Auld Licht Antiburghers – joined the Free Church and twenty-four years later, they were joined by almost all of the Reformed Presbyterians.

Leaving aside for the time being the small groups left behind by their refusal to take part in these reunions, Presbyterians in the last quarter of the nineteenth century were divided into three organizations. About half were in the national Kirk and the rest were divided fairly equally between the conservative evangelical Free Church and the more liberal 'voluntary' United Presbyterian Church. The Kirk was the established church, the Free Church wanted to be the established church, and the United Presbyterians wanted the end of establishment.

Summary: dissenting advocates of toleration

There is no difficulty in explaining why the Relief Presbytery argued for religious toleration. After all, its founder was a visionary who was expelled from the Kirk precisely because he rejected the idea of an established church with legal powers to enforce religious conformity. Presumably as a result of his association with English Independents, he had become a convinced voluntary. Thus the Relief stands as an example of deliberate ideological innovation, and can be explained by reference to the resonance between the class and status interests of the emerging bourgeoisie and the theology of what was in effect the first non-Calvinist evangelical movement in Scotland. What is of greater sociological interest is the 'unintended' and unexpected shift of the Seceders from establishmentarianism to voluntarism.

On its own, one movement in this intricate dance of church history might be dismissed as being of no particular analytical importance. What makes it significant is that it was repeated a hundred years later, to a slightly faster tempo, by a second wave of conservative dissenters – the Free Churchmen – among whom were to be found those Seceders who had 'sat out' the first time the dance was performed. By the last quarter of the nineteenth century, the Free Churchmen had so completely abandoned their

Disruption claim to be supporters of the idea of a state church that they could promote union with the liberal branch of the Secession which was now fully committed to voluntarism.

The shift can be explained partly as a result of the direct impact of new ideas. Both the New Licht Seceders and the liberal wing of the Free Church were influenced by changes in the cultural currency. However, an explanation which looks only at the influence of ideas has difficulty in explaining why the changes took place when they did, and why they repeated themselves. After all, religious toleration was not that much of a new idea, and if it was a new idea in the 1770s, it was not ninety years later. One thus has to explain why certain people should, at certain times, have proved more or less receptive.

In part, the initial act of dissent, almost irrespective of its causes, had a general liberating effect. Although the first thing that both the Seceders and the Free Church did with their freedom was to assert an ultra-conservative position on church/state relations and on theology, by breaking free from the dominant establishment and its suffocating organization, the dissenters could, if they so chose, follow the wishes of their congregations.

There is no doubt that the shift towards liberalism was related to the class base of Scottish dissent. Their increasing wealth and mobility gave the dissenters new and extended cultural horizons. At the same time, the rise in social status and economic power gave them increased opportunities for personal gratification and made the narrow restrictions of Calvinism a more onerous burden than they had been on their parents and grandparents.[1]

However, equally important was their own failure to convert the majority of the people to their dissenting movement. In order to justify and protect their own freedoms as members of a religious minority, they had to argue for religious freedom as a general principle. It is not impossible to remain committed to an idea under which one can only suffer – the Seceders and the Covenanters denounced Queen Anne's Toleration Act despite the fact that it gave them increased freedom – but as time passes, it becomes more and more difficult to do this with enthusiasm and conviction. Opposition political parties can remain committed to the judgment of the ballot box so long as they believe that they will, some day, form the governing party. Similarly, dissenting movements can remain committed to establishment so long as it is possible that they might one day become the established church.

To suggest that the majority of dissenters became advocates of toleration in order to protect their own position is to suggest unfairly a narrow and mean source of motivation. A more generous way of putting it would be to say that their failure to become more than a minority gave them both need and opportunity to re-examine their theories of church and state relationships. Their own interests predisposed them to accepting general democratic theories which, although not yet popular, had become widespread since the French Revolution. Furthermore, the gradual abandonment of sectarian self-images was one sensible way in which they could make sense, not just of their own failure, but of the general increasing diversity of the religious culture. The more enlightened sections of Scottish dissent could not help but notice that not all good men believed the same things. The deviation of Episcopalians and Catholics could be dismissed; these people were after all rebels who were beyond the pale. The divergence of beliefs among other decent Scottish Presbyterians could not be so lightly dismissed. The reality of fragmentation meant that major disagreements about religion were combined with positive or at least neutral evaluations of those holding divergent views. The result was the beginning of what later developed into full blown 'denominationalism': the notion that while one's own beliefs might be true, other quite different beliefs might also be true. Thus the nonconformists pioneered the dissenting minority route to tolerance.

THE RISE OF THE SECULAR STATE

Causally linked to increasing religious fragmentation is the rise of the secular state. The discussion here is largely limited to democratic societies. A ruling elite of one religious persuasion may choose to 'ignore' considerable pluralism. Even in democracies it is possible for one confessional group which enjoys an electoral majority to continue to accord its co-religionists various privileges. But even in oligarchies and 'divided society' democracies such as Northern Ireland, increased religious pluralism creates considerable pressure for the state to assume various functions previously performed by the dominant religious establishment.

It is all too easy to suppose that the separation of social

institutions from religion and their incorporation into the secular state represented a victory for the secular state over the church, but to view the development in this way is to miss a more subtle cause of state expansion. In the Scottish case battle-lines were never really drawn in this way. In the first place, the Kirk was largely the state. In some respects Scotland differs from other Protestant countries in that the union of the Scottish and English crowns and then, in 1707, of the parliaments, had left Scotland without a state. But in England, which will be discussed shortly, there was a similar closeness between church and state. A more accurate picture than church versus state is one of the church initially acting as the local agent of social control and social administration but gradually giving up areas of competence to secular institutions.

A second danger lies in assuming that the marginalization of the churches was a result of the increasing power of an active secularist body of opinion which positively desired to remove powers from the church. This was certainly not the case in Scotland, and was hardly the case in many other Protestant societies. The church was not pushed back by the state. Under the increasing weight of demands made on it by a growing and mobile population in a rapidly changing society, it gave way, like a bookcase in which all the joints had worked loose. Far from fighting to retain their many roles, leading Scottish Presbyterians knew they could not sustain their social functions, and themselves called for increased state intervention. To illustrate this, three areas in which competence passed from the Kirk to the secular state will now be considered.

State expansion (1): education

Changes in the organization and content of education are clearly crucial to any account of secularization, both as symptom and as cause of the hastened decline of religiosity. The clerics of the Christian Church were the intellectuals. They were responsible for writing and for training the ruling classes. The rise of popular schooling was also very much a result of church activity. The evangelical stress on the Bible as the sufficient source of salvational knowledge was a considerable impetus to educating the masses. The French Revolution, with its threat of militant revolutionary atheism, gave an additional fillip to mass schooling as evangelicals, such as Wilberforce and Hannah More, argued that limited amounts of education (enough to read improving literature but not enough to write socialist tracts!) could prevent the masses being recruited to the cause of revolution.[2]

Initially most education was provided by the Church; it was institutionally integrated with religion. One can offer a variety of reasons why an industrializing society should wish to break that link.

As knowledge itself became increasingly secular so priests became less appropriate as teachers, and as the content of education shifted from a religious–moral concern (developed at least partially in the interests of the maintenance of social control) to an increasingly instrumental–technical concern (developed in the interest of increased economic productivity), so education emerged into an institutional order in its own right.

(Wilson 1966: 58)

Although it is convenient to describe the secularization of education in a shorthand which treats abstractions such as education and the economy as actors, it remains to answer the question of who did what and why. In parts of colonial America, secular public education was consciously promoted by secularists, deists, and Protestant dissenters keen to reduce the influence of the established Churches. In England and Wales, debates about education also often involved arguments about the status of the established Anglican Church. However, there was little secularist influence in Scotland where the impetus to state intervention resulted from the Church's own inability to maintain and expand educational provision for a growing and shifting population.

John Knox's Reformation ideal had been a church, manse, and school in every parish. Although there were considerable problems in implementing this policy (not least the failure of the reformed Church to have much initial impact on the Scottish highlands) by the early nineteenth century, the Kirk did provide something like a national parish-based elementary school system which was widely admired for its educational standards (Mechie 1960: 136–53).

At the Disruption in 1843, 400 parish school teachers came out and joined the Free Church. By 1851 the Free Church had built

712 schools. Although this considerably increased total educational provision, it did so in a chaotic and inefficient manner which mirrored the Free Church's general expansion. Instead of locating itself in the places where population shifts had created the greatest need, the Free Church tended to site itself close to the Kirk. They competed. Of the fifty-two Free Churches built between 1879 and 1891, a full third were put in exactly the wrong place: in areas with declining populations. The union of the Free and United Presbyterian Churches in 1900 simply exaggerated the process. In 1881 the parish of Duirinish in Skye had five churches for a population of 4,319. Thirty years later, the population had declined to just over 3,000 but the number of churches had increased to ten. Most of the people belonged to the Free Presbyterian and the Free Church, the two conservative remnants of the 1900 merger. The Church of Scotland had thirty-three members in two congregations and the United Free Church had fifty-nine in two congregations (Sjolinder 1962: 49–55). This is an extreme example but the spread of dissent generally took that form. So that they could compete effectively and thumb their noses, the dissenters built their church across the road from the Kirk.

Furthermore, even in the uncommon circumstance of the expansion of religious provision which followed the Free Church schism having given any particular town or city a reasonable number of church places, the dependence of the dissenting ministry on voluntary giving caused that provision to be badly skewed. There was a marked tendency for Free Church congregations to abandon their first locations and move to areas where they would draw a 'better' (and hence more generous) class of customer. In Disruption Aberdeen, two of the newly formed Free Church congregations moved from poorer areas and set up close to each other in order to compete for the support of the same affluent class (MacLaren 1974: 109).

Thus expansion failed to fill the gaps. And it was not just religious offices which became inefficiently distributed. As the churches provided much of Scotland's education, some places were over-supplied while others had hardly any supply at all. 'Matters appeared at their worst in the slums of the industrial towns where the children of the poor were often neglected, many of them starving and homeless' (Ferguson 1978: 314). There was also nothing by way of co-ordinating supervision. Thomas Guthrie, a leading Free Churchman, attempted to remedy the situation with his 'ragged school' movement, but – and this is the crucial point – even he realized that the problem could only be solved through state intervention.

> The slow but sure trend was towards a national system supervised by the state, and in 1861 this was reinforced when the established church lost its legal powers over the parish schools. Increasingly rules were laid down by government inspectors. The ground was thus well prepared for the Education Act of 1872 which set up a national system under the newly created Scottish Education Department. Popularly elected school boards were given wide discretion in running the public schools.
>
> (Ferguson 1978: 315)

The reason for the removal of the Kirk's legal control over the parish schools can be traced back to the increase of religious dissent. When there was a genuinely national Church, paid for by what amounted to a form of rating, and when there was general public agreement that the Kirk represented the will of the majority of the people, it made sense for the Church to administer education, just as it made sense for the Kirk session to act as the local force of social discipline. The increase of dissent meant that the Kirk was no longer a representative national body. Hence even its own members could be found arguing that the state should take over its 'non religious' activities. Furthermore, once the 1872 Education Act had created the precedent of state financing of schools, the churches were quick to abandon even their better schools (Roxborough 1971). Whatever the legal position, the fact was that widespread dissent created considerable resentment in the Kirk as many members saw themselves as 'involuntarily' shouldering national responsibilities, and they became only too willing to see a heavy financial burden removed.

The nearest thing one finds to organized anti-clericalism in the debates about education in Scotland was the appearance in the first elections to the Glasgow School Board of an Anti-Catechism League slate of candidates. This was a very mild form of secularism. The League did not object to simple non-denominational Bible teaching; it objected only to the instruction of children in the

Presbyterian Shorter Catechism. The League's candidates were comprehensively beaten. After a brief debate about the Catechism in one of the first meetings of the Board, all discussion of religious issues was set aside as the Board faced the far more pressing issue of providing enough places in decent schools for the city's population (Roxborough 1971: 218). Although the churches retained some influence through ministerial membership of boards, they did nothing to ensure a continued Protestant ethos in the schools. Religious education remained on the curriculum but, with no one church being able to control its contents (again a consequence of fragmentation), all soon lost interest.

In the state of Virginia, non-denominational education was actively promoted by Thomas Jefferson, who was at best a deist, and in other American states, other opponents of church-based education were also influential. But in Scotland it was not a body of convinced state interventionists that took education away from the Church. Rather, the growth and movement of population exposed the poverty of the existing system. In 1834, Dundee minister George Lewis collated the evidence of educational need to argue that 'private enterprise, even with all the ecclesiastical aids, is not enough. The nation must pay' (Douglas 1985: 64). He wanted the nation to pay by giving money to the Kirk to finance expansion of its facilities. However, the fragmentation of the Church, which was considerable then, and insurmountable after 1843, led even active Presbyterians to argue for state intervention. The state did not willingly intervene to push back the frontiers of religion, to break the institutional links between education and religion. The actions of competing and fractious religious organizations made it inevitable that, if there were to be a return to even and coordinated provision of education, it would have to be provided by the secular state.

State expansion (2): social control

The gradual erosion of the Kirk's role in social control, and the state's assumption of the organization of discipline, differed from the secularization of education in that class stratification rather than religious competition seems to have been the first cause of delegitimation. Discipline, one of the distinguishing features of Calvinistic Presbyterianism, had degenerated into something approaching a system of class oppression. Instead of maintaining social cohesion, it had become concerned almost solely with the sexual misconduct of the lower classes, 'leaving among the class which produced its victims the conviction that it was no more than narrow-minded tyranny' (Drummond and Bulloch 1973: 86). Even when the Church was prepared to discipline the powerful (and the powerful willing to accept such discipline), they were permitted to avoid such humiliating punishments as having to stand in front of the congregation in wet sackcloth. Their sins were heard by the Kirk Session in private and their punishment commuted to a monetary fine.

The rise of the towns and cities, and the decline of the rural community played their parts in hastening the decline of the Kirk's authority. *Gemeinschaftliche* forms of control collapsed in the face of geographical mobility. Offenders could avoid punishment simply by moving. But denominational fragmentation was also involved. The Kirk tried to prevent malefactors from escaping their punishment by promoting the use of 'references' and 'transfers'. Although the insistence on written 'characters' from one's previous parish did something to stop the mobile evading social control, it only worked for those willing to accept it and those who wanted something, such as poor relief, from the parish. Those who wished to stay in the same area could escape the censure of the Kirk by transferring their allegiance to a dissenting organization. Sects could control and discipline their own members but they could not discipline the nation.

State expansion (3): social administration

Such welfare provisions as existed were the responsibility of the Kirk. Under laws which dated back to James VI, the local Kirk Session licensed a certain number of beggars to ply their trade in the parish. Only people who had resided in the parish for three years were entitled to be licensed; the wandering poor of other parishes were moved on. Believing there was a danger of a large and growing vagabond population, General Assemblies frequently exhorted parishes to ensure that 'care be taken in receiving servants that they have testimonials of their honesty and Christian behaviour, and that the same be required of all others who flit or remove from one parish to another' (Graham 1937: 236).

Money for poor relief was initially raised by church collections. The vices of some benefited others as the fines levied as punishment for misdemeanours augmented parochial funds. Private marriages and baptisms provided another source of income. Initially to exert some control over sexual activity, the Church insisted that marriage and baptism be publicly solemnized. Ministers reacted to the increasing fashion for private events by making small fines; in effect, charging for their offices. However, the ability to raise money from the members of the congregation was reduced as dissent increased in the second half of the eighteenth century. Seceders not only avoided making any contribution to the parochial funds for poor relief, but were also not averse to claiming from the parish when they themselves fell on hard times (Graham 1937: 256), as they were perfectly entitled to do so long as the Kirk claimed to administer a national and universal system of relief.

The changes in the economy which reduced the number of people employed on the land presented the same problem for social welfare provision as it did for the provision of religious offices: the Kirk was unable to move speedily enough to maintain an even national provision.

Although his tone is one of romantic attachment to an almost certainly over-idealized view of the village community, Graham makes an important point which demonstrates the close interconnection between the class nature of dissent and social relations within a community.

> The landlords and their families were intimate with, and interested in, the concerns and fortunes of the humbler classes near their doors, who had lived in the same quarters for generations, in days when there was no trade to attract them away, and no 'improvements' to turn them out. The children, rich and poor, the sons of laird, farmer, ploughman, sat on the same forms at the parish school, sharing its teaching and its not quite impartial discipline. After the middle of the century and onwards to its close, however, there was a transformation for the worse in these relations, and there appeared a widening gulf between each rank . . . . A similar process . . . went on in the towns, notably in Edinburgh . . . about 1775 the fashionable and the wealthy began to migrate to the suburbs and stately

houses in the New Town; they withdrew from the ill-flavoured wynds in the High Street where high and low had for ages dwelt companionably together.

(Graham 1937: 263)

The fragmentation of the Church contributed to these divisions:

Now it happened that instead of laird and people all being of one religious body, all meeting together in the same kirk and having intercourse in the kirkyard, the Seceder, without a touch of his bonnet, passed the laird on the road, and stalked on with satisfaction of superiority of conviction to the meeting-house of the 'body' he belonged to.

(Ibid.: 264)

The decline of communal solidarity – undermined by social differentiation and religious fragmentation – meant that, when poverty came, voluntary giving had to be supplemented with compulsory assessments and levys, and when beggars became more numerous the law was enforced to suppress them. Voluntary aid and informal control were replaced by compulsion, and compulsion required a national institution. With something like 1,000 dissenting congregations of one sort or another in 1840 (and that was before the Free Church split) the Kirk could no longer be regarded as that institution and, reasonably, many members resented bearing the weight of national burdens. While still in the Kirk, Thomas Chalmers had tried to demonstrate that a well-organized inner city parish could cope with the demands of urban industrialization by providing poor relief, education, and moral uplift in addition to the more obvious religious offices (Brown 1987: 144). His critics were not convinced that his scheme for St John's in Glasgow lived up to its claims and made the obvious point that its apparent success might simply be a result of exporting its destitute to neighbouring parishes. Anyway, come 1843, 'the Disruption ... finally extinguished the faint possibility that Dr Chalmers' St John's scheme might become generally operative throughout the country' (Mechie 1960: 78). An Act of 1845 created a statutory obligation to provide for the sick poor, and although the geographical units of the parishes provided the framework for its implementation, the work was supervised, not by the Kirk, but by local boards. It is true that members of Kirk Sessions formed a part of the boards for almost fifty years but they were now there because they were respectable citizens and community leaders; a halfway stage to the time when they would not be there at all. As Mechie bluntly concludes: 'The most radical change made by the Act of 1845 was that it took responsibility for the care of the poor out of the hands of the Church' (Mechie 1960: 79).

Those who wish to insist that denominational fragmentation was inconsequential and epiphenomenal may argue that the growth of the cities and the increase of social distance between classes would have been enough to create the same crises and hence to encourage the expansion of the secular state. It is difficult to find comparisons which would settle the issue. The development of states involves a complex interrelation of so many elements, many of them specific to only one or two countries, that is it almost impossible to isolate genuinely comparative material. None the less, there seems good reason to suppose that the decline of religious cohesion was implicated. If one considers the example of education, it is clear that education in many Catholic countries remains considerably more religious than does schooling in Protestant states. Although Catholic schools tend to have class characteristics which divide them, they continue to have far more in common than do secular state schools, and they continue to share their Catholicism. Similarly, one might note that in the Irish Republic, a considerably modernized country, much health care and welfare is still provided by or channelled through the Catholic Church.

CONCLUSION

The moral which I wish to draw from the career of Scottish dissent is simple. Two related major cultural changes – the rise of religious toleration and the transfer of important areas of social life to a secular state – were in large part inadvertent and unintended consequences of a series of schismatic actions which were initially designed to promote, rather than undermine, state enforcement of religious orthodoxy. The failure of any particular schism to carry with it the majority of the Scottish people caused massive fragmentation of the religious culture. This had two related sets of consequences. The self-image of most of the dissenters shifted from sectarian exclusivity to something approaching denominationalism. Slightly behind in time-scale, there was a gradual expansion of the secular state as even those active in administering the Kirk's various social functions came to realize that the divisions in Scottish Presbyterianism had left it unable to act as the schoolmaster, magistrate, and poor law administrator of the Scottish people.

If the changes in Scottish dissent exemplify the minority dissent route to tolerance, there is a corresponding and related 'establishment' route, which can be illustrated from the English case.

Chapter Four

ESTABLISHMENTS AND TOLERATION

The development of religious toleration in England was an ultimate and wholly unintended consequence of the Reformation.

(Henriques 1961: 1)

In the late nineteenth century one finds examples of countries which had maintained relatively homogeneous Protestant cultures espousing the principle of religious liberty as part of a wider package of constitutional reforms. Examples of this can be found in the case of the Scandinavian Lutheran churches which will be discussed at the end of this chapter. But prior to the spread of modern democratic government, established churches were naturally loath to relinquish their positions, and it was only their failure to prevent significant dissent which led them to moderate their claims. In challenging the position of established churches, enduring dissenting movements also presented their governments with problems in maintaining punitive sanctions against nonconformity. Although one can occasionally find examples of perceptive leaders of establishments promoting religious toleration, it is generally the case that the relaxation of the legal superiority of the establishment resulted from the government's need to acquire wide popular support (and hence to cultivate nonconformists) rather than from the established church's willing abandonment of its privileges. In this sense, the rise of dissent both precedes and causes the corresponding changes in the claims of the religious establishment. This process will be illustrated with material drawn from English Protestantism.

PROTESTANTISM IN ENGLAND

Henriques (1961) suggests that the growth of toleration in England can be described in three phases. In the first, from Henry VIII's break with Rome to the Civil War, the practical conditions for toleration were created, although few people appreciated the enormity of the changes that had taken place or espoused the obvious ideological legitimation for those changes. The rejection of Rome had changed the English Church from a branch of Catholicism into a national church headed by the monarch and thus, as in other European countries, made it possible for the political interests of the monarch to override the religious interests of the Church, which suffered a considerable loss of economic and political power through the confiscation of its property. This did not, of course, immediately mean greater tolerance or diversity. It simply made subsequent changes in priorities more likely. As Henriques notes (1961: 2), none of the competing parties – Church, Protestant dissent, or Catholic remnant – was willing to accept diversity until attempts to enforce uniformity had failed. The Scots Presbyterians and their English supporters failed, during the Commonwealth, to remake the English Church in their own image and the Restoration church leaders failed in their counter-attempt to eliminate Protestant dissent. These failures were followed by a period – from the Toleration Act of 1688 to the repeal of the Test and Corporation Acts, and the passing of the Catholic Emancipation Act in the early nineteenth century – in which dissenters were permitted to worship but still suffered civil and political restrictions: 'a strict Nonconformist, one who would not take the Anglican sacrament, could neither hold office under the crown nor in the Municipalities, and was excluded from the Universities' (Bebb 1980: 71). But with one or two reverses (such as the hostility to dissenters which followed the French Revolution and the European wars), this period saw the slow and steady removal of restrictions on nonconformists. By the middle of the nineteenth century, religious affiliation had ceased to be of any great significance for civil and political rights, and the periodic outbreaks of church and chapel conflict – despite the energy which the protagonists expended – concerned relatively minor matters of mostly symbolic advantage.

73

From the Reformation to the Civil War

For our purposes, the story of English Protestantism can begin
with the Anglicanism which was pioneered by Henry VIII, when he
broke with Rome, and consolidated by Elizabeth. In this form, the
structure of the Church remained hierarchical and episcopal while
much of the doctrine became Protestant. The Church became a
state church but it did not develop the strong element of 'prince-
worship' which characterized European Lutheran Churches
(possibly because the Anglican Church, although stripped of
much of its wealth, was considerably less financially dependent on
the state than did its Lutheran counterparts). To what extent
Protestant Christianity really informed the lives of the common
people is not clear. The writings of clerical critics certainly testify
to widespread ignorance and indifference (Thomas 1971:
189–99).[1] Cases brought before ecclesiastical courts show that
many of even those who did attend church services were a little
short of appropriate reverence: 'Members of the congregation
jostled for pews, nudged their neighbours, hawked and spat,
knitted, made coarse remarks, told jokes, fell asleep and even let
off guns' (Thomas 1971: 191). There certainly seems good reason
to question Laslett's view that 'all of our ancestors were literal
Christian believers all of the time' when, as Collinson (1982: 198)
points out, almost every page of *The World We Have Lost* contains
evidence to undermine it. Yet we need to be cautious of the claims
of contemporary clerics, many of whom had a very narrow
definition of religion and a vested interest in painting as bleak a
picture as possible. There were many parts of the country in which
religious offices were rare and religious knowledge still rarer. It
was also the case that a considerable culture of magical and
superstitious practices continued and that many villagers resisted
the attempts of the more zealous to control their lewd and
licentious amusements. Detailed evaluation of the evidence of
popular religion in Elizabethan England would be out of place in
this study but the material presented by Collinson (1982, 1983)
suggests that the Church had considerable popular compliance, if
not active support, in those areas where it provided offices, and
that 'the godly people' were growing in number even among the
lower ranks of village and town life.[2]

The first significant element of dissent came from members of the Church who felt that Henry's reforms had not been pushed far enough. Usually designated Puritans, these Churchmen were not themselves united behind any clear alternative notion of what the Church should look like. As Collinson correctly points out, the position of the Puritans was for a long time an ambiguous one within the Elizabethan Church (1983: 6–16). Although the Puritan ministers with parishes and settled charges tried at first to see their mission as a mission to the whole people of their parish, the logic of their stress on religious experience, tests, and exercises meant that their followers tended to form a gathered remnant. In some areas, Puritan ministers maintained fraternal links with each other in a vaguely presbyterian manner while working in their parishes and relating to their followers in a congregational or 'independent' fashion. A detail which is relevant here, although more germane to the early Hanoverian period, is that, while deviation was often tolerated from individual ministers and congregations, dissenting organizations were not. Hence early dissent had only the most rudimentary and amorphous structure beyond each incidence of deviation, and one must therefore be cautious of too readily accepting as accurate descriptions of early dissenters, labels later used to identify separate denominations.

It is important to the thesis of this book to note that the English Puritans, like the Scottish Covenanters, were not advocates of toleration. As Skeats and Miall put it: 'they held to a purer doctrine than their opponents, but none the less, did they require it to be enforced by "the authority of the civil magistrate"' (Skeats and Miall 1891: 16). So that there will be no mistake about this, I will quote at length the views of Thomas Cartwright, one of the leading Elizabethan Calvinists, on the correct attitude towards atheists, the disobedient, and other unregenerate people:

> therefore the church having nothing to do with such, the magistrate ought to see that they join to hear the sermons in the place where they are made, whether it be in those parishes where there is a church, and so preaching, or where else he shall think best, and cause them to be examined how they profit, and if they profit not, to punish them; and, as their contempt groweth, so to increase the punishment, until such times as they declare manifest tokens of unrepentantness; and

then, as rotten members that do not only no good or service in
the body, but also corrupt and infect others, cut them off; and,
if they do profit in hearing, then to be joined unto that church
which is the next place of their dwelling.

(Quoted in Little 1970: 99)

Note the magnificent reach which Cartwright wishes for the civil
magistrate. It is not enough for the state to enforce attendance. He
wants the magistrate to ensure that the unregenerate are listening
and learning. Little makes an interesting distinction between the
defensive intolerance of Anglicans such as Whitgift, Bancroft, and
Laud who wished to maintain the existing order, and the offensive
intolerance of the Elizabethan Puritans who wanted to impose
their new order. In this brave new world 'idolaters, blasphemers,
contemners of true religion and of the service of God' would be
executed.

The Puritans were the spiritual fathers of the Presbyterians and
the Independents, although both terms are difficult to apply
consistently in this period. While those who were called
Presbyterians were more fond than were the Independents of
some sort of collective and centralized authority over individual
congregations, there was considerable shifting of views, and very
few of the English Presbyterians were wholeheartedly committed
to the Scottish model. Nevertheless, in the first three decades of
the seventeenth century, many of those divines who were later
claimed as the founders of Independency were really non-
separating congregationalists who combined what was essentially a
congregational practice with a willingness to remain within the
Church and to condemn those who advocated separation. In
addition, even some of the divines who could sensibly be seen as
Independents were convinced of the virtue of the Scottish notion
of the civil magistrate enforcing religious orthodoxy.

Of the more popular and influential elements of the first wave
of English dissent, only some of the Baptists could realistically be
described as conscious advocates of religious toleration: a position
which followed rather obviously from their views on baptism and
membership of the Church.[3] If only individuals who had come to
some personal apprehension of the truth of Christian doctrine,
and who had been baptized in such a knowledge were 'real'
Christians, the idea of state enforced orthodoxy was ridiculous.

The element of personal choice in Baptist thinking made it very difficult for its advocates to continue to believe in state churches, Lutheran or Calvinist.[4] Collinson's argument, which seems unobjectionable, is that the religious beliefs of the English reformers led inevitably towards something like Independency (Collinson 1983: 5–10). In the absence of the sort of social order which Calvin tried to create in Geneva, the religious impulses of the godly were bound to become turned inwards: from the parish to the family hearth: from society to the saved individual.

As was often the case, what turned these Anglican 'congregationalists' into outright separatists was not simply the working out of the logic of their own beliefs but also the actions of their opponents. In this case, Archbishop Laud's attempts to reintroduce elements of pre-Reformation liturgical worship to the Church of England, and his unwillingness to tolerate the presence of proto-dissenters, led some to reason that it was more convenient (and consistent) to leave the Church than to remain within it.

AN ASIDE ON SERIAL PLURALISM

Although it complicates the issue slightly, it is worth adding a brief but interesting note. The problem of knowing just how religious the people of pre-Civil War England were has already been introduced. For many historians the problem is one of assessing the extent of 'the Reformation'. We know what sort of changes occurred in the official ideology, practice, and structure of the Church but we clearly cannot simply assume that popular religion changed in step with official religion. Hill offers an important caution:

> at the time men must have thought of themselves simply as members of the English Church, which was undergoing some modifications. It is only in retrospect that reform becomes 'the Reformation'. The majority of clergymen retained their livings throughout these three decades, and we should be wrong to think of them as merely time-serving. Most of the laity must altogether have missed what seems to us the point.
>
> (Hill 1969: 36)

It is certainly true that 'the Reformation' is an observer's construct. It is likely, as Hill suggests, that a good part of the laity and the

lower ranks of the clergy (as distinct from the leading protagonists) had little sense that they were part of a series of related
changes which would later be seen as radically separating what
came after from what had gone before. None the less, the
observer's construct has not been cut from whole cloth and
changes in offical ideology must have had some impact on
ordinary people. After all, in Norwich and Chester in the 1630s, at
least three and possibly four different catechisms were used in
succession (Reay 1985a: 96). Anyone who was more than
minimally involved in the life of the Church must have felt that the
world, even if it was not yet turned upside down, was shaking a bit.

An important argument developed below the delegitimating
and secularizing effects of pluralism. Until now, and hereafter, it
has been and will be 'contemporary' pluralism – the simultaneous
existence of competing alternatives – which is the main focus. But
Reay's example of changing catechisms suggests another sort of
pluralism which, following the practice of describing the present
American pattern of marriage, divorce, and re-marriage as serial
monogamy, we might call serial pluralism. In those parishes which
were affected by the offically sponsored changes, the religious
career of any active church member would have had similarities
with that of someone in the twentieth century who moved from the
Church to Methodism to a pentecostal church and back to
Methodism. But there is an important difference. People who
choose to move from one organization to another, although they
are disillusioned with each one that they leave and may eventually
give up searching for a church that suits them, presumably take up
each new commitment with enthusiasm. People who stay in the
same organization and have it change around them might be
expected to have far less enthusiasm for each new development.
One might expect, and it would be an interesting topic for
research, that such alternation had delegitimating effects. I do not
intend to pursue the notion of serial pluralism beyond pointing
out that the gross destabilizing changes in the religious life of the
nation, which can be seen in factionalism, schism, and expulsion,
had their harmonic resonances in internal upheavals. It is a truism
to say that all things change but there are degrees of instability.
The involvement of many people in the life of the Anglican
Church was so slight that, as Hill reminds us, they may have been
unaware of the strangeness of the times in which they lived. But for

active Anglicans, the changes must have been disturbing. They were nothing as compared to the upheavals of the Civil War.

The Civil War and its aftermath

The outbreak of the Civil War not only called into question the nature of the state; it also challenged the nature of the church.[5] In order to produce some agreed and accepted scheme for the order of religion, in 1643 the Long Parliament summoned the Westminster Assembly of thirty lay assessors and 121 divines of varying views. However, this gathering of the godly was always unlikely to produce a scheme acceptable to the whole of England and Scotland. In the first place, the Baptists were excluded from its deliberations. In the second, the more Presbyterian elements refused to accommodate those who preferred a more independent or congregational organization (Bradley 1982). Furthermore, a major element of political strategy entered into these deliberations, with the Scottish model being promoted by some politicians anxious to win Scottish support for the Parliamentary Army in the war. In one significant respect, the proposals of the Assembly were even less tolerant of religious diversity than the previous Anglicanism. The Prayer Book and the Thirty-Nine Articles of the Anglican Church had been enforced only on the *clergy*. The Westminster divines wished to impose the Scottish Solemn League and Covenant on the whole population.

The majority of the English public (meaning by that, those people whose views counted) did not accept Scottish Presbyterianism. Cromwell and other leading parliamentarians grew tired of the Presbyterians' refusal to produce a broadly acceptable and comprehensive scheme and the Assembly was brought to an end. Thus the already existing fragmentation of the more reformed Protestants into three competing factions effectively ruined the last opportunity for a consistent and popular reformation of the national Church of England. To return to the major theme of these chapters, the fissiparousness of dissent produced further fragmentation.

The period of the Commonwealth was one of unprecedented religious freedom. Episcopalians were permitted to continue in their parishes and, even after he had defeated them at the battle of Dunbar, Cromwell was prepared to allow the Scots Presbyterians to maintain their rhetorical support for the League and Covenant. An Order of the Council of state of 1653 allowed 'That none be compelled to conform to the public religion by penalties or otherwise; but that endeavours be used to win them with sound doctrine, and the example of a good conversation' (in Skeats and Miall 1891: 44). However, this was not religious *laissez-faire*. Popery and prelacy were forbidden, as was anything likely to lead to licentiousness, although how one was to recognize such a thing was not explained!

Given that they were later hailed as the fathers of toleration, it is ironic that the persecution of this period was largely the work of Presbyterians and Independents, who were responsible for the incarceration of many of the 3,000 Quakers imprisoned during the Protectorate. It required Cromwell's personal intervention on behalf of the Friends to secure the release from prison of George Fox and a relaxation of the harassment of Quakers, but they were still denied permission to meet in public for worship.

The restoration of the Stuarts brought mixed consequences for dissenters. As usual, the Presbyterians were to be found arguing against their own interests. At the Savoy Conference of Episcopalians and Presbyterians, supposedly called to discuss a comprehensive scheme for a state church which both sides could accept (but suspected of being designed to keep the Puritans out), they repeated their demand for the reform of the establishment and only limited toleration for Independents and Baptists. In the interests of political stability, Charles II preferred to return to an Episcopal Anglicanism, and through the 1660s a series of Acts against dissenters was passed.[6] The Corporation Act made it impossible for them to hold municipal office, the Act of Uniformity silenced their ministers, the Conventicle Act outlawed meetings of more than five people in addition to the members of one family, and the Five Mile Act kept dissenting ministers that distance from any corporate borough. Finally, the 1673 Test Act made all civil, naval, and military employment dependent on having taken the sacraments in a parish church (Bebb 1980: 69–71).

Although these measures were designed as a major assault on the freedoms of dissenters, the actual situation in many areas was slightly more liberal. In the first place, it was always possible for dissenters to engage in occasional conformity; they could take the sacrament once in a parish church but could continue to worship with a dissenting group. In the second, Charles II had some notion of freeing himself from the Anglican Tory party by building an alliance of Catholics, Protestant dissenters, and ex-Cromwellians. He was thus less than enthusiastic in his support for punitive measures against dissenters and had often to be encouraged by his ministers. As a result relaxation and restriction see-sawed. Early 1662 was restriction; December 1662 was indulgence. The three years after 1664 saw restrictions; 1667 to 1669 saw relaxation. The passing of the second Conventicle Act in 1670 heralded one of the worst years for dissenters, but in 1672 a Declaration of Indulgence granted freedom of public worship to nonconformists (Bebb 1980: 39–41).

There was also a strong lobby in the Anglican Church which wanted to strengthen the establishment by broadening the Church to encompass the more moderate dissenters and thus reserve penal measures for only the most obdurate sectarians. Those more interested in the stability of the state than in the fortunes of the Church shared such an aim. Foreign and domestic policy would have been well served by uniting Protestants against the threat of popery. There were also complex internal pressures on religious alliances. While Protestant dissenters shared some common interest with Catholics, their anti-popery gave them common cause with Anglicans. When the Anglican establishment was in the ascendancy, the dissenters were at odds with the Church, but under the reign of Charles's less cautious brother, James VII and II, 'even High Church bishops found a common cause with Dissenters against a King who used royal prerogative to romanize the country' (Henriques 1961: 3).

The final departure of the House of Stuart brought William and Mary and further relaxation of restrictions on dissent. It was not the Protestant millennium which some had expected – William had too much need of the support of the Church to disestablish it – but it did confirm the general trend towards greater toleration and made it difficult for Queen Anne's Tory ministers to turn the clock back. They tried to do just that with one Act to prevent occasional conformity and another to force dissenters to raise their children as Anglicans, but without any great success.   .

In terms of organized efforts to improve their position, dissenters were relatively quiet during the first quarter of the eighteenth century. While the Dissenting Deputies – representatives of most English dissenters except the Quakers – performed a useful function in protecting the civil and religious rights of dissenters at local level, they hardly agitated for the repeal of the Test and Corporation Acts, seemingly willing to accept Prime Minister Walpole's claim that, although he was on their side, the time was not right to begin any agitation which would again raise the cry of 'The Church in danger!' Probably because they suffered the greatest disabilities, the Quakers were more persistent. Their refusal to pay tithes to the Church led them to suffer severe penalties. Not only were they fined for non-payment, but their cases were tried in expensive superior courts. Many were imprisoned and more were ruined by the judicial process. Under skilled political leadership, the Friends painstakingly put together petitions to promote an Act which would not free them from fines (that would have been going too fast) but which would lessen the costs of their dissent by having their cases dealt with by faster and less expensive procedures. For once, Walpole responded and pushed the Bill through the Commons, only to see it thrown out by the House of Lords, led, hardly surprisingly, by the bishops. This humiliation seems to have been a major reason why Walpole was thereafter unwilling to risk his prestige by further moves to accommodate the dissenters.

As was the case in Scotland, the 1745 Jacobite rising inadvertently improved the reputation of the dissenters. Only Roman Catholics and High Church Anglicans (and only some of them) rejoiced in the arrival of the Young Pretender. English dissenters followed the example of the Seceders in Scotland and proved their loyalty to the Protestant Succession by actively mobilizing against Charles Edward Stuart. Like Ebenezer Erskine in Stirling, Philip Doddridge encouraged his supporters to enlist in, and to organize, volunteer companies, and many dissenters were sufficiently keen to act on their Protestantism that they violated the terms of the Test Act by accepting commissions in the volunteer forces. After that display of loyalty, it was increasingly difficult for Anglicans to claim that dissent was dangerous because it encouraged rebellion.

Changes in ideology

In this period both dissent and establishment views of the civil magistrate changed. Some English Presbyterians and Congregationalists began to follow the Baptist lead and argue that the state had no obligation or right to support a particular religious organization. Others, almost certainly the majority, had moved some way in this direction but had stopped short of advocating religious *laissez-faire*. Thus one finds Doddridge, probably the most influential dissenting leader of the period, arguing that the state could, if it so chose, establish a church and expect even those who did not accept its teachings to support it financially. He justified this position from the analogy with wars. A representative government could expect people to pay their taxes and use those funds to support a war which many of the tax-payers might not wish to see fought. Only if the majority of the people opposed the war could it be legitimately opposed and taxes withheld. Similarly, only if the majority of the English people dissented from the Church, could nonconformists withhold their tithes.

Doddridge's position is important for the novelty of his grounds for religious establishment. Unlike the Puritans or the Scottish Seceders, he did not regard the religious obligations imposed by the civil magistrate as divinely ordained but as matters of democratic will. The legitimacy of a state church now came from its popular support. It was no longer God's will but the people's will which was crucial.

There was a similar and reciprocal shift in the arguments of churchmen for establishment. Although some continued to argue from theories of divine right and apostolic succession, many were offering a new and pragmatic defence. Church and state should form a constructive partnership, not because God demanded it, but because it was socially useful. In return for the state granting the Church various privileges, the Church promoted social order, morality, and loyalty. Such a utilitarian position may initially have seemed appropriate to the age but it was highly precarious because it could be undermined by evidence either that the Church was failing to be socially useful or that nonconformity was as good as Anglicanism at performing these social functions. The combination of the display of loyalty of the dissenters during the two Jacobite adventures, and the parlous moral state of many parts of the national Church, rotten as it was with plural holdings, absenteeism, placemen, and plain corruption, made it ever easier for dissenters to insist, on pragmatic grounds, that the state would benefit as much from even-handedness as it did from supporting the Church. Where a dissenting body was strong, the argument for social order disposed the government seriously to consider dividing its support. In Australia, the government first supported the Anglican Church and then, in the 1836 Church Act, divided its affections between the Church *and* the dissenting bodies (Turner 1972). To give an example from South Carolina after the colonial war, the ruling classes, while themselves mostly members and active supporters of the established Anglican Church, followed the logic of the functionalist argument and disestablished the Anglican Church in order to consolidate the support of the other Protestant churches which were stronger in the inland parts of the colony (Bolton 1982).

Methodism

In 1736, the year that Walpole effectively killed a bill to repeal the Test and Corporation Acts by refusing to support it in the Commons, George Whitefield was ordained. Three years later John Wesley began open-air preaching. The Methodist movement had begun.

The rise of a new dissenting movement was much helped by the stagnation of the establishment and the decline of old dissent. The reasons for these conditions need not concern us, but the former can be explained briefly as a result of the Church's refusal to think in terms of competing in a 'market'. Although it was obvious that the Church had lost the support of large parts of its constituency, there was little serious thought given to the need to adapt its structure and practice to face the new situation. In part, the Church had never really recovered from the depletion of its resources first under Henry and again under the Commonwealth. Many of the legal pressures to conform had gone, and only in those lowland arable areas with small settled rural communities headed by a resident squire was there strong informal social pressure to conform to the establishment. It is not coincidence that, outside the growing cities, the Methodists (and other dissenters) made their greatest inroads in places where the Church had large parishes, where there was no effective squirearchy, and where there were large numbers of freehold small farmers (see Gilbert 1976: 94–126). Why old dissent should have declined is a more complex question. In the half century before 1740 'first the socially distinguished and then the economically powerful sections of early nonconformity almost disappeared, having been for the most part reabsorbed into the Anglican Communion' (Bebb in Gilbert 1976: 16). At its peak around 1700, some 300,000 people had been dissenters. By 1740 this number had been halved.[7] The loss of the elite support could have been compensated for by the recruitment of what Doddridge called 'the plain people of low education and vulgar taste', but by then dissent had become elitist and introverted, and had lost its evangelistic impulse. There was thus a clear place in the market for a movement which could fill the gaps left by the stagnation of the Church and the ossification of old dissent. Wesley, Whitefield, and other Methodists seized the opportunity.

Attracting huge crowds and considerable public support, the Methodists were soon forced to abandon their equivocal attitude towards the Church. While Whitefield was tolerant of any man who preached what he believed to be the truth, the Wesleys had always insisted that they were churchmen. Although he may have been employing hyperbole, Charles Wesley did remark that 'he would sooner see his children Roman Catholic than Protestant dissenters' (Skeats and Miall 1891: 307), and John Wesley was similarly critical of dissent. In their own minds, the Wesleys were promoting a revitalization movement within the establishment. However, the practice of preaching and arranging meetings wherever there was an audience undermined the authority of the parish system and challenged the hierarchical structure of the Church. Furthermore, the failure of large numbers of Anglican clergymen to rally to the Wesleyan standard meant that, as the movement expanded, it had to develop its own organization and recruit its own functionaries. In 1744 Wesley called the first conference of Methodist clergymen and lay leaders. The rift with the establishment was deepened by the gradual expansion of the role of unordained men from reading scripture in meetings to preaching. Despite their claims to the contrary, the Methodists were becoming dissenters.

Some indication of the growth of Methodism can be given from statistics of Wesleyan membership, which grew from 22,410 to 77,402 between 1767 and 1796 (Gilbert 1976: 31). In the same period there was a revitalization and a considerable increase in the active support for Baptist and Congregational congregations. The 'new dissent' Baptists had largely broken with Calvinist predestinarian theology and acquired a new zeal for evangelism. The Congregationalism of this period was also discontinuous with the old Independency and much closer to the Arminian evangelicalism of the Wesleys. The net result of these movements was to increase considerably the number of dissenters and to undermine further the viability of the religious establishment.

Although English reaction to the French Revolution involved yet another attempt to construe dissenters as an internal fifth column and inspired politically motivated attacks on dissenters, the end of the eighteenth and start of the nineteenth centuries saw the gradual removal of all legal restrictions on dissent. The Conventicle and Five Mile Acts were repealed and the oath required of Quakers was dropped. Although they had ignored it with impunity, the Unitarians were offended by the existence on the statute books of a law which made it an offence to deny the doctrine of the Trinity; in 1813, the statute was removed. Finally on 9 May 1828, the offensive Test and Corporation Acts were repealed, this time with the active support of the majority of the Anglican bishops, who had finally accepted that unpopular legislation could not turn dissenters into Anglicans.

The political power of the dissenters was increasing all the time. Not only were they becoming relatively more numerous but the social strata which supported them were becoming richer and more powerful. The 1832 Reform Act brought more dissenters into parliament and their power in the major urban centres was considerable. In the late 1830s a number of cities refused to set church rates and thus forced the issue of dissenting financial support for the established Church.

> Where the Dissenters were strong enough to do so, they forced the injustice of their position on public attention by frustrating the operation of the law and taking the consequences. One notorious case at Braintree in Essex resulted in legal proceedings that went on for sixteen years! There were other cases in

which nonconformists were sent to prison for contempt of court.

(Vidler 1974: 137)

It is common for a dominant group which has recently and reluctantly accepted the need to give up some of its privileges to become *more* rather than less tenacious in the defence of its remaining advantages. Those whose position has been allowed to improve are supposed to be grateful for what they have received and not press further. Given the obvious presence and stability of dissent and the growth in economic and political power of the nonconformists, the removal of the final hurdles seems to have taken an unconscionable amount of time and effort: church rates, for example, were not abolished until 1868.

Another site of conflict was education. Although popular schooling had been pioneered by the Free Churches (and evangelicals within the Church whose denominational affiliation did not prevent them working outside its structures), once the established Church realised the appeal of the schools, it became active. As happened in Scotland, bills to improve schooling were often taken by churchmen as opportunities to repeat their claims to state favour. However, such attempts to constrain social innovations within a crumbling framework of outdated relationships regularly failed. An attempt in 1843 by conservative churchmen to monopolize factory schools was soundly defeated by nonconformists. In 1870 the Foster Education Act created a network of state Board schools to work alongside the voluntary schools. The Church wanted Anglican religious teaching in such schools, while nonconformists argued for a secular education with religious instruction being provided outside the school system. The solution was a compromise which permitted undenominational or 'simple Bible teaching' and barred the use of distinctive formularies such as the Church Catechism (Vidler 1974: 138).

Far more space could be given to the arguments between Victorian churchmen and nonconformists, but the end point is so clear that further detail of the renegotiation of relations between church and state would be superfluous. Nonconformists had won the removal of all restrictions on their civil and political rights. The expansion of elements of the secular state (such as mass education) was so great that the relative advantages enjoyed by the Church of England in, for example, retaining its own schools became trivial. Like the Church of Scotland, the Church of England retained a patina of establishment but real privilege had gone, leaving only pomp and ceremony.

SUMMARY: THE ESTABLISHMENT ROUTE TO TOLERATION

Enough historical detail has been given to allow me to sketch the key elements of the establishment route to toleration. The story can be clarified with the separation of two different sorts of cause: those related to changes in religious affiliation and those which resulted more directly from changes in the state. The initial establishment reaction to dissent was to outlaw it and to coerce waverers into conformity. The ineffectiveness of this quickly became clear when those dissenters who were most vigorously persecuted – the Quakers, for example – thrived. Not long after the failure of the Elizabethan settlement to create a united and coherent Church, the more far sighted Church leaders appreciated the failure of persecution. They sought a basis for 'comprehending' the majority of dissenters which would allow them to reserve punitive action for a small, and hopefully unpopular, minority. When this strategy also failed, some churchmen began to abandon altogether the notion of enforced conformity.

It would be a mistake to accept too readily the view that pre-revolutionary Protestantism was built on a class fracture of society, with the Puritans and the high Episcopalians representing two competing classes: the old and the new. There were religious divisions within as well as between social strata and, where they were strong, the Puritans were firmly on the side of social order. While Walzer (1965) is right to see the overthrow of the traditional order as the obvious long-term consequence of Puritan doctrine, Collinson deploys considerable evidence to show that the non-sectarian Calvinists were considerable respecters and consolidators of traditional authority (Collinson 1982: 180–8). Clearly one needs to specify more accurately just which group of dissenters one is considering in any identification of political tendencies, but such detail is unnecessary for my argument. It is enough that there is a general element of truth in the picture of

England as a society in which most of the aristocracy and the gentry at the top and the peasants at the bottom sided with the established Church, while the dissenters, as in Scotland, drew their support from the rising middle and artisan classes (this is especially true of Methodism).[8] The changes in the economy which brought a shift in political power thus favoured nonconformity and made it more and more difficult for the politicians to rule by relying on the support of 'Church and King'. But even before political expediency made it necessary to incorporate the growing body of urban dissenters into the body politic, changes in the political arena had undermined the moral authority of the established Church. One could almost return to the Henrican Reformation and point to the delegitimating effects of the confiscation of Church property. To use the title of an excellent brief discussion by Hill (1986a: 41–57), the 'Social and Economic Consequences of the Henrican Reformation' were the most immediate and obvious, but the very fact of deliberately organized change in the structure of the Church called into question the legitimacy of any future structure: 'in temporarily solving the economic problems of the ruling class it gave a stimulus to ideas which were ultimately to overthrow the old order' (ibid.: 47).

As if Henry's reforms and later changes in the relations between church and state had not been enough, the Williamite revolution caused further and massive problems for the leaders of the establishment. Until then it had been possible (with some gnat-swallowing over Henry's break with Rome) to maintain that the doctrines of the divine right of kings and the apostolic succession of bishops were inexorably linked. Their experiences in the Commonwealth and Protectorate periods gave conservative churchmen and politicians, in the reign of the 'restored' Charles II, very good reason to preach Church and King.

> As a class the clergy became deeply committed to a high religious theory of kingship. Each 30 January, the anniversary of the execution of Charles I, and each 29 May, the day of his son's return, the pulpits thundered for the doctrines of the divine hereditary right of kings and the utter sinfulness of resistance to his commands.
>
> (Bennett 1969: 156)

89

But desire to believe and ability to do so are not the same and the expulsion of the Stuarts and the invitation to William and Mary to accept a 'contractual' monarchy made it very difficult to argue that God rather than the people determined monarch selection. As Stromberg put it: 'The truth is that for both Whig and Tory, *jus divinum* became irrevocably obsolete.' In the words of some bad contemporary verse:

> I would by no means Church and King destroy
> And yet the doctrine taught me when a boy
> By Crab the Curate now seems wondrous odd
> That either came immediately from God.
>
> (Quoted in Stromberg 1954: 131)

The irony of the Revolution settlement and its implications for an established Church was that it was precisely the most consistent believers in the divine ordering of church and state – the nine bishops and some 400 clergymen who refused to accept William and Mary – who were deposed. Although post-Revolution monarchs continued to maintain a state church, they had to do so without the support of the very people who believed that such an institution was divinely ordained. The new breed of Whig bishops gradually shifted to a more pragmatic justification for a state church and, with it, a more tolerant attitude towards dissenters. Nonconformists could now be regarded as socially disruptive but they could hardly be judged to be acting against God's will. Although Hoadly was one of the more Whiggish of the new bishops, his view that 'mutual charity, not . . . a pretense of uniformity of opinions' was the correct foundation of religious harmony, although a little premature, was a foretaste of future pragmatism (ibid.: 91). This is not to say that the High Church party did not resist; they frequently did. Between 1702 and 1704, for example, Rochester and Nottingham introduced bills to outlaw the common practice of dissenters avoiding civil restrictions by engaging in 'occasional conformity'. The bills were rightly seen as an attempt to turn back to a more robust interpretation of the Toleration Act than was then common, and were defeated. An act did make it to the statute books in 1711 but it was rarely used (Bennett 1969: 172).

Hopes for religious uniformity were additionally undermined by the expansion of the English state and its failure to convert the

Presbyterians of Scotland and Ulster, and the Catholics of the rest of Ireland, to Anglican Episcopalianism. Although it took a long time to be recognized:

> there lurked an inherent contradiction in the circumstance that within the single British polity established in 1707 there existed not one but two established churches, different to some extent in their theology and still more different in their form of government. If Ireland, still a separate kingdom up to 1801, did not also present a contradiction, it did furnish an anomaly.
>
> (Christie 1982: 33)

Initially Protestant dissent had to be accommodated to present a united front against the papist threat of Britain's European enemies and, finally, British Catholics had to be accommodated in the hope of defusing the Irish problem.

Thus one sees two principles working together to create a secular state tolerant of religious diversity. On the one hand, the establishment had to learn to live with its failure to retain the dissenters; the costs of enforcing conformity became too high and penal sanctions counter-productive. At the same time, various exigencies forced the political establishment to reduce gradually its commitment to promoting conformity to a state church. Although the Episcopal Church remained the legally established Church of England and Wales, the real advantages which it enjoyed over the Free Churches were reduced to the point where many nonconformists could ignore them.

THE FINAL IRONY: PROTESTANTS AND CATHOLICS

The English Independents and Scots Seceders who objected to Queen Anne's Toleration Act on the grounds that it paved the way for the acceptance of Roman Catholicism were right, although they failed to see the part their own dissent would play in the process. The debates among seventeenth- and eighteenth-century Protestants about the limits of toleration always assumed that Catholics were beyond the pale, and the various political intrigues engaged in by some Catholics did nothing to change that perception. The gradual abandonment of the idea of state-enforced religious conformity benefited the Protestant dissenters first, and only in the nineteenth century were there serious moves to incorporate Roman Catholics fully into the body civil. Although many conservative Protestants campaigned against Catholic emancipation, their previous efforts to argue on universalistic democratic principles for their own rights made it difficult for them to appear consistent when proposing the denial of the same rights to some other dissenting group. And the government had good reason to want to indulge Catholics. Lord North was willing to provoke the anti-Catholicism expressed in the Gordon riots of 1778 because he wanted to enlist the Scottish highlanders (who had not yet converted from Catholicism and Episcopalianism to evangelical Protestantism) to fight in the American colonial and French wars. The full emancipation of English and Scottish Catholics was a result, not of their own agitations, which tended to be of a very moderate and unassuming nature, but of attempts to stabilize government in Ireland. Just as the 1707 union of the Scottish and English Parliaments called into question the allocation of political rights on the basis of religious affiliation, so the 1801 union of the British and Irish parliaments created further pressure for Catholic emancipation, which was granted in 1829. As Otto Hintze has argued (in Hechter 1975: 61), the British government's need to develop some sort of stability in Ireland led it to grant citizenship to Irish Catholics. English and Scottish Catholics also benefited. Thus one sees the final fulfilment of what had been latent since Henry's break with Rome: the subordination of the religious interests of the Church to the political interests of the state.

One suspects that even concerted opposition to Catholic emancipation from conservative Protestants would have been ignored by the government but the Protestants were too fragmented to present a united front. There were those who followed the establishment logic to argue that, as Roman Catholics existed, their further persecution would only cause more problems than it solved. Furthermore, the threat of French Jacobinism seemed more potent than that of British popery. Given that religious conformity was long dead, social cohesion became a more pressing cause. There were also versions of the dissenting reasoning. Although some conservative Protestants wanted to draw the line of permitted variation at their own dissent, others were driven to support the Emancipation Act, both by a desire for consistency and because it was another stick with which to beat the religious establishments.

If some supported emancipation out of a genuine respect for the religious and civil rights of Catholics, others did so in order to convert Catholics from their unchristian ways. Thomas Chalmers, who was then still an evangelical within the Kirk, thought that the conversion of the Irish would be aided by putting all religions on the same legal footing. In his view, it was only natural resentment at the privileged position of Protestantism which prevented the poor wretches from seeing the superiority of evangelicalism. Although he did not endorse voluntary principles, Chalmers suspected that establishment devalued the established religion by implying that it *needed* state support. Such an argument was, of course, only necessary and possible in those conditions of pluralism which the conservative Protestants had done so much to create and which Chalmers was about to extend by leading the Disruption.

Thus conservative evangelical dissenters, evangelicals within the establishment (but not convinced establishmentarians), and liberal dissenters could all, for their various reasons, support the Catholic Emancipation Bill. But those who did so remained a minority. Although the supporters could draw on the cultured elites, they could not claim to have the country with them. However, opposition to Irish Catholics was weakened by regional variations in both religious affiliation and Catholic settlement. For the national churches of Scotland and England, Catholics were not a general problem because they were concentrated in particular areas (on England, see Gay 1971; on Scotland, see Bruce 1985a). As those areas were generally the growing urban centres, which were under-represented in the national churches, relations with Catholics were only an issue for a minority of officers of the churches. This was even more the case for the increasingly centralized state which gave little attention to regional issues.

Whether they liked it or not – and most of them did not – the actions of schismatic conservative Protestants had created religious pluralism and thus made possible a climate of opinion which endorsed that reality by promoting private conscience and religious *laissez-faire* as valued principles. That the climate they had created inadvertently benefited Rome, the old enemy, was much regretted but there was little or nothing conservative Protestants could do about it. The chance to create a reformed and popular national church had been offered by the Long Parliament. The failure of the Westminster Assembly to seize that chance had permitted the fragmentation of the religious culture to increase to the point where it could not be reversed by the insignificant threat of British Catholicism or the distant conflict with Irish Catholics.

The unintended nature of the rise of religious toleration is made clear by Dickens in the epilogue to his study of *The English Reformation.* He lists the one or two pious Protestants – William Turner, the physician to Protector Somerset and John Foxe, for example – who openly espoused toleration, but clearly has trouble finding many representatives. The best he can say of Cranmer, for instance, is that 'he persecuted only a few extremists' (Dickens 1983: 440). For the times, Cranmer's self-denial may have been unusual and laudatory, but there is something bone-chilling about that 'only'. In his last paragraph, Dickens comes very close to the point I am arguing in these chapters:

> While the Reformation was slow to produce genuine tolerance among its devotees, it soon destroyed the more solid psychological bases for religious persecution. Once Catholic Christendom had been succeeded by a multiplicity of national churches and dissenting groups, persecution began to occasion practical disadvantages which could be seen, intermittently at least, to outweigh the advantages of uniformity. Such situations inevitably led to practical experiments in toleration, and where it was proved that such toleration could subsist without disaster, the more positive appeals of religious liberty were bound sooner or later to make their appeal.
>
> (Ibid.: 441)

It is a measure of Dickens's skill that, although the *consequences* of pluralism are not the focus of his work, he none the less concludes with an observation which could be taken as a text for the rest of this book: 'At varying rates most of the people bought their freedom. The price in terms of spiritual confusion often proved high, for history is usually a hard bargainer with men' (ibid. 1983: 441).

THE THIRD WAY: SCANDINAVIAN LUTHERANISM

This and the previous chapter have offered detailed illustrations from Scottish and English church history to support the argument that a major contributing factor to the rise of religious toleration was the essential fissiparousness of Protestantism. Although it may be argued that class differentiation and the expansion of the British state would eventually have caused the abandonment of religious affiliation as an important criterion for the allocation of social, political, and economic rights, the material presented above suggests that the fundamentally democratic nature of Protestantism, by permitting the fragmentation of the religious culture, was a significant factor in three related developments: the gradual shift among dissenters from a sectarian to a denominational self-image; the establishment's gradual acceptance of the rights of nonconformists; and the rise of a secular state.

There are two important Protestant cultures in which religious toleration did not result from internal fragmentation producing religious pluralism: those of America and Scandinavia. The pluralism of American Protestantism was a natural consequence of the settlement of the continent. Each ethnic group brought its own variation and, even before the attack on privilege popularized by the colonies' revolt against English rule had fuelled widespread opposition to religious establishment, the imported fragmentation made anything other than denominationalism difficult to sustain outside small areas. If America differs from Britain in the source of its pluralism, the Scandinavian situation differs in the comparative lateness of its espousal of toleration and the source of the ideology of religious freedom. The cases of Denmark, Finland, Sweden, Norway, and Iceland will be used to introduce the third route to toleration: the modern democratic impulse.

Although there are interesting differences between the Scandinavian countries, they may, for most of our purposes, be treated as a single case. Around the 1550s, all the Christian churches in Scandinavia were reformed along the lines established by Martin Luther. However, what Vogt says of Norway could be repeated for the other countries: 'There is a profound continuity, both in the faith of the people and in the institutions, territorial divisions, etc. between the Medieval Catholic Church in Norway, and the modern Lutheran Norwegian Church. Many phenomena today are virtually unchanged' (Vogt 1972: 381). There was very little Calvinist influence. The Church Assembly in Uppsala in 1593 rejected as heretical both Catholicism and Calvinism. For almost 250 years from the end of the sixteenth century, Lutheranism enjoyed a state enforced and state supported monopoly in Scandinavia. It was only in the middle and late nineteenth century that basic religious freedoms were introduced. In 1845, Norway permitted all Christian bodies to practise and evangelize. Even then civil servants were excluded from the provision that allowed Norwegian citizens to leave the national church. After 1849, Danes were allowed freedom of worship. Eleven years later, Swedes were permitted to leave the national Lutheran Church but until 1951 they were legally obliged to affiliate to another recognized Christian body.

What is significant about the Scandinavian countries is that religious toleration came to be recognized as a fundamental characteristic of modern democracies (and was usually introduced as part of a major constitutional change from absolutist monarchy to parliamentary democracy) without there being much by way of preceding religious dissent. That is, toleration was accepted more as a 'good thing' in its own right than as a necessary accommodation to *de facto* pluralism. Given the crucial role which pluralism played in other Protestant settings, this requires explanation.

The lack of fragmentation can be explained by the relative absence of the two factors which explain British fragmentation: the individualistic ethos of reformed Protestantism and social diferentiation. As Vogt (1972) makes clear, the Scandinavian Lutheran Churches were less 'Protestant' than either Calvinist Presbyterianism or Anglicanism. In sociological terms, there was far less emphasis on individual judgement and far more weight given to the community that was the Church. In this sense, Scandinavian Lutheranism lay somewhere between reformed Protestantism and Roman Catholicism. The less radically reformed Lutheran Churches remained national churches. To return to the classificatory typology presented in the first chapter, while Calvinism drew heavily on the Bible as its source of authority,

96

Lutheranism retained greater reliance on the Church. It was thus less ideologically prone to factionalism and schism.

As late as 1870, only 10 per cent of Swedes worked in industry or craft occupations. In the most developed of the Scandinavian countries – Denmark – it was only 25 per cent. In Norway, Finland, and Iceland it was considerably less. Norway remained a rural society until the twentieth century. Christiania (later Oslo) had only 9,000 residents in 1880. There was thus far less social differentiation in the Scandinavian countries in the eighteenth and early nineteenth centuries than there was in Britain. This is not to say that social differentiation causes religious fragment- ation, but it is to recognize that the increase in social distance between classes is a major factor in the development of different emphases within the same dominant religious tradition, as different classes alter the faith to suit their new interests and perspectives.

Even when regional and elementary class divisions did produce revivals similar to those which attended the Seceder and Free Church splits in Scotland, they did not cause serious fragmen- tation. 'At a time when revivalism in some other Protestant societies led to separatism and to new religious organizations, the Church in Finland was able to assimilate these movements' (Seppanen 1972: 145). Like enthusiastic movements in Catholicism, Lutheran revitalization movements tended to remain within the Church. Hauge, the leader of the first major revival in Norway, was far more consistent (and successful) than Wesley in imploring his followers to remain within the Lutheran Church. The second Norwegian revival – the 'firm believers' – also 'decried all sectarian departures from confessional Lutheranism' (Hale 1981: 51)

A third reason for the greater homogeneity of Lutheranism in Scandinavia was that, unlike the British establishments, it was totally reliant on the state. The Henrican Reformation in England had deprived the English Church of a lot of its wealth, and hence much of its independence, but it was never entirely Erastian. Bishops and clergy retained important elements of financial and legal independence. The Scottish Presbyterians were even less dependent on the state. Even in those periods when the right to appoint the clergy was removed from congregations, the clergy enjoyed considerable legal security and were subordinate, not to a centralized state authority, but to the local state of heritors and patrons. The Scandinavian Lutheran national churches were completely subordinate to the state in the training and appointment of the clergy and were heavily dependent on the state for financial support. Such conditions were not conducive to independent thinking and, combined with the Lutheran tendency to reject independency and voluntarism, explain why tensions within the dominant religious traditions did not blossom into full-blown dissent.

The first pressures in the Norwegian Parliament to relax legal control of dissent concerned restrictions on lay-led conventicles and came from the supporters of Hauge. The rural Haugean members of the Parliament supported greater toleration within confessional Lutheranism but when other legislators pushed for the legalization of dissent from the Church, they voted against the moves. However, by the middle of the nineteenth century the example of other European societies was becoming increasingly attractive as a model for a modern democracy. It is important that nearly all the government officials – those members of the elites with the widest international contacts and with the professional responsibility for running the state – voted for the liberalizing dissenter law. Similarly, twelve of the sixteen pastors who held seats in the Storting also voted for the changes. Their reasoning was that of Thomas Chalmers: if there was going to be market competition, the true religion was so self-evidently superior that it did not need artificial support.

In some places, there was an element of French Revolution and Enlightenment inspired anti-clericalism but this was far more muted than it was in those Roman Catholic countries where the rise of a labour movement and social democracy divided the society into strong clerical and anti-clerical blocs. However, the left–right division was stronger in Scandinavia than it was in England where the considerable body of dissenters who aligned themselves on the left (and the small but influential number of Anglican clergymen who promoted liberal and leftist causes) prevented the development of a firm association between the church and the right.

The arrival of religious toleration in the Scandinavian countries comes then, not as a consequence of religious struggles (which, because of the cohesion of Lutheranism and the relative lack of social differentiation, remained muted), but as part of a general re-evaluation of civil rights in the light of the rise of democracy across Europe. In this it resembles the Catholic model more than it does the British experience. This observation allows us to complete this analytical account of the rise of religious toleration.

THE RISE OF TOLERATION: A SUMMARY

To recapitulate the argument of this and the previous chapter, it is suggested that the view which stresses the influence of Enlightenment and modern democratic notions of individual liberty as a cause of religious toleration is really correct only for the last of three stages. The chronologically and causally primary route to toleration comes from the inadvertent and unintended consequences of Protestant dissent. The early Baptists advocated religious liberty from the first but they were an exception, driven out of most of Europe, unknown in Scotland, and far less numerous in England than the Puritans, who mostly followed Thomas Cartwright's view that idolaters, blasphemers, and other ecclesiastical ne'er-do-wells should be executed. Most schismatic Protestant groups accepted the idea of state enforced orthodoxy and wished to lead a legally established national church. Far from wishing to see greater toleration, they wanted their own narrower orthodoxy to become the creed of a *more* authoritarian state church. Only after they had failed to win their ideological battles with the establishment did they begin to see the sense in the positions taken by the very early liberals whom they had persecuted.

In the second stage, religious establishments were forced – by their failure to prevent dissent – to moderate their claims, and the state moved to a position of ever-increasing toleration. First, Protestant dissent was grudgingly permitted, and then all claims to distribute civil and political rights according to religious affiliation were abandoned. The failure of the established churches to remain national popular institutions forced the state to expand its activities to take over functions previously performed by the churches.

The third element of this account concerns those Protestant societies where the establishment was Lutheran and where industrialization and urbanization came late. Once religious liberty had become firmly established as part of the nature of modern democracies, those countries which had maintained a relatively homogeneous Protestant establishment also adopted the practice of religious toleration.

Where this account differs from that offered by other sociologists and historians is in its stress on the fissiparous nature of Protestantism. Class fragmentation and regional tensions within developing nation states provided a major part of the thrust towards religious pluralism, but the impact of such social differentiation was mediated and amplified by the individualism of conservative Protestantism which made it possible for different social groups to develop the dominant religious tradition to suit their own interests. Although one might suppose that the separation of religious affiliation and civil rights is such a necessary element of any industrial democracy that it must eventually have come to pass, it is the case that Protestant schism hastened the process. The related point which I have stressed is the unintended nature of the rise of religious toleration. While one can identify small groups of innovators who dissented in order to advocate religious liberty, it is generally the case that the publics which they addressed were unreceptive. It was only when the advocates of competing religious orthodoxies failed to impose their doctrines and standards on the population at large that they began to accept, reluctantly at first, an ideology which legitimated the reality created by their own failures. The Covenanters, Seceders, Puritans, and Independents were not pioneering liberals or early proponents of denominationalism, and the established churches did not willingly give up their legal privileges. Very few religious innovators wanted denominationalism. It was thrust upon them by their failure to convince or suppress their rivals. That there were so many rivals is explained by the essentially individualistic nature of Protestantism.

Chapter Five

THE RISE OF LIBERAL PROTESTANTISM

The previous two chapters described the social and cultural changes which provided both the opportunity and the need for the widespread adoption of liberal Protestantism. At various times in the history of the Christian Church, there have been movements which have promoted some element of what is now termed 'liberal Protestantism'. In one sense, there is a cyclical pattern to the rise and fall of heresies; universalism, for example, is not new. As the cultural anthropology of scholars such as Eliade (1971) has demonstrated, there are only a limited number of possibilities in the religious lexicon. What is at issue in charting cultural change is not the invention or the occurrence of deviant perspectives and heretical opinions; the same ones eternally return. What is important is the relative popularity of such alternatives. An obvious point is that periods of religious enthusiasm tend to alternate with periods of moderation. In the Scottish Church the Secession followed one period of stagnation, the Disruption another. In the Anglican Church, the parlous spiritual condition of much of early nineteenth-century church-manship was followed by the High Church and evangelical revivals. Although there is a general pattern of alternation, modern liberal Protestantism does seem qualitatively different to other turns of the wheel. In the second half of the nineteenth, and in the twentieth, century various strands coalesced and achieved sufficient popularity to amount to a major shift in Protestant thinking which can be described most simply as the triumph of relativism. The two main differences between the present position of the major Protestant denominations and that of, say, the moderates of the Church of Scotland of the 1760s, are (a) that, rather than advocating a new theology, the latter were largely indifferent to theological disputes, being more concerned to maintain the appearance of cohesion; and (b) that the extent of theological disagreement within the Kirk was considerably less than the variation now permitted by most major Protestant churches. The theologians of the present ecumenical movement are tolerant of diversity, not because it makes for an easy life, but because they believe that diversity is itself a 'good thing', and they accept a far wider range of conflicting views. Where most Church of Scotland moderates were reluctant and foot-dragging in accommodating to the cultural standards of their age, one has the sense that modern liberals are enthusiastic pioneers of the 'post-Christian' age.

While the edges of the movement may be hard to locate, the essence of liberal Protestantism can be fairly simply identified. It is a tendency which regards human reason as paramount and which begins its theologizing from the agenda of the secular world. It thus appears as a continual impulse to modernize the faith, to abandon the confines of the historic creeds, and to accommodate the thought and practice of the churches to those of the secular world. Although it is distinct from ecumenism (in that one can imagine a limited ecumenism within the confines of one particular ideology), it is historically and sociologically close, and was essential for the development of the modern ecumenical movement. While the extreme liberal position is one of endorsing the secular world, more moderate liberalism involves the reduction of the importance of the boundaries between previously competing organizations. The belief in 'new light' becomes the belief in different lights. Where the hermeneutic perspective allowed one generation of Christians to believe something radically at odds with what previous generations believed without having to assert their superiority publicly (however much they may privately have rejoiced in it), it now allows one group of Christians to accept as 'equally valid' the different traditions of another group. In much of what follows, and where it is not important to separate theology from attitudes towards other organizations, liberalism will connote not just liberal theology but ecumenism.

The first point which needs to be made about modern liberal Protestantism is that it evolved gradually. It is anachronistic to assume that the post-1920s division between conservatives and liberals has always existed so starkly. At the end of the last century and the start of this, one finds considerable overlap between those who later became identified as fundamentalists and those who became firmly associated with 'the social gospel'. At the 1887 Evangelical Alliance conference in Washington, there were mainstream conservatives who 'were manifestly pious, sincere, and supportive of middle-class sensibilities' (Wacker 1985: 47). There was a second group which 'embodied a growing liberal impulse widely known as the new theology'. And there were committed evangelicals who were supporters of 'higher life' theology.[1] Although the view that the conversion of individuals was a precondition for social improvement and the notion that the amelioration of social problems should precede evangelism are now taken to be competing alternatives, for a considerable period there was no radical divide between the spokesmen for these claims. Differences of emphasis took some time to develop into competing positions embodied in discrete movements. As Wacker has cogently argued, the stress on the later fundamentalist controversy period has caused us to overlook the considerable similarities between the new theology and the higher life. Both social reformers and pre-millennialists were convinced of the spiritual maturity of the age. 'Both were certain that God's unfolding truth, richer and fuller than ever before, had rendered the time ripe for the Lord's harvesting' (ibid.: 58). The general point worth emphasizing here is that it was not just the liberals who were being influenced by new currents in their culture. Those who were later dubbed fundamentalists were not motionless in the cultural sea of change. Not only in their reaction to change but also in the 'progressive' and optimistic elements which they incorporated into their rejection of the liberal alternative, the conservatives were also very much products of their times (Marsden 1982). A good organizational example would be the network of people who clustered around Dwight L. Moody, the most prominent American evangelist of the Victorian era. Moody was patron of both the Scot, Henry Drummond, who pioneered a synthesis of New Testament Christianity and Darwinian evolution, and of Reuben Torrey, who after Moody's death turned the Chicago Bible Institute into a major base for fundamentalism. Moody's Northfield Conferences were also a major influence on John R. Mott, the pioneer of ecumenism in America who was largely responsible for bringing the Orthodox Churches into contact with the major Protestant denominations.

Another example of a mixing of what later become liberal and conservative positions can be seen in the attitudes of the late nineteenth-century students at the Free Church of Scotland College in Edinburgh. Many of them were coming increasingly under the influence of German rationalist higher criticism but they were also enthusiastic assistants in the Moody and Sankey crusades. They saw no contradiction between higher critical approaches to the Bible and mass evangelism. In the 1870s, the battle-lines had not yet been clearly drawn.

The Student Christian Movement as a case study

As a methodological preliminary, it is worth offering some justification for the frequent reference in this chapter to the British and American Student Christian Movement (SCM). There are two separate sets of reasons why the SCM should be used to illustrate observations about liberalism and ecumenism. In the first place, the SCM was far more than a student Christian organization. Many twentieth-century Protestant Church leaders (and not just those of British and American churches) first became active in church life through the SCM. Until the 1960s, there was hardly a major bureaucrat in the interdenominational organizations which make up the ecumenical movement who did not graduate from the staff of the SCM, and many Church leaders first came to prominence through their activities in the student movement. Furthermore, many ideological and organizational innovations in British and American Protestantism were first introduced in the universities.

If the above are substantive reasons for paying attention to the SCM, there are also analytical reasons. The main focus of this book is not any particular church, sect, or denomination, but belief-systems and patterns of behaviour that are not coterminous with any particular worshipping community. Here, organizations like the SCM are useful because they existed to represent these broader concerns rather than to promote a particular confessional identity. The final reason for attending to the SCM is that, after the conservative evangelicals left it and formed the Inter-Varsity Fellowship of Christian Unions, there existed in British universities two Protestant organizations with identical organizational structures and similar modes of operation, which recruited in the same market place. The major differences between them were that one was liberal while the other was conservative evangelical, and one declined while the other prospered. The neatness of the contrast allows us to observe the consequences of the different belief-systems.[2]

TACTICAL ACCOMMODATION

To return to the main themes of this chapter, a second important point about the development of British liberal Protestantism (something similar could be said of all previous liberal movements) is that many Protestants initially accommodated to the intellectual standards of the secular world for tactical purposes. As one might expect, very few converted to rationalism or universalism. There was no one point at which they suddenly woke up to the realization that, for example, the Westminster Confession was outdated or wrong and that they could no longer stand where their forefathers had stood. Rather, they saw their shifts as being vital to the preservation of the essentials of what their forefathers had believed. Schleiermacher wrote his *Speeches On Religion* in order to address what he saw as the ever-increasing number of 'cultured despisers'. It is not coincidental that many of the pioneers of liberalism and ecumenism were active in missionary work, and that 'comity' arrangements in the mission field were among the first instances of 'fraternal relations' between competing denominations (Latourette 1954). Apart from its economic irrationality, competition was seen as harmful to the image of Christianity. Many missionaries initially accepted the strategic value of good relations with others and gradually came to see ecumenism as a positive value in its own right.

Similarly liberal Protestantism was initially promoted, not for its own sake, but as a device for attracting the attention of the unchurched. This emerges very clearly from the letters, diaries, and internal memoranda of the early leaders of the Student Christian Movement. They believed that the heathen, who could not be attracted by the 'old time gospel', might be tempted by something less radically distinct from what they already believed.

Once their interest was aroused, they could gradually be socialized into the real Christian gospel.

This can clearly be seen in the biography of Tissington Tatlow. Tatlow has been sorely neglected by church historians but he, more than any one man, deserves to be regarded as the founder of modern British ecumenism. As a student in Dublin in the early 1890s, he was an intense Church of Ireland evangelical. His diary shows a constant round of prayer meetings, Bible studies, and church services. Mentions of friends and acquaintances are almost always followed by 'I had a talk with her about the things of the Lord' or some such reference. He underwent a typical Victorian evangelical conversion experience at his first student missionary conference at Keswick. He even records the date in his diary: 28 May 1896; 'Had today definite dealings with the Lord'.[3]

Tatlow spent a year as an organizer for the Student Volunteer Missionary Union (SVMU). He toured universities encouraging students to become 'Volunteers' for overseas missionary work and to form branches of the SVMU. At the same time as the SVMU was growing, evangelical students in a number of colleges were forming Christian Unions to promote and maintain the evangelical faith among students. The national umbrella organization created from these – the British Colleges Christian Union – was so closely connected with the SVMU, sharing staff and members, that a union was effected and Tatlow became the full-time General Secretary of what was then called the Student Christian Movement. Having been forced to postpone his planned retirement because of the havoc wreaked on the organization by the First World war, Tatlow effectively ran the SCM from the late 1890s until the 1930s. It was while trying to build the SCM as a popular, national, and influential movement that his attitude to other Protestant, and later other Christian, traditions, changed.

In 1896, as a good evangelical, he described 'High Church' Anglican worship as a mockery. But he and the other SCM leaders had a vision of a united student movement with a presence in every college in the land, including the Anglican theology colleges, many of which were Anglo-Catholic. Given that the SCM had its roots in evangelical and missionary circles, it is not surprising that the Anglicans should have been suspicious of what was seen as a 'Protestant' and Free Church movement, and given it a rather frosty reception. An idea of the temperature of the Anglican response can be gained from an extract from the notes of one early SVMU travelling secretary on his 1895 tour of theology colleges:

> I walked about six miles to Cuddesdon Church of England College. I saw the Principal but could get no promise of an opportunity to address the students. Next Salisbury, I could not enter the college . . . . Lichfield, on the evening of my arrival I saw two students who I think would have arranged a meeting for me in the theological college but the Principal withheld his consent. The case at Lincoln was very similar and no opening offered . . . . At Leeds I was unable to get an opening in the Clergy School.
>
> (Quoted in Bruce 1980:131)

Tatlow and the other student movement leaders systematically set out to woo the Anglicans. An indicator both of tension between the competing Protestant churches and of the SCM leaders' appreciation of the problems that faced them was the fact that the first move towards ecumenism had to be a step backwards from the easy relationship which had existed in the movement when it had been entirely evangelical. So that non-evangelical Anglicans might not be immediately offended, the SCM dropped the practice of holding a combined communion service at its annual conferences. The next stage was the setting up of a Church of England subcommittee which persuaded six leading Anglican intellectuals to sign their names to an open letter commending the annual SCM conference. Then the most influential of the Movement's few non-evangelical Anglican sympathizers were persuaded to sign a letter, to be sent to all college principals, explaining the nature of the SCM and offering them a private interview with the travelling secretary. Tatlow then arranged to have himself invited to the Conference of College Principals, where he explained the nature of the movement and smoothed feathers of various hues. Having been persuaded that the SCM was not negligent of denominational identity, the principals dropped their objections and the SCM was able to build a secure base in the Anglican colleges.

The important point is that the SCM had begun life as a missionary recruiting organization. The travelling secretaries for the SVMU became convinced that, in an increasingly secular environment, missionaries could not be recruited unless there was some established student Christian presence in the universities. So the missionary activity became first associated with, and then subordinated to, the establishment of Christian Unions in universities and colleges. More than anywhere, it should have been in the theology colleges that the movement had its strongest presence; it could not maintain its self-image as a student 'Christian' movement if it only recruited from the Free Churches and the very low wing of the Anglican Church. Hence the need to woo the Anglicans and the quite conscious changes in policy which were made during that wooing process. At its most general, the same process occurred wherever Protestants had to deal with pluralism and refused to practise sectarian isolationism. If they were to work with representatives of other positions, then not only those representatives but the positions they represented had to be accepted as legitimate.

Tatlow's experience of winning over the initially suspicious Anglo-Catholics stood him in good stead when he became involved in the organization of the Edinburgh 1910 World Missionary Conference (Gairdner 1910). The previous conferences had been exclusively 'Protestant' affairs. Considerably aided by John Mott, the leader of the American student movement, Tatlow was able to use the contacts he had made in the SCM to bring the Anglo-Catholic Society for the Propagation of the Gospel to the meeting which can sensibly be regarded as the start of the ecumenical movement.

The evolution of the SCM was matched by Tatlow's own personal transformation from evangelical to relatively liberal ecumenist. In both cases, the shifts were initially strategic. The emphasis on organizing Christian Unions rather than recruiting missionary volunteers was designed to make it easier to recruit missionaries in an increasingly secular environment; there was no conscious decision to stop recruiting missionaries. But the early decision to concentrate on building Christian Unions meant the creation of a broad base for the movement. The success in building such a base (and the expansion and changes in the student population) made the Missionary Department, as the SVMU had become, less and less important, until it was closed down.

Tatlow's first contacts with people outside narrow Protestant circles came about as a result of his interest in *promoting* narrow Protestantism. Only later, as he developed strong personal friendships and working relationships with other sorts of Christian, did he come to appreciate the intrinsic merits of the positions he promoted.

My suggestion is that a major source of the shift towards liberalism is the need to accommodate to pluralism. This is not offered as a monocausal alternative to previous explanations. There are clearly elements of Protestant ideology which themselves made liberalism attractive, and there are an array of cultural and social structural forces which disposed an increasing proportion of people in the late nineteenth century to shift in that direction. My point is that, if we want to see how such factors combined in the actual lives of people who became liberal Protestants in this period, an important point to notice is that such people were actively involved in religiously pluralistic settings. Those Christians who wished to work with representatives of other traditions (rather than just dismiss them) needed to find some ideology which would justify accepting people with apparently competing beliefs as also being 'in the faith': liberalism did just that. The second main reason for the reconsideration of the doctrinal basis of the faith has also already been suggested in the reference to Schleiermacher's 'cultured despisers'. A major influence on Tatlow's development – and something similar appears in the biography of many liberals – was a course of lectures he gave to women art students in London. He quickly discovered that the exposition of orthodox evangelical doctrine was having little impact on people whose Christian faith was not 'taken for granted'. As Schleiermacher found, the need to engage in apologetics for an interested but unconverted audience gave good incentive to seek ways of remodelling the faith to make it appealing to urban sophisticates. That the new religion could be attractive to doubters on the fringes of the churches and yet have no appeal to the thoroughly unchurched was not yet clear.

THE DEPENDENT NATURE OF LIBERALISM

Although no value judgement is implied, it seems accurate to describe liberalism as being parasitic on evangelicalism. No large popular movement has converted non-believers to a liberal Protestantism. The development of nineteenth-century Unitarianism, for example, was 'not the kind of growth being experienced by the New Dissent during the same period: it involved the metamorphosis of existing congregations rather than the creation of new ones' (Gilbert 1976: 41). The heterodox elements of Presbyterianism and the General Baptist traditions were united but showed little capacity for growth. While evangelical nonconformity showed a considerable net increase in a growing population, Unitarianism initially remained stable and then declined.

In asserting that liberalism (and its modern organizational expression in ecumenism) is dependent on an earlier period of conservative evangelical Protestantism, I mean more than that liberalism followed evangelicalism in time. I will argue that the appeal of liberalism was that of a release from a conservative strait-jacket, and that it was the years in the strait-jacket which gave liberalism its shape and delayed its collapse.

That Tatlow was not unique can be demonstrated from the biography of any number of late Victorian Christians. Alexander Whyte was a leading figure in the Scottish Free Church and a principal architect of the union of the Free Church and the United Presbyterians, the heirs to the liberal wing of the Secession. Despite pastoring what had been the congregation of R. S. Candlish, widely regarded as one of the leading Scottish Victorian evangelicals, Whyte was on the liberal wing of the Free Church. When Robertson Smith was tried for heresy for his 'higher critical' views (which included the radical claim for those days that Moses did not write all of the Pentateuch), Whyte was outspoken in Smith's defence. Yet Whyte had been raised in conservative Presbyterian orthodoxy. As a boy in Kirriemuir, he had attended the Free Church Sunday school. His grandmother took him to the more liberal Relief Presbytery Church in the afternoon, but on Sunday evenings Whyte went on his own to worship with the ultra-conservative Auld Licht Seceders. His adolescent reading had included the extremely orthodox *British and Foreign Evangelical Review* (Barbour 1924).

Henry Drummond has already been mentioned as a personal friend of the American evangelist D. L. Moody. He was also a keen supporter of the early student movement. In the early period of his career, he was regarded as sufficiently evangelical to be invited to speak at Moody's Northfield conferences. Yet he was also keenly interested in natural science and he wrote a number of books, of which *Ascent of Man* was the best known, which argued that Protestantism could, be wed happily to Darwinian evolution. Drummond had been raised in an 'evangelical Christianity of a doctrinal form, strict in its adherence to a somewhat dry routine of preaching and teaching' (Smith 1902: 26). John R. Mott, the pioneer of ecumenism in America, had similarly been socialized into conservative orthodoxy before broadening in later life.

What these men and their less well-known counterparts shared was a thoroughly orthodox upbringing which had steeped them in the fundamentals of a highly conservative Protestantism. It was their own personal certainty which made it possible for them to argue for the abandonment of creeds and membership tests. The first written 'statement of faith' for the student movement had declared 'A belief in Jesus Christ, God the Son and only Saviour of the World'. In 1899 there was considerable discussion about the status of this declaration. Was it an exclusive membership test? Against those who argued that it be used as a test, others insisted that it would prevent young seekers from becoming associated with the movement. Interestingly, the strongest opposition to the use of any creed or doctrinal basis came from the Scottish Free Church students, the very people who had been raised in the most orthodox tradition. They could afford to argue against tests because they knew what they believed! It is clear from his correspondence and memoranda that when, in the 1920s, Tatlow was engineering a change in the SCM's basis to a statement which would permit all non-Roman trinitarian Christians to join the movement, he did not envisage a time when Unitarians and Roman Catholics would be acceptable. The Americans, such as Mott, who had a greater acquaintance with religious diversity, were much more cautious about abandoning creeds.

The psychology of the individuals involved and the attitudes of some organizations show considerable similarity. In both cases, the strength of the traditions of the past was taken to be the guarantor of future orthodoxy. Those who had been fully socialized into evangelicalism could, with security, abandon the narrower aspects of their faith and engage in liberal and ecumenical experiment because their personal past had been so firmly orthodox that it gave protection against anomie. It provided such a strong pull that their experimentation was limited naturally, without the imposition of the ideological equivalents of perimeter fences.

111

Much the same could be said for the attitude of the Scottish Presbyterian Churches when they handed over their schools to the state. The Roman Catholic and Episcopalian Churches in Scotland refused to enter the national school system in the 1870s and were only brought in under the 1918 Education Act which offered them considerable safeguards (Brown 1987: 201–6). They were effectively allowed to run their schools much as they liked. Most importantly, they retained control over staff appointments and could thus ensure that only teachers who would promote the Catholic or Episcopalian faith would be hired. The Protestants handed over their schools for far weaker guarantees and seem to have assumed that, because Scotland was a predominantly Presbyterian country, the schools would remain Presbyterian. They were content that religious education in the schools given over to state control would continue to use the Bible and the Shorter Catechism according to 'wont and usage'. The past would guarantee the future. It did not do so. What this suggests is that where, as in America, conservative Protestants early see themselves threatened, they can take preventative action by constructing distinct social institutions to preserve their faith. When the conservatives, who split from the SCM, began to build their alternative Inter-Varsity Fellowship (IVF), they wrote a long and detailed creed which they used as a membership test and as a 'boundary maintainer'.[4] They had learnt the lesson of the SCM. But when the first generation of late Victorian liberals were pioneering the ecumenical movement they did not anticipate the future problems.

At both the individual and organizational level, there was the tacit assumption that the orthodoxy of the past was itself, without further organizational safeguards, sufficient guarantee that future changes would be kept within the bounds of what was tolerable. That meant, in effect, within a liberalism which challenged particular evangelical orthodoxies but which continued to hold that there was a God, that the Bible in some sense exclusively represented His Word, that Protestantism was superior to other Christian traditions and categorically different to non-Christian traditions, and so on. In ecumenical terms, that meant that good relations should be cultivated with all trinitarian Protestant denominations, with the Orthodox Churches, and, just possibly, with the less imperialist elements of Roman Catholicism. What no one involved envisaged was the wholesale capitulation to the agenda of the secular world which occurred in the 1960s.

Perhaps the best way of appreciating the dependence of liberalism and ecumenism on the orthodox pasts of the people involved is to recognize the extent to which evangelical socialization provided the coherence for the twin movements. From the last quarter of the nineteenth century to the 1940s, liberal Protestantism built on the orthodox past of its supporters. The secular world provided so many symbolic resources that, in trying to find a new expression for the faith which would appeal to 'modern man', the experimenters would quickly have ceased to have much in common had they not all started their voyages of discovery from the same small plot of ideological land. The problem, of course, was that the amount of variety in what liberal Protestants believed gradually and steadily increased so that those younger people who had not been raised in conservative evangelicalism began to challenge the orthodoxies of their parents. The amount of specific doctrine which was shared decreased in proportion, and the seeds were sown for the debacle of the post-war period.

The temporary revival of denominational identities

The contemporary period in Church history has been repeatedly described as an era of ecumenicity. Within American Protestantism this contention is easily borne out by looking at the most obvious organized manifestations of ecumenicity, such as the development of a variety of cooperative agencies across denominational lines and a marked tendency for denominations to merge .... Yet side by side with this development of a new ecumenical spirit there has occurred a resurgence of denominationalism which has been marked by a renewed emphasis on the historical heritage and peculiar theological position of each denomination in question.

(Berger 1963: 77)

Although written in America in the 1960s, this could perfectly well have been said about Britain and other European Protestant countries in the 1940s and 1950s. The explanation for the paradox will be presented shortly. First, the British situation will be described. Like so many developments, this was both part produced by, and best illustrated with, the SCM. The movement had initially been 'undenominational': a term originally used by evangelicals to describe events such as crusades which were constructed around the highest common factor of shared belief. Baptists, Methodists, Brethren, and others could cooperate in evangelistic crusades in which they confined themselves to presenting those theological elements which all participants agreed about. Beliefs and practices specific to particular denominations were temporarily left aside. Given the high degree of conservative Protestant orthodoxy in these organizations in the late Victorian era, this was a viable approach.

It was the undenominational identity of the SCM which the Anglo-Catholics found objectionable. They refused to see their faith divided into elements, some of which they were supposed to leave at the door. Tatlow's crowning achievement in the SCM was the production of the 'interdenominational' basis which expressed what became the ideological foundation for the ecumenical movement. It argued that students should bring with them, into the SCM, their specific denominational identities which could be appreciated as part of the Christian equivalent of life's rich and varied tapestry.

> The Student Christian Movement is interdenominational, in that while it unites persons of different religious denominations in a single organization for certain definite aims and activities, it recognizes their allegiance to any of the various Christian bodies into which the Body of Christ is divided. It believes that loyalty to their own denomination is the first duty of Christian students and welcomes them into the fellowship of the Movement as those whose privilege it is to bring into it, as their contribution, all that they as members of their own religious body have discovered or will discover of Christian truth.
>
> (Tatlow 1933: 400)

This dual focus – Christian unity and denominational identity – was reflected in the interests of the members and activists, many of whom progressed to become leaders of their own denominations,

as well as senior figures in ecumenical bodies such as the World
Council of Churches. The new basis was designed to avoid the
rocky harbours of outright sectarianism and the uncharted open
waters of innovative syncretism. Although only its critics described
it as such, it was essentially relativist. It implied that what appeared
to be competing claims were, somehow, complementary.

As Berger notes, the very structure of ecumenical contact
brought with it an impetus to the reassertion of denominational
identity:

> Increasing contact between denominations brings about an
> increasing number of situations where denominational
> representatives, both clerical and lay, face each other in a
> variety of subcommittees, conferences, consultations, and so
> on. These situations are commonly defined explicity in terms
> of this interdenominational confrontation: that is, each
> representative is expected to play a role appropriate to the
> denomination he represents. At this point some fundamental
> social psychological processes are set in motion that could be
> summarized somewhat pithily by saying that, if a de-
> nominational identity does not already exist, it will have to be
> invented in accordance with the role expectations of the
> situation.
>
> (Berger 1963: 78)

Berger goes on to add another element to his explanation of the
apparent paradox of heightened denominationalism in the
ecumenical movement. He makes the telling point that little of
serious theological substance now divides the main
denominations. Like companies marketing detergent, they are
forced to spend money on creating and maintaining 'brand
loyalty' because, with so little separating them, brand switching
would be easy. The stress on denominational identity is thus a
sensible response to product standardization.

One element of the recommitment to denominational
identities is the social construction of tradition. Parts of the
histories of the particular organizations are rediscovered and
reworked to make them both distinct and suitable for present
circumstances. For example, the Reformed Presbyterians, or
Covenanters, have been presented for most of this century rather

inaccurately, but none the less fashionably, as founders of democracy. The fact that they were keen on the suppression of (other people's) heresies is conveniently overlooked. Only their rebellion against tyranny is remembered and they are reconstructed as part of the Scottish Presbyterian contribution to the development of democracy. Although denominational historians vary in the willingness with which they fall prey to the temptation to reconstruct those they wish to claim as ancestors, many partisan histories (Skeats and Miall 1891, for example) show the tendency only too clearly.

A development allied to the rediscovery of denominational identities was the rise of Barthian 'neo-orthodoxy', which became popular in reformed churches in the post-war period. Ronald Preston, who was active in SCM in the 1950s, has privately taken me to task for decribing the SCM as a liberal Protestant organization. In denying the appropriateness of the liberal label, he stressed not only the strength of denominational feeling in the movement but also his generation's commitment to Karl Barth's theology. Professor Preston is absolutely right but I would argue that, despite appearances, Barthian 'neo-orthodoxy' was not a major departure from liberalism. Rather, it was a diversion, briefly fashionable with some theologians, which had little long term impact. To summarize Barth (doubtless in caricature), neo-orthodoxy rejected the implied liberal idea that man was essentially good, rejected liberal subjectivism, and reasserted the centrality of God as *subject*, not as object of our theological speculations.[5] Barth stressed the transcendent nature of God and the centrality of Christ. But although he believed in the primacy of God's Word in Christ, this was not the same as the primacy of scripture. Indeed, the neo-orthodox treatment of historical facts tends to remove from them religious or theological significance. The historicity of events recorded in the Bible can be denied, while their significance in *heilsgeschichte* (or salvational history) is maintained.

Although Barthianism began as an outright rejection of the man-centred theology of existentialist Christian theologians such as Bultmann and Tillich, it was not fundamentalism and it was not orthodox conservative Protestantism. By the late 1950s, it had either been rejected or assimilated to the subjectivism and relativism which it had initially repudiated.

CONCLUSION

As with the conclusion of the previous chapter, the purpose here is not so much to repudiate the more common accounts of the rise of liberal Protestantism as to add to them a previously neglected element. The rise of liberal Protestantism is usually, and quite rightly, seen as a response to a series of major social and cultural changes. New forms of knowledge were undermining the plausibility of traditional Christian beliefs. The churches were either losing members or waking up to the fact that they had already lost them. Late nineteenth- and early twentieth-century modern industrial societies were almost 'post-Christian'. Although Christian language and symbolism were still common, and although many people in Europe and America were church members, Protestantism was rapidly losing conviction. Liberal Protestantism was promoted as a retrenchment, a movement to retain what could be salvaged, while changing or abandoning peripheral elements of the faith to make it more attractive to modern man. What is missing from many accounts of the rise of liberalism is a sense of the part played by the fragmentation of the religious culture in the process. It is the argument of this discussion that the nature of the movement can be seen more clearly if it is recognized that it was one of the two poles on an axis of possible reactions to the increased fragmentation of the dominant religious tradition.

The example of the SCM has been used because it faced the problem of pluralism more starkly than many churches. As a relatively new voluntary organization working in an environment with a constantly changing market, the impact of its encounter was not cushioned by its members having strong traditional attachments to the SCM. Given its image as a student 'Christian' movement, it could not restrict its appeal to just one confessional tradition. But many within the churches faced a similar situation. They had the choice of either endorsing the diversity which existed and making a virtue out of necessity, or rejecting the legitimacy of competing Protestant variations. To put it in the language of church, sect, and denomination, once internal fragmentation had destroyed the claims of Protestants to having a church, they had to choose between being a sect and being a denomination.

The denominational road was initially chosen grudgingly, not for its own intrinsic merits but as a route by which the wolf of the old sectarian certainties could be slipped into the fold. However, it soon became accepted as worthwhile in its own right, as what God wanted of his people in that generation.

The other pole on the axis of reactions – the sectarian rejection of pluralism – will be the subject of Chapter 7. Before going on, in the next chapter, to discuss the decline of liberal Protestantism, it is worth noting that liberalism and the romance of the ecumenical movement did help at least two generations of Protestants to maintain some vestige of their Christian faith in what they saw as an overwhelmingly hostile environment. Clearly, one can only make weak 'if A, then perhaps B' guesses about what might otherwise have been the case, but it does seem likely that, before the corrosive effects described in the next chapter set in, liberal Protestantism had the effect of preventing the intelligentsia from being converted to secularism. Particularly for those who were engaged in justifying their faith to the heathen (both at home and abroad), liberalism was a sensible response to the rationalism of the modern world and ecumenism was the best reaction to the fragmentation of the Protestant tradition. In many ways, liberal Protestantism was a noble attempt to create an intellectually supportable version of Christianity, in the face of the massive divisions within the body of those who claimed to worship the same God. Its proponents can hardly be blamed for failing to see that such appeal as it had was confined to those who felt suffocated by narrow doctrinal orthodoxy and embarrassed by ancient dogma.

Chapter Six

THE DECLINE OF LIBERAL PROTESTANTISM

INTRODUCTION: PLURALISM AND FAITH

The discussion of secularization in Chapter 1 gave some indication of why it is that religious pluralism undermines the plausibility of religious belief, or, to rephrase it, why religious toleration becomes religious indifference. This brief section will consider the corrosive effects of pluralism in more analytical detail before going on to consider the viability of the liberal Protestant response.

A major problem for the religious believer in a religiously pluralistic society is the relative absence of institutional support. The state either refuses to endorse the once-dominant religion or, characteristic of the transitional phase, gives only limited support, and increasingly does so for pragmatic rather than ideological reasons. More damaging than the actual absence of institutional confirmation of the veracity of one's own religious beliefs is the state's implied rejection of the notion that there is such a thing as a true religion. An even-handed approach to competing religious traditions is tantamount to the assertion that religion is a matter of personal preference. As Martin (1978a: 3) rightly notes, there are different consequences depending on whether the state permits entirely free competition or itself takes an interest in promoting a 'civil religion', but for the general question of plausibility both have the consequence of suggesting that, at least at the public level, the traditional premise of religion – that it is true because God said so – is no longer acceptable.

A second observation about pluralism concerns interactions with the 'heathen'. At the same time as reducing the extent to which believers interact with fellow believers (and thus acquire implicit confirmation of their world-view), pluralism increases interaction with people who see the world differently. In the early stages of the growth of religious heterogeneity, such interaction will be infrequent and can be compartmentalized because the bearers of alternative religious views will usually be 'foreigners' and often enemies. This was the case for British Protestants when the threats of the Spanish, the French, the rebellious Irish, and the Jacobites gave good reason to live in fear of popery. Even when the carriers of alternative beliefs cannot be plausibly construed as dangerous enemies, they, and hence their beliefs, can be devalued by stereotyping. For example, the belief of most British Protestants that Roman Catholicism was anti-Christian was bolstered by the maintenance of invidious stereotypes of Roman Catholics. The low social and economic status of the Irish immigrants in mainland Britain was taken as proof of the falsity of their religion.

When pluralism has resulted from the internal fragmentation of a dominant culture rather than from the import of a foreign religion, it is less easy to dismiss the carriers of alternative beliefs as foreigners who know no better, as disloyal rebels, or as a shiftless social underclass. Pluralism of the sort produced by Scottish and English dissent meant that competing beliefs were being advanced by people of the same ethnos and relatively similar class position. Such infidels were more difficult to sanitize mentally or 'bracket' out of consideration. For the ordinary member of the Church of Scotland, those Covenanters, Auld and New Licht Seceders and Episcopalians (not to mention the odd representative of English dissent) whom he met in the course of his daily round were his own people: people who, in most respects except religious affiliation, were like him.

Of course, increased interaction does not necessarily increase amity. If there are enough sources of tension and conflict, closeness produces more ill-feeling and offers more opportunity for displays of hostility, as it did in the Ayrshire mines in the early nineteenth century when Irish Catholics were imported as strike-breakers (Campbell 1979). However, the most frequent consequence of increased interaction with representatives of other faiths is the gradual modification of invidious stereotypes. The biographies and letters of the pioneers of ecumenism testify to the considerable changes they had to make to their images of those they had previously despised, derided, or distrusted, as they came to recognize that people could hold quite different religious beliefs and still be decent citizens and nice people. In her history of the ecumenical movement, Ruth Rouse relates the following story of Dr V. Stukey Coles, the Head of the High Church Pusey House, who,

> came to a Student Movement conference to find out why and how this movement had been the means of conversion of an Oxford undergraduate whom he had entirely failed to help. The author has a vivid memory of seeing this stalwart Anglo-Catholic seated at the foot of a staircase in earnest talk with Mary Hodgkin, a Quaker, finding spiritual fellowship in unexpected quarters. Friendship with her brother, Henry Hodgkin, followed. From that time on he supported the Student Movement.
>
> (Rouse 1967: 344)

The division of the 'life world' into discrete compartments can initially blunt the impact of such contact and prevent it from triggering a revaluation of beliefs. At work, the Vale of Leven Orangeman cooperates perfectly well with Catholics. At home and in his leisure time, he continues to subscribe to a conservative Protestant faith in which Catholics are not Christians. The problem, of course, is that such compartments are not watertight. To put it another way, one may continue to assert (as most evangelicals do) that one is opposed to the system of Catholicism but not to individual Catholics. But because a great deal of how we evaluate beliefs rests on how we judge the carriers of those beliefs, the more one engages in successful and rewarding interaction with individual Catholics, the less easy it is to maintain the distinction between acceptance of the person and rejection of their beliefs. One particular kind of rewarding interaction which has major consequences is marriage. Although the direction of cause remains an open question, there is a strong correlation between cross-denominational marriage and low church attendance rates. In one survey of adult Protestants, 62 per cent of those who married within the same denomination attended church monthly, while only 33 per cent of adults who married members of another denomination went to church once a month or more often (Roozen and Carroll 1979: 25–8).

Related to interaction, but analytically distinct from it, is the general availability of alternatives in the cultural supermarket. The existence of a wide variety of cultural choices will mean that some of these will be chosen, irrespective of their merits. However, as will be argued in a later discussion of religious pluralism in America, the simple availability of alternatives does not immediately mean that these will often be chosen. Considerations such as the status of the proponents, the resonance of the substance of alternatives with the interests of potential consumers, the degree of fit between already held beliefs and new alternatives, and the costs and benefits attached to alternatives, will all play a part in determining 'take-up'.

As people come to grips with the existence of decent people who believe different things, and with the fact that the state will give their own beliefs little institutional validation, they may move to the denominational position of implicit relativism. Alternative belief systems are no longer seen as competing but as being equally true, for those who choose to accept them. The problem with this attitude is that it is logically, ideologically, psychologically, and sociologically unstable.

The logical problem is that denominationalism requires believers to abandon the law of non-contradiction, which is probably a universal but even if it is not, certainly lies at the heart of western thought and culture. The relativism which is found in Buddhism, for example, is foreign to us and especially foreign to our notions of the divinity. Either there is a God or there is not. Either God made the world in six days or he did not. It requires a radical break with the way we think to sustain the possibility that God made my world, but not yours, in six days, or that a number of Gods may or may not have made the world in six days, depending on the tradition into which one has been born.

The logical problem can be avoided by radically changing the nature of the epistemological claims made for the faith – which is what liberal Protestantism does – but this introduces the ideological problem. Until the late nineteenth century, the majority opinion within Christianity made *exclusive* claims. The Christian God was a jealous God; there were to be no other Gods. The non-exclusive brand of Christianity pursued by the more radical modernizers receives no support from the mainstream Christian tradition. It is a bastard with disreputable and usually heretical forefathers. It thus lacks strong ideological support from the tradition.

Even if these problems can be overcome, the psychological consequences remain real. Religion is concerned with certainty. It is about discovering the Archimedean point which allows us to escape the ambiguity and confusion of the mundane world. It is difficult to develop or maintain a high level of commitment to something which may or may not be true, which may only be partially true, or which may be true for only some people.

The above may be contested, but even if the claim that the denominational attitude is logically, ideologically, and psychologically precarious is doubted, it is possible to demonstrate that it is organizationally precarious. The rest of this chapter will examine the problems of maintaining liberal Protestantism as a shared belief-system.

THE DECLINE OF LIBERAL PROTESTANTISM

The first thing which needs to be established is that a worthwhile problem has been identified correctly. There is general agreement among sociologists writing about Britain (Bruce 1983b), Canada (Bibby 1978), and America (Kelley 1972) that conservative varieties of Protestantism have recently proved more resilient than liberal versions. Since the publication of Dean Kelley's *Why the Conservative Churches Are Growing* there has been considerable debate about the relative weightings of different causal factors.[1] More recent considerations of the evidence argue that the conservative Protestant Churches have been growing, not so much by conversion as by retaining a greater proportion of their offspring. Hence attention has shifted from conservative growth to liberal decline, but no one has seriously contested Kelley's basic claim about the relative strengths of conservative and liberal Protestantism.

A few examples may be presented. Almost all American denominations grew between 1955 and 1965. The greatest percentage increases were shown by the more conservative churches such as the Assemblies of God, the Missouri Synod Lutherans, the Church of the Nazarene, and the Southern Baptists (who have sustained their growth so that the Southern Baptist

Convention is now the largest American Protestant organization). The period from 1960 and 1965 saw the first net decline in a major organization, the United Church of Christ (UCC). Some of the loss was due to the departure of conservative members of the constituent denominations, which had merged to form the UCC in 1957.

> In the other major liberal denominations the rate of growth slowed, while the conservative bodies, large and small, continued to grow at a more rapid rate. It was in the latter half of the 1960s, continuing into the middle 1970s, that all of the theologically liberal denominations began to experience membership decline.
>
> (Roozen and Carroll 1979: 13)

Presenting the same data in another way, the highest growth rates between 1950 and 1975 were sustained by the two most conservative major churches: the Southern Baptist Convention (80 per cent) and the Lutheran Church-Missouri Synod (60 per cent). The two lowest growth rates were recorded by the two most liberal major churches: the United Methodist Church (3 per cent) and the United Church of Christ (–7 per cent).

Bibby's extensive researches of religiosity in Canada show considerable decline in active adherence to the churches. Some conservative organizations have shown no growth relative to the total population, while others, in particular the Pentecostalists, the Christian and Missionary Alliance, and the Salvation Army, have grown faster than the population. But although conservative Protestantism's 'cumulative proportional population gain over the century has been negligible' (Bibby 1985: 288), liberal and broad Protestantism has shown a considerable and marked decline. The extent of differences in liberal and conservative support can be illustrated with data on church attendance. In one of his surveys, Bibby asked people to compare their attendance at church when they were children with their adult attendance patterns. He found that the rate of 'fall-out' correlated clearly with theological conservatism. The greatest decline was among the Presbyterians (53 per cent), the United Church (42 per cent), and the Anglican Church (42 per cent). Lutherans had a fall-out of 23 per cent, the Baptists came next with only 15 per cent fall-out, and a variety of evangelical denominations lost just 10 per cent of their attenders (Bibby 1979: 109).

The situation of British Protestant churches appears to be similar. It should be noted, however, that British church membership statistics are less readily available and less reliable than those for the American churches. Although the excellent work of Peter Brierley and his associates has provided good statistical material for the last decade, it is very often impossible to make long-term comparisons because the starting-line data are badly flawed. None the less, sufficiently good data are available to give us confidence in the very general outline of the pattern.[2]

The United Reformed Church (URC), formed in 1972 from the merger of the Presbyterian Church of England, and the majority of the English congregations in the Congregational Union of England and Wales, showed a faster rate of membership decline after the merger than the component units had shown before. The dissident Congregationalists, most of whom rejected the merger because of the theological liberalism of the new organization, as well as its centralized polity, performed considerably better (see below, p. 129).[3]

It might be argued that decline is a consequence of size: small organizations grow while large organizations lose members. But there seems no good reason why the size of the overall organization, rather than congregation size, should be an important independent variable. If overall size is relevant, it is most likely to be a mediating variable between theology and commitment. As sects grow most tend to moderate, accommodate to the prevailing culture, and relax the behavioural standards that made the organization distinctive in the first place. Thus in so far as size is important, it is probably because growth tends to go hand-in-hand with increased liberalism.

However, it is not the case that only large denominations decline. The 30,000 members in 1943 made the Unitarian/Universalist Church small but between then and 1980, it still managed a decline rate of 63 per cent – to 11,000 members.

Scottish Protestantism offers an excellent field for comparison because there are a number of organizations with a common history, very similar styles of worship and structure, but with quite different theologies and careers, competing in the same market place. Between 1956 and 1986, the membership of the more liberal United Free Church (UFC) went from 24,800 to 10,500: a decline of more than 50 per cent. In the same period, the membership of the Church of Scotland declined by 36 per cent: from 1,319,600 to 840,000. The two conservative churches – Free Church and Free Presbyterian Church – remained stable. The difference in fates is probably greater than these figures suggest. While the Church of Scotland and the United Free Church recruit from all of Scotland (with a bias to the urban lowlands in the case of the UFC), the two conservative churches, despite their best efforts, recruit primarily from the highlands. Although the overall adult population of Scotland has declined by about 4 per cent over the last thirty years, it is the highlands which has suffered the most marked depopulation, ranging in parts from 10 to 30 per cent.

If the argument is that liberal Protestantism is more precarious than its conservative counterpart, the comparison of churches should be complemented by the consideration of changes *within* churches.[4] After all, many of the larger denominations, such as the Church of Scotland and the Church of England, have within them liberal and conservative Protestants (compounded in the Anglican case by 'High Churchmen'). Unfortunately little other than anecdotal evidence is available for comparisons within churches. For example, it is the case that three conservative clergy associations within the Church of Scotland have all increased their membership over the last two decades, while the total number of clergymen has fallen by a third. In the absence of data on the age of the clergy in question this is at best suggestive. There are, however, two studies of English Baptist congregations. A survey of some 100 congregations found that it was generally 'the smaller churches, by and large, [which] are growing while the larger ones are declining' (Briggs 1979: 15). The report goes on to add that the smaller ones are usually more conservative than larger congregations. A second survey controlled for size by comparing only those with more than fifty members. Radical and 'middle of the road' ministers tended to have declining congregations, while conservative evangelical ministers had growing congregations (Beasley-Murray and Wilkinson 1981: 36).

THE STARK AND BAINBRIDGE EXPLANATION OF LIBERAL DECLINE

Before presenting my explanation of liberal decline, with its stress on the organizational precariousness of diffuse belief-systems, I will consider a recent alternative. Stark and Bainbridge's 'rewards and compensators' theory of religion (1985) includes an explanation for the failure of liberal Protestantism. If it is the case that we all want rewards which we cannot have (if only for Durkheim's reason that once we get what we presently want, our aspirations increase), we are in the market for compensators, which Stark and Bainbridge rather confusingly define as both substitutes for rewards and explanations of how rewards might be attained at some future date. A detailed critique of the Stark and Bainbridge theory has been presented elsewhere (Wallis and Bruce 1986: 47–80; Wallis and Bruce 1984). This discussion will concentrate on their account of liberal Protestant decline.

For Stark and Bainbridge, only supernatural belief-systems can offer compensators that are both sufficiently satisfying (the meek inherit the earth, not just a job promotion) and safe from refutation (there is no way of here and now knowing what, if anything, the meek will inherit). Naturalistic compensators are generally both petty and testable. Hence belief-systems which claim to deal with the big things in life will become more popular if they become more supernaturalistic, as Dianetics did in changing from a secular psychotherapy to the religion of the Church of Scientology (Wallis 1976). Those religions which reduce their supernaturalism will decline fastest: the fate of liberal Protestantism. A number of the theoretical assumptions built into the explanation are dubious. As I have already suggested, there is clearly some difference in the testability of theories about the natural and supernatural worlds, but Stark and Bainbridge exaggerate it. It should be clear that many propositions about the natural world are, for most people, taken on faith. On the other hand, it is equally obvious that, for those people who believe that sort of thing, the proposition that, for example, getting right with Jesus makes us happier and better people, is every bit as testable as the claim that what appear to be solid objects are really full of

127

space. However, detailed criticism of the theoretical assumptions can be found elsewhere. The discussion here will confine itself to an examination of the evidence which relates to the proposition that liberal Protestantism has declined in popularity because it has failed to satisfy a desire for compensators.

If it is the case that people have abandoned liberal Protestantism because it does not offer sufficiently powerful compensators, they should have moved to a more supernaturalistic form of religion: either conservative Protestantism or something quite different, such as Roman Catholicism or a new religious movement. Unfortunately for Stark and Bainbridge, there is no evidence that the new religious movements have been swollen by dissatisfied liberal Protestants. At a rough estimate, the major British Protestant denominations lost half a million members between 1970 and 1975 alone. In 1980 there were 588 Moonies resident in Britain. There were 536 British Children of God in 1981 (Wallis and Bruce 1986: 20). This hardly suggests that people leaving major denominations are going to new religions. A longitudinal study of changing religious affiliation in Canada similarly shows no evidence of switching to new religious movements (Bibby and Weaver 1985).

Furthermore, Stark and Bainbridge's own data are unimpressive. A major piece of evidence suffers from the ecological fallacy. They demonstrate that the popularity of new religious movements (which curiously they measure by counting the number of organizations rather than by the total membership of such movements) is greatest in those areas where the traditional Christian denominations are weakest. But this, of course, tells us nothing about the numbers of people involved in new religions or their reasons for such involvement. We can accept that there is a positive correlation, between secularization and the presence of new religious movements, without accepting the Stark and Bainbridge conclusion that secularization is a self-limiting process. It could simply be that the decline of older religions makes a larger number of people available for recruitment to alternatives. What are important are the numbers of the unchurched who make use of their new found freedom to affiliate to an alternative (very few!) – and their reasons for becoming unchurched in the first place.

If the Stark and Bainbridge theory is to be taken seriously, it should be the case that those who left mainstream churches which became thoroughly liberal went to more conservative churches. Actually, some of them did, but not for the reasons Stark and Bainbridge suggest. Dissent from the merger which created the United Reformed Church has already been mentioned. Most of it came from Congregationalists. Of 2,370 Congregational groups, 1,815 joined the URC, 300 joined the Congregational Federation, 110 joined the Evangelical Fellowship of Congregational Churches, and 140 remained independent. By 1984, a further twelve churches had left the URC for eithe the Federation or the EFCC, five had left the Federation for the EFCC; and five new congregations had been formed and affiliated to the EFCC.

The crucial point about the URC relocations was made to me in a number of interviews with Congregational leaders. The people who refused to join were conservative evangelicals whose position, within the theologically mixed Congregationalists, had been precarious for some time and who refused to enter an organization which would be predominantly liberal. They left in order to *remain*, rather than to become, conservatives. There is no reason at all to suppose that they had previously been committed to the liberal Protestantism which became the dominant ethos of the URC, and suddenly discovered themselves to be dissatisfied with liberalism. Precisely the same point can be made about the conservatives who refused to stay in the denominations which formed the American United Church of Christ in 1957.

The political conflict gives added dimensions to religion in Northern Ireland but a similar, albeit exaggerated, pattern is evident there. Those people who have been recruited to Ian Paisley's Free Presbyterian Church since its foundation in 1951 have very largely been the most conservative Presbyterians and Baptists in Ulster, not unhappy liberals (Bruce 1986). Like those who refused to join the URC, they have shifted allegiance in order to prevent further dilution of what was left of their reformed Protestantism. They were conservatives who finally concluded that the denomination with which they were associated had become too apostate to deserve their continued support.

A major area of conservative Protestant growth in Britain has been the usually misnamed 'house church movement' (Walker 1985). As yet there are no good survey data which bear on the motives of those who have become active in this amorphous movement, and one can only speak from personal observation and anecdote, but it is my impression that the majority of these new pentecostalists were previously active in other conservative Protestant organizations (surprisingly, there seem to have been more defectors from the Brethren and Baptist groups than from the last wave of pentecostal organizations).[5]

Stark and Bainbridge, as if aware of the poverty of data to support their argument, shift tack from suggesting that it is disaffected liberals who move to conservative Protestant churches, to claiming that the *children* of the now atheistic defectors from the liberal churches will be recruited to conservative Protestantism. Hardly suprisingly, given the large number of potential candidates, there has been the odd celebrity conversion. Bill Murray, the son of Madeline Murray O'Hair, the leading American secularist campaigner whose lawsuit in the 1960s was crucial in having public prayer in schools adjudged to be unconstitutional, is now a leading campaigner for school prayer. But the odd celebrity apart, there is little or no evidence for the revised Stark and Bainbridge claim. As will be made clear in the next chapter, conservative Protestant churches primarily recruit from the families of existing members.

AN ALTERNATIVE EXPLANATION: ORGANIZATIONAL PRECARIOUSNESS

The major problem with the Stark and Bainbridge theory is that it rests on assumptions about why people leave or join churches for which they, and most of us, have no evidence. They have neither longitudinal nor biographical data which would allow evaluation of customer satisfaction. In the absence of such data, I would like to suggest an alternative explanation for the decline of liberal Protestantism which makes far fewer assumptions about consumer reactions, and which does not rest on a highly contentious theory. Rather than consider the potential to satisfy inherent in any belief-system, I wish to explore the organizational or structural consequences of liberal Protestant beliefs.

In Chapter 2 the different epistemological assumptions which underlie the four main traditions of authority within Christianity were described. It was suggested that the traditions which base themselves on the Bible, Culture/Reason, and the Spirit will all have problems of maintaining order. All three are inherently democratic, in that they are what Wallis called 'epistemologically individualistic' (Wallis 1976: 11–18). Anybody can claim to have insight into the will of God, as expressed through these three channels. The schismatic consequences of the reformed Protestant stress on the Bible as the sole source of authoritative knowledge have been described and explained.

What saves liberal Protestantism from the fractiousness of either conservative Protestantism or the charismatic/pentecostal tradition is its comparative indifference to doctrine. Liberals are relativists, explicit or implicit. They no longer believe that there is one way to salvation. The willingness to tolerate, or the enthusiasm to embrace, diversity, saves liberalism from organizational fragmentation, but it has its own costs. Building on the observations of Demerath and Thiessen (1966), Budd (1967), and Wallis (1980), we can develop an understanding of the organizational problems of a diffuse belief-system which goes a long way to explaining the decline of liberal Protestantism.

Product profile

The first problem of diffuseness is a lack of a strong 'product profile'. There is little by way of an agreed body of doctrine to define the faith, and what identity a liberal Protestant church retains is largely based on peripheral characteristics, such as the regional or class identity of its supporters, or on a memory of a time when it did have a clear identity. In the public perception, Methodists have good hymns and tend to be professional people. The Episcopalian Church in Scotland has a more refined sense of liturgy than its Presbyterian competition, and is the natural home for English émigrés in Scotland, and so on. To assert that liberal Protestantism does not have a clear shared body of belief is not to suggest that liberal theologians do not know what they believe. Clearly they do, but the complexity of professional liberal theology does not easily translate into a language which ordinary people can appreciate. To take a recent and controversial example, David Jenkins, who became Bishop of Durham in 1984, has a highly complex theology, but his own best efforts have failed to prevent the general public from seeing his position as one of rejecting traditional Christian beliefs. To the ordinary Anglican, Jenkins is the man who does not believe in the Virgin Birth, the bodily resurrection, the life-everlasting, eternal damnation, and so on. Evangelicals like to recount the story that Rudolph Bultmann, when he was in the pulpit, preached a conservative evangelical gospel. True or not, the tale has the merit that it neatly reflects the difficulties of translating what Bultmann wrote on the need for 'de-mythologizing' into terms which ordinary Christians can comprehend as being something other than a rejection of the Christian tradition. There may be a difference between calling the gospel stories myths and saying that they are not true, but the difference does not travel well and is not widely appreciated.

Boundary maintenance and goal selection

A lack of a clear product profile or identity brings with it the problem of boundary maintenance. To use a territorial analogy, belief-systems, like countries, call for boundaries between themselves and other belief-systems. Conservative Protestants know just who is on the Lord's side and who is not. Liberal Protestants are unable to describe their boundaries. Many go so far as to denounce the activity of boundary maintenance itself, seeing it as a sign of insecurity or immaturity, and are fond of describing their mission, in the language of a second Enlightenment, as one of bringing the faith to a world which has 'come of age'. It is significant that John Bowden, the editor of the SCM Press, a leading publisher of liberal Protestant theology, does not think 'that there is any point in trying to draw distinctions between Christians and non-Christians for most practical purposes' (Bowden 1970: 12). He concludes his book *Who Is a Christian?* by saying: 'It should be clear by now that there is not going to be a straight answer. It is difficult to see how there could be' (ibid.: 111).

An inability to maintain the boundaries of the faith creates serious organizational problems. To liberal Protestants, it might seem unchristian to be concerned about safeguarding resources, but there are basic difficulties for organizations which do not operate membership tests. Churches and other religious organizations require funds to maintain and promote their beliefs. Ministers have to be paid and buildings have to be maintained. Recruiting drives, of whatever nature, need funding. Even a movement as organizationally unsophisticated as the Cooneyites needs some idea of who is a valid member and who is not. The 'two by twos', as they were known, relied on an unpaid ministry of evangelists who travelled in pairs (Parker and Parker 1982). They lived entirely by faith, which effectively meant that supporters were expected to house, clothe, and feed the evangelists. If they were to conserve and use their resources efficiently, they needed to confine their support of itinerant missionaries to those who held their beliefs. Every cuckoo is a corresponding loss to the movement.

The allocation of resources cannot usually be separated from the issue of selecting goals, and this brings us back to the problem of shared identity. Diffuse belief-systems do not readily produce goals which the majority of believers will agree to support. The last days of the Student Christian Movement saw a number of disputes which neatly demonstrate the difficulties liberal Protestants have in producing an agreed purpose and programme. By the late 1960s and 1970s, the SCM had become so broad that only the most inclusive definition of Christianity would have made its name an accurate description. Both in an attempt to attract new student interest, and because it was felt to be the right thing to do, the SCM began to invest its staff and financial resources in novel projects. One was the funding of communes. Until the early 1970s, SCM full-time staff had operated with the conventional separation of home and work. They lived in ordinary houses and went to work organizing local branches, holding meetings, planning evangelistic crusades, editing magazines, and so on. Influenced by the hippy commune movement, the SCM decided to purchase a number of large houses which would serve as homes and offices for the regional staff and as centres of spirituality. People who sympathized with the aims of the SCM would be encouraged to share the houses. Communal meals and informal acts of worship would give the movement 'living bases'. The central office staff also moved from London to a large crumbling mansion in the Bristol countryside which was intended to be office, commune, and conference centre. The problem, of course, is that this expensive investment of resources was not – could not – be kept solely for committed supporters or directed solely towards the promotion of the goals of the SCM, because the diffuse belief-system did not readily produce goals. Being unable to define its mission in any but the loosest terms, the SCM could not determine who should have the benefit of its resources.

Boundary maintenance problems dogged the Movement's relationship with a wide variety of interest groups. Money was given as unsecured loans to Third World liberation, feminist, radical, and ethnic minority organizations. A 'community education centre' was funded and money was promised for a 'Free University of Black Studies'. The SCM's willingness to give its money to such projects may have been commendable but it amounted to a redistribution of the Movement's resources to a variety of interests which had only the most tenuous connection with organized Christianity. Although such investment was regarded as 'evangelistic' in the sense that it demonstrated the relevance of Christianity, it did not result in any identifiable increase in recruitment or commitment to the SCM's version of the Christian faith. I make this point, not to criticize the movement but to make clear that the SCM had little choice but to be uncritical and inclusive in consideration of what sorts of activity to fund; it had no criteria for determining its purpose. Those who had been active in earlier eras tended to blame the Movement's lack of direction and financial mismanagement on the 1970s generation of staffers, but the roots of the problem can be traced back at least to the post-war period.

When the Movement was theologically conservative, it had no problem in knowing what it ought to do. When it first became liberal and ecumenical, it still had little difficulty because it was working within a theologically conservative Christian environment and gaining considerable cohesion from the conservative backgrounds of many members and activists. The serious problems began when it tried to take its liberal and ecumenical faith to people outside the churches. In its anxiety to demonstrate to the secular world that Christianity was indeed relevant, it ended up doing little more than endorsing the interests and positions of the secular world.

Because its rapid turnover of members and activists made it a sensitive barometer, the SCM displayed, in a particularly dramatic fashion, the problems which follow from diffuse beliefs, but they are common to all organizational expressions of liberal Protestantism. With support for traditional religious activities apparently waning (and being unable to agree on what doctrines should be presented in such activities), activists seek a new direction. But any new goals (a) may already be in the domain of

134

other better established secular organizations and (b) may be divisive.

To take the problem of competing with secular organizations first, although Christian Aid undoubtedly does an excellent job, it is difficult to see in what respect it differs from secular relief organizations. Those churches which have invested in community ministries in new housing estates and deprived inner city areas have quickly found that the clergy are acting as untrained social workers rather than propagators of the gospel.[6] Church members may resent their donations being used for things which are not obviously their business or which are done better by more specialized organizations. The rapid hand-over to the state of Church of Scotland schools showed that financially hard-pressed congregations were keen to move to a restricted view of what the Church should be and do. Similar reasoning will make them reluctant to endorse an expansionist clergy's search for new purpose.

Works of a non-political or charitable nature may command general support within the liberal denomination. There is always, however, the danger that one section of the denomination will pursue goals which offend another. For the SCM, the promotion of communes and the Free University for Black Studies seriously alienated some supporters. Within the British liberal denominations, support for the World Council of Churches Programme to Combat Racism has been a contentious issue, as has clergy support for the Campaign for Nuclear Disarmament and criticism of the social and economic policies of the Thatcher government. .

To summarize, liberal Protestant churches (in common with other sorts of movements with diffuse belief-systems) have general problems of identifying goals and mobilizing people to support them (a) because there is little consensus about goals; (b) because the search for new goals may take them into competition with better established agencies; and (c) because any new interests are likely to alienate some section of the membership.

Given that goal selection is primarily in the hands of the clergy, the above discussion suggests a complex link between the declining membership and influence of the major Protestant churches, and their search for new relevance. It might be supposed that 'trendy vicars' have taken to politics or social work because the clergy 'are being edged out of the old secure role in an understood social structure' (Martin 1979: 17). It is certainly the case that the decline of demand for, and the importance of, traditional clerical roles has been part of the impetus to find new relevance. I would add that, in the Protestant case, a general expansion of clerical roles was made both possible and inevitable by the inability of liberal Protestantism to clearly define its nature and its purpose. The diffuse belief-system has built into it enormous potential for role spillage.[7]

Recruitment

Members are the key resource for the organizational base of any belief-system. The inability of liberal Protestantism to define its boundaries seriously impaired its ability to recruit. In the first place, an ecumenical mission is a socio-psychological absurdity: the drive to proselytize comes from the conviction that one possesses knowledge which others do not possess and which is vital to their salvation. The more that one allows that there are other ways to salvation, and the greater the number of such other ways that one permits, the less reason one has for promoting one's own beliefs. When Tatlow formulated the SCM's interdenominational basis of faith, he intended to comprehend trinitarian Christians. Already in the post-war period, that inclusive definition had been extended to take in the Unitarians. In 1982, Richard Zipfel, an American Catholic ex-General Secretary of SCM then working for a Catholic Church bureaucracy, authored a report which argued that Rastafarianism was a valid religion which should be permitted the use of Catholic Church facilities. Although each generation of liberals tends to maintain boundaries which are just a little more inclusive than the ones it grew up with, the logic of liberalism is universalism. Universalism can only proselytize in the sense of arguing for further inclusiveness and relaxation of boundaries. It cannot recruit outsiders because, instead of challenging, it endorses what the outsiders are already doing.

But even if liberal Protestants could individually have maintained the degree of conviction required to devote energy to trying to convert others to their faith, the organizational problems of diffuseness would have remained. Individual liberal 'evangelists' would have had either to contradict each other or confine themselves to increasingly empty pieties.

Recruitment can in turn be related to the problem of goal selection. In part, people join organizations because they want to see the organization's aims and ambitions realized. This is less the case with a church than with, for example, a social movement organization such as the Campaign for Nuclear Disarmament; church membership is more an expression of a commitment to an ideology and a type of worship than it is an instrumental goal-directed activity. None the less, goals influence recruitment. As already suggested, any denomination's search for new relevance and purpose may be self-defeating, either because the new goals are regarded by some members as undesirable or because the goals are accepted as valuable, and members suspect they are better pursued in another organization. In the first case, members alienated by the new direction leave. In the second case, members sympathetic to the new direction may divert their energies to working with CND, feminist groups, anti-racist groups, inner-city housing cooperatives, and so on.

Recruitment: mass media

An important sub-theme of any discussion of modern proselytizing is mass evangelism and the use of the electronic media. The point will be returned to in the later discussion of religious revivals, but mass evangelism, be it of the more traditional stadium variety or the modern television version, does little to recruit the heathen to Christianity (Ward 1980; Clelland *et al.* 1974). These means of spreading the gospel serve more to reinforce the beliefs of existing believers, and to maintain a network which can be used for alerting believers to new threats or needs. But even if mass evangelism does not extend conservative Protestantism, the near monopoly of the electronic church which evangelicals possess has been useful, if only in giving evangelicalism a high public profile and considerable fund-raising capacity.

It is worth thinking about the failure of liberal Protestants to make use of the mass media. They complain about the trivializing of the gospel, which such presentations generally involve, and imply that they would not want to compete in what Hadden and Swann (1981) call 'televangelism'. However, there are good reasons to suppose that, even if liberals wished to compete, they would be less successful than conservative Protestants. Fundamentalism and evangelicalism can be readily reduced to simple dogmas and presented in brief and telling homilies. The creed of the liberal Protestant does not carry well on radio and television to an audience which has become accustomed to sensation and which has a short attention span. 'Get saved or go to hell' is a message ideally suited to modern methods of communication. It probably does not convince many people who do not start out with a predisposition to believe it, but it holds the interest of those who do.

Recruitment: the next generation

Liberal Protestantism has difficulty in recruiting by socialization, and socialization is vital. Bibby and Brinkerhoff's study of recruitment to twenty evangelical Protestant churches in a western Canadian city shows that 72 per cent of those who joined in a four-year period were reaffiliates from other evangelical denominations or congregations. Only 28 per cent were 'converts', and of these, 68 per cent were the children of evangelicals (Bibby and Brinkerhoff 1974). In concluding his explanation of the growth of the evangelical Christian Reformed Church, Bouma says it 'grows primarily by retaining those who were born into it' (Bouma 1979: 135). As these are churches which pride themselves on their outreach activities, it would be difficult to exaggerate the importance of the recruitment of members' children.

The socialization of the children of believers into the faith is a problem for all faiths. The rise of liberal Protestantism demonstrates, in the biographies of Tatlow, Drummond, Whyte, and the countless others who could have been offered as examples, that conservative evangelical parents do not always succeed in raising their children to stay in the faith of the fathers. However, a diffuse belief-system is especially disadvantaged in two respects. The first, already mentioned, is the lack of will to indoctrinate children, which comes from the same source as the lack of interest in converting outsiders. The second concerns the breadth of options that are left open by early socialization. Let us assume that childhood socialization lays a foundation of basic ideas which have considerable influence on (although they do not completely determine) later receptivity to competing ideas. Conservative Protestant children may remain in the faith, become more liberal, or convert to something quite different (which would include atheism). But any of these except the first requires a considerable change and a rejection of their childhood socialization. The offspring of liberal Protestants can become almost anything with hardly any rebellion against the culture of their parents. Because liberal Protestantism permits, and even encourages, diversity, the foundation which it establishes for children is barely restricting. The only possibility which is unlikely is conversion to a more conservative variety of Protestantism; a move which is made difficult by the lack of belief in the possibility of one true religion. Liberal children are socialized into tolerance and something approaching relativism.

There is a technical problem for those interested in transmitting liberal Protestantism to children. Liberal critics may be right to see fundamentalist preaching as trivializing, but something like trivializing is exactly what is needed for the education of young children. The socialization of young children necessarily involves bowdlerizing and simplifying. The virtue of conservative Protestantism is that it survives such treatment better. Children can understand and believe in a God with the white beard who actually did make the world in six days and who dictated the Bible, to faithful stenographers. Apart from anything else, conservative Protestantism has the advantage that its treatment of the Bible, as containing true stories of miraculous occurrences, makes for appealing presentation to children. Because conservative Protestantism is realistic and dogmatic, what is left after it has been reduced to the level of the comic book is still consistent with the mature product. When it suffers the same translation, liberalism appears either empty or uncertain and ambiguous. The 'de-mythologizing' liberal has the choice of either attempting a sophisticated presentation from the start or teaching the Bible in the same way as the conservative does, and then having to disabuse the child of simplistic notions in the late teenage years. The first way is technically very difficult, and the second runs the risk of disillusioning the adolescent at just the time when he or she is becoming aware of alternative cultures and belief-systems.

Maintaining commitment

Closely related to recruitment is commitment. The direction of my argument may be better signposted if it is introduced with a brief discussion of a view of commitment which is antithetical to my own. In her study of the longevity of a variety of communitarian movements, Kanter (1968, 1972a, 1972b) offers some interesting observations about the value of 'commitment mechanisms'. Movements which demanded considerable sacrifice, renunciation (often involving celibacy and child–parent separation), the abandonment of personal property, involvement in shared ritual, the mortification of the self, and the subordination of the individual to the community, survived longer than those which had few such 'commitment mechanisms'. Putting it simply, those movements which demand most from their members get the most commitment. However, in her concentration on the way in which organizations deploy 'devices' for extracting and retaining commitment, Kanter loses sight of the possibility that such devices reflect, rather than produce, commitment, and implies that such mechanisms can be deployed by any movement irrespective of its goals or belief-system.

McGaw tends to a similar view in his comparison of two American Presbyterian congregations: one 'mainstream', the other 'charismatic'. He explains that the more conservative congregation has the more committed members because it is better able to provide its members with 'meaning' and 'a sense of belonging' but then divorces the ability to do this from the congregation's ideology. He advances three arguments. First, he suggests that 'primary group bonds with members of one's religious community are instrumental in bringing about religious commitment'. Second, he argues that 'the greater the extent to which the local religious community and its leaders serve as a reference group for the members, exclusive of a wider religious or secular community, the greater the intensity of religious commitment in the group'. Finally, he claims that 'the more close-knit the community, the more likely are the beliefs to be strong, consensually agreed upon and reasonably uniform. The combination of strong similar beliefs and community will reinforce the intensity of commitment' (McGaw 1979: 146–63). In his final paragraph, McGaw takes issue with the claim that it is

140

conservative beliefs which explain the success of conservative denominations.

> There is little reason to suppose, on the basis of the evidence presented here, that in a hundred years or in less tumultuous times the liberals and mainliners may not find a way to be the dominant providers of meaning and belonging, much as they were a hundred years ago. The *nature* of the belief[s] ... seems no more important than the *social context* in which they are presented.
>
> (McGaw1979: 161)

What McGaw is forgetting is that 100 years ago the dominant providers of meaning were not liberal. The mainstream churches were considerably more conservative then than they are now. I do not want to overemphasize the role of beliefs, but McGaw is posing a false duality of belief and social context, and by so doing, suggesting, as does Kanter, that social context is efficacious, independent of beliefs. He offers causal relations without justifying the supposed direction of cause, and he supposes the less likely of the alternatives. For example, the claim that the more religious leaders serve as a reference group for members, the greater the degree of commitment, is taken to show that 'serving as a reference group' causes commitment. Firstly, some sleight of hand (or misleading grammar) needs to be exposed. Reference groups do not offer themselves to 'serve' as reference groups. A reference group only exists by virtue of some other people regarding it as a reference group. Religious leaders only become a reference group when members look to them for leadership and guidance and use them as standards by which to measure and evaluate their own performance. That is, the attitudes of the members, the led, are logically and temporally prior. So, with much more sense, we can invert McGaw's causal connection and say 'the more committed members are, the more they will regard their religious leaders as a reference group'.

The curious thing about McGaw's position is that it is not internally consistent. Before the conclusion in which he suggests that the mainline churches may yet again have highly committed memberships, McGaw clearly says that the degree of commitment is related to the strength of interpersonal ties in the believing community, and he lists 'strong similar beliefs' as a factor in the maintenance of such ties. Precisely; it is the obvious absence of beliefs, which are either strong or shared, which explains why liberal Protestantism attracts and sustains far less commitment than its conservative competitor.

In criticizing Kanter and McGaw for supposing that social context or commitment mechanisms can be regarded as causes of commitment (rather than expressions and reinforcers of commitment), I do not want to argue that conservative Protestant beliefs are intrinsically more satisfying than the liberal alternatives (although that may well be the case). What I do want to suggest is that the epistemological assumptions of belief-systems have important consequences for both the ways in which individuals can hold such beliefs and for the ways in which organizations can organize to maintain and promote them. Even if liberals wanted to, they could not with conviction adopt Kanter's commitment mechanisms or construct McGaw's social context. The essential diffuseness of liberal Protestantism prevents it from deploying a wide range of commitment mechanisms.

The correct causal connection between commitment 'mechanisms' and commitment is that the former are an expression of the latter which may serve to reinforce it. Evangelistic outreach, for example, is engaged in by conservative Protestants because they believe it is the duty of right-believing Christians. It is a consequence of their religious commitment. At the same time, evangelistic work often reinforces members' commitment. The very act of advertising the faith, and the constant harping on its virtues so entailed, will either consolidate faith or expose their own uncertainty to the people engaged in outreach. Promoting the faith will either deepen or destroy it.

Evangelism thus has the consequence of increasing the individual and personal commitment of those members who do it (Bromley and Shupe 1979). It can also serve to increase the cohesion of a group of believers through a more roundabout route. The stress on the need to maintain a 'Christian witness' can be used by members to discipline themselves and each other. A study of a small group of young evangelical Christians noticed that the word 'witness' was usually used in the context of censuring or gossiping about some member who was deviating from accepted norms of behaviour (Bruce 1978). It is common in evangelical and fundamentalist circles for 'backsliding' members to be accused of not keeping up a good witness'. Even if witnessing is, if taken literally, pointless in that the performances are only witnessed by other believers, it still has value in contributing to internal cohesion. When part of the believers' claim to superiority rests on their willingness to make a public stand for the faith, then the behavioural consequences of such a claim can become a useful vehicle for social control within the believing community. But to return to the debate with Kanter, witnessing can only be part of a system of social control because members believe that God wants Christians to live their lives in a manner which makes those lives a testimony to his saving work; belief first, then commitment mechanism.

Organized crusades and outreach meetings can also have latent functions' in providing work for church members and thus creating a sense of usefulness independent of the results of such work. If large numbers are not brought to the Lord through some endeavour, this does not mean that the work was a failure. A seed may have been planted which the Holy Spirit will work on in God's good time. And such crusades are less of an obvious failure than the recruitment statistics might suggest. They provide excellent opportunities for the children of members to announce their commitment. Many evangelical outreach services are similar in consequence to the confirmation services of mainstream denominations. A similar point can be made about fund-raising. Critics of mass evangelism (especially that which uses television) have often complained that a high proportion of funds raised are spent on either maintaining the bureaucracies of evangelistic organizations or preaching to the converted (Bruce forthcoming). However, my interviews with Christians who tithe to church work suggest that even if such funding is at first sight economically irrational, it has the important 'latent function' of making the donors feel good that they are contributing to the Lord's work.

To summarize the point, it may seem that the failure of evangelistic activities to markedly increase the size of conservative Protestant denominations refutes my claim that liberal Protestantism is undermined by its inability to recruit. Far from it; irrespective of their value as means of attracting outsiders, the evangelistic endeavours of conservative denominations produce a number of what are largely unintended consequences, of which

the most important are an enhancment of each member's sense o
commitment, and an increase in the organization's cohesion.

Defection

The metaphor of boundary maintenance is a good one because i
reminds us that belief-systems and movements do not operate in a
vacuum. Generally, they compete for the time and attention o
potential followers. What makes diffuse belief-systems particularly
precarious is their weakness relative to other better defined and
more coherent belief-systems. Speaking of humanist organ
izations, Wallis pointed to the damaging competition from:

> other movements and organisations established to pursue
> specific and limited goals relating to morality, education, civi
> rights etc. which, being able to mobilise a more consensually
> based membership, often seem more likely to achieve succes:
> than the Humanist movement in that particular field. Such
> competing allegiances are always likely to draw away members
> who feel the need to 'do something' rather than constantly to
> discuss what should be done.

(Wallis 1980: 132)

Again, the SCM can offer in miniature good examples of the
problem as it affects liberal Protestantism generally. The SCM's
response to a decline of student interest in Christianity was to
identify those things which students were interested in and present
Christianity as being similar and complementary to that interest.
Thus conferences were organized on Christ and Marx, and Christ
and Freud. If students were interested in communes, then the
SCM would organize a conference on Christian communitar-
ianism and set up Christian communes. The danger of building
bridges, of course, is that bridges can carry traffic in both
directions. On one shore, one has the diffuse belief-system, of
which Demerath and Thiessen say: 'With such vague goals, passion
dissipates. There are no concrete actions, no gauges by which to
measure progress' (Demerath and Thiessen 1966: 685). At the
other end of the various bridges that the SCM built were
movement organizations which were narrower in their goals and
hence much more likely to attain them. The membership of the
Edinburgh SCM commune house went off *en masse* to join the local

Trotskyite party: a highly rational response to the then fashionable SCM claim that Marxism was really Christian.

It is also likely that the organizations on the other shore will have better credentials for whatever arena or activity the liberal Protestants are attempting to 'invade'. Social work is done by trained social workers. Politics is better done by skilled and experienced politicians. The church in the modern industrial society has superior credentials in only one area: the mediation of the supernatural. To say this is not, as Pinder (1971) has misleadingly suggested in his criticisms of some of Wilson's observations of diversification in liberal churches, to tell the churches what they ought to do or to give sociologists the right to establish the goals of religious organizations. It is only to recognize the reality of the differential distribution of credentials in modern societies. When churches move away from the mediation of the supernatural, they face competition from other organizations which are taken to be better qualified and which, having narrower goals, are seen as more likely to succeed.

Far more could be said to illustrate the precariousness of a diffuse belief-system, but enough has been done to establish the main point. Having no agreed ideological centre, the beliefs cannot be given the organizational base which is necessary to maintain and promote them.

AN ASIDE ON LITURGY

Although it is tangential to the main argument, it is interesting that the rise of liberalism and ecumenism has also been accompanied in places by a revival of interest in liturgy. Wilson has explained this (and the more general revival of denominational identities) as a consequence of the erosion of the significance of the Christian ministry in a modern secular climate. As clergymen have seen the importance of the beliefs they represent being diminished, some have reacted by becoming increasingly 'professional':

> The Free Churches now resist further secularization, they see in ritual a protection, a necessary and indispensable expression of religiosity . . . . Their plain old liturgies develop and are elaborated. The aesthetic appeal is added to the higher status and the

145

centrality (within contemporary religious discourse) of more
elaborate and traditional liturgical forms. So in all the Free
Churches we see the growth of sacramentalism, the heightened
authority and apartness of the minister, who increasingly
approximates to the position of a priest of a Church of higher
persuasion.

(Wilson 1966: 160)

This observation can be extended to incorporate the problem of
public perceptions of religion in a secular age. In a strongly
religious Protestant culture, clergymen were set aside (as were
believers generally) by their beliefs and the behavioural patterns to
which such beliefs gave rise. One could recognize religion by its
ideological content. As unbelief has spread, Protestantism has lost
that quality of being recognized as a distinct set of true beliefs
about the world. The conservative variety has lost some recogniz-
ability because the audience are less and less familiar with it and
now see it primarily as a puritan moral discipline. The liberal
variety has become even less distinct because its representatives
have reduced the behavioural differences which separated them
from the surrounding environment. The result is that when
film-makers wish to show 'religion being done', they bring on
priests or rabbis, professionals who look religious and do visibly
religious things. A rediscovery of liturgy permits the religious
professional to be visible against the secular environment because
it provides uniquely religious activities.

Another point about the value of sacramentalism can be added.
The last days of the SCM, when its relativistic impulses had to be
taken to the logical conclusion of having no restriction of
membership, were accompanied by a revived interest in worship.
The Wick Court commune, which housed the central office and
conference centre, had a small bare room set aside as a chapel, and
adorned, I recall, with only a Celtic cross. Two staff members wrote
an 'Order Book' before going off to join a single-minded religious
community (another example of bridge-building defection). For
an organization that was almost totally devoid of shared ideology,
there was a considerable interest in shared acts of worship. There
was also an interest in reinventing 'traditional' forms of worship.
There were even 'services' with parts in Latin. The value of this
renewed interest in archaic, if ersatz, forms of liturgy seems to have

been that it allowed the participants to avoid recognizing and confronting their lack of consensus. The rediscovery of Celtic Christianity allowed young Protestants and Catholics to overlook the Reformation and to ignore the fact that, if they believed anything at all, they believed different things. Similarly the avoidance of the vernacular allowed them to evade the problem of stating clearly, in a language they could all understand, what it was that they believed. To have faced that would have been to discover that there was little or nothing shared.

The social construction of tradition is not a particularly new response to fragmentation and uncertainty. In 1938, George McLeod, a gifted Church of Scotland leader and First World War hero turned pacifist, founded the Iona Community. The Cathedral on Iona, the cradle of Celtic Christianity, was restored. Young ministers were invited to spend three months with the Community: half on the island and half working in a factory. This was followed by a two-year assistantship in an inner city parish interspersed with refresher visits to Iona. An admirer of McLeod had the insight to see the logic behind his mixture of a radical, modern ministry to the secular world, an island retreat, and the revival of Celtic Christianity: 'one suspects, perhaps wrongly, that the emphasis on Celtic Christianity is a device to gain a standpoint independent of Geneva, Canterbury or Rome' (Henderson 1969: 17). I do not want to impugn the motives of Mcleod and others, but 'fudge the issues' might be a more accurate description than 'gain a standpoint'. The great value of Celtic Christianity was that nobody actually knew anything about it. Hence, as with a Rorschach ink blot, they could impute to it almost anything they liked. They could thus retain some sense of community and solidarity in the absence of shared beliefs.

THE PROBLEMS OF CHURCH REUNION

Thus far, this chapter has been concerned with the precariousness of liberal Protestantism as a diffuse belief-system. In so far as ecumenism has been discussed, it has been treated as an aspect of liberalism. There is one observation about ecumenism, however, which should be separated out for particular consideration.

In the introductory discussion of secularization, the importance of radical breaks was mentioned. Any individual's religious commitment is a complex matter. Some evidence of a decline in that commitment will be gradual; donations to church work become smaller and less frequent, and church is attended less often. From the point of statistical evidence of religious commitment, the clearest change is seen, not in such signs of gradual withdrawal but in disaffiliation. The point was made earlier that certain sorts of changes present people with opportunities to abandon, to change or to renew their church membership. The more common are such opportunities in a society in which religion is of diminishing significance, the more rapid will be the decline of church membership.

This is important because it introduces a point which has usually been absent from discussions of the consequences of church reunions. Although a short-term response to ecumenism is to exaggerate what separates the denominations, as each seeks to maintain some sort of identity, the long-term aim of the ecumenical movement is the reunification of the Christian Church. From the point of view of the organizations, there are good reasons for merger. Many members feel that the divided nature of the churches is an obstacle to evangelism. It is no accident that the biggest cross-confessional merger – that which led to the creation of the Church of South India – was strongly promoted by missionaries who felt that the divisions in the Christian Church gave non-Christians too good a reason to be unimpressed by their claims for the superiority of their religion. Especially in a hostile or indifferent world, a common front was seen as essential for the growth (or survival) of the churches.

A second good reason for merger is rationalization and the reduction of 'fixed costs' that would follow. Although all the churches together still do not provide enough places for the total population of the societies in which they operate, most religious organizations have spare capacity given the present demand for, and interest in, their offices. Merger would permit the concentration of resources. Where two buildings are half-full, the same services can be provided in one at half the cost. Such calculations have led a number of local congregations in new housing developments to cooperate in funding a building which can be used by all. Even greater savings could be achieved if such local ventures are repeated at the level of the national organizations.

Such considerations have led sociologists to view church reunion as a response to declining membership. To make the organizations more efficient in a declining market was clearly part of the intentions of those who promoted such schemes but, as I will argue, church merger may well be counter-productive. The evidence at this stage is difficult to assess because, to date, there has been a lot of talk and little actual reunification. Most mergers have been of denominations within the same confessional tradition. In two stages – in 1900 and 1927 – the majority of Scottish Presbyterians regrouped in the national Church of Scotland. In America, there has been a tidying up within Presbyterian and Lutheran traditions. In England, the Bible Christians, the Methodist New Connexion, and the United Methodist Free Churches merged in 1907 to form the United Methodist Church, which united with the Wesleyan Methodists and the Primitive Methodists to form the Methodist Church in 1932. More dramatic schemes to unite Christians of different traditions have so far not borne fruit. Although a committee of the Church of Scotland's General Assembly produced a 'Bishops in Presbytery' model for union with the Scottish Episcopal Church, it was roundly rejected by the Assembly. The long-running discussions in England between the Methodists, the United Reformed Church, and the Anglicans have so far failed to produce agreement. The even more audacious schemes to reverse the Reformation and reunite Protestants and Catholics have so far failed to produce anything other than documents which express varieties of pious goodwill and provoke considerable dissension. Why this should be the case is obvious. If one considers the position of the Church of England, it is clear that the sorts of change which would permit the Anglicans to unite with the Methodists and the United Reform Church are in direct conflict with the changes which would make the Anglicans more acceptable to Rome.

Although there have not yet been cross-confessional mergers, the consequences for membership decline of more limited mergers can be evaluated. In 1955 there were 69,700 members of the Presbyterian Church of England, 209,600 English Congregationalists and 144,000 Welsh Congregationalists. Thus there were 423,300 members in those organizations which planned to merge in 1972 to form the United Reformed Church. Between 1955 and

1970 the combined membership had declined by 107,100: a drop of about a quarter over fifteen years.

The majority of the Welsh Congregationalists did not join the URC but continued as the Union of Welsh Independents. The total claimed membership of the URC at the merger was 192,100. By 1985 it had fallen to 133,000: a decline of 31 per cent in only thirteen years. It might be supposed that the apparently faster rate of decline was due to the withdrawal of the Welsh Congregationalists, but this cannot be a complete explanation. Extrapolation from these numbers is an extremely dubious operation, but in the absence of alternative sources of information, it is worth trying. If one works out the annual membership loss for the English Presbyterians and English Congregationalists (allowing for some 15,000 who opted out in 1972), and projects from the 1970 figures for these two organizations to what size they would have been if they had remained separate and continued to decline at the same rate, then one arrives at a total of 49,300 Presbyterians and 81,300 English Congregationalists. Together they would have totalled some 130,600 members in 1985. The membership of the URC in 1985 was 135,000, which includes about 2,000 members of the Reformed Association of the Churches of Christ who joined the URC in 1981.

Although the absolute totals are not sufficiently reliable to be categorical about the rate of membership decline, the calculations certainly suggest that the formation of the URC did very little to slow down the decline of the organizations that joined it. On the best estimate, they were less than 2 per cent 'less badly off' than they would have been if the merger had not taken place. In contrast, the English Congregationalists who refused to join have shown a smaller proportional decline. The majority of the dissenters joined the Congregational Union of England or the Evangelical Federation of Congregational Churches. Membership figures for these organizations are available for 1975 and 1985 and show that the Congregational Union declined by only 4 per cent over the decade while the Evangelical Federation grew from 5,000 to 7,600 members: an increase of more than 50 per cent (but, note, from a small base). Again, one has to view all of these numbers with a certain degree of scepticism but they do suggest that the organizations which merged to form the URC performed less well than those which stayed out, and that the merger did not have the desired effect of stemming the flow of defectors.

The case of the United Church of Christ in the United states is similar. A merger in 1961 of two liberal denominations caused the most committed conservative section to withdraw and the decline continued after the merger. The percentage changes in membership for five-year periods for the denominations which merged and for the new body were as follows (Doyle and Kelly 1979: 146):

	Percentage and direction membership change
1950-55	+ 8
1955-60	+ 6
1960-65 (merger 1961)	− 8
1965-70	− 5
1970-75	− 7

The merger brought with it a change from growth roughly in line with the growth in the population as a whole to absolute decline.

In the cases of the URC and the UCC, the mergers were accompanied by the withdrawal of the most conservative congregations; precisely the ones that were most successful. Hence we would expect further decline in the now more liberal new organizations. But centrist reunions have another problem in addition to the loss of their conservative and resilient congregations.

A little reflection on what it is that people are members of may explain why reunion does not have the rejuvenating effect that its most enthusiastic exponents expect. Professional church leaders with a strong sense of history may rejoice in the reunification of separated elements of a strong tradition. The two mergers of Presbyterian churches in Scotland were, for activists, emotionally charged and romantic events. Unfortunately, it is only the professionals who leave records of such events and we have to guess about the reactions of ordinary members. My guess is that rank-and-file members draw most of their satisfactions of membership from the building in which they worship and the nature of the congregation of which they are members. Their reference group is the local meeting and not the over-arching organization. After all, only a small number of members will ever attend Presbyteries, Synods, General Assemblies, Annual Meetings, and Conferences. If the purpose of a merger between two denominations is to reduce operating cost, congregations will have to merge and some will have to move. The greater the differences between the two organizations, the greater the change which will be forced on the members of the merging bodies and the greater the likelihood that some members will be offended by such changes. While a merger may be rational for the organizations involved, it has no obvious benefits for many members, who see it simply as unwarranted interference in their religious lives. In such circumstances it is not surprising that a decline is not reversed.

The issue of what consequences follow church reunions is clearly complex and a detailed examination is beyond the scope of this treatment. Any serious theory of church growth and decline has to involve a number of variables which have not been mentioned here: the change in size and age profile of the total population, theological changes, and changes in the socio-economic status of the constituencies involved. One would also have to consider the amount of change which any particular reunion forces on members. My expectation is that ecumenical moves in a declining market will either have no impact on membership or be counter-productive. While the closing of church buildings may be accepted by members as necessary and may even, by taking people out of a building they cannot fill, remove one source of a sense of failure, it is hard to see how amalgamation can lead to any increase in the commitment of members. Whatever gloss religious professionals put on mergers in a declining market, they can hardly be seen as great victories and their purpose will only be achieved if the new body proves more attractive to outsiders than did any of the old denominations. As such mergers are always in the direction of a less distinctive 'product profile' it is hard to see why the new body should succeed where the old ones failed.

CONCLUSION

The reasons for the decline of liberal Protestantism can be stated briefly. In their various ways, Stark and Bainbridge, Kelley, and others have explained the weakness of liberal Protestantism as a result of its failure to satisfy the customers. The contentious compensator notion of Stark and Bainbridge can be replaced with the observation that liberal Protestantism demands very little from its adherents and offers little in return. The problem with comparing the rewards and costs of different belief-systems is that it is not the objective outsider's evaluation which explains whether such belief-systems are maintained: it is the views of believers and potential believers which are important. While I take the view that conservative Protestantism is both more demanding and more satisfying, I am an outsider. Given the ability of one culture to maintain beliefs which another finds fanciful, it is dangerous to suppose that liberal Protestantism is intrinsically unsatisfying (independently of the believers showing us, by their actions, that this is the case). Hence there is a need for caution in attributing the decline of liberalism to its failure to satisfy fundamental needs and desires.

It is possible that Stark and Bainbridge and others have missed an alternative explanation of the decline of liberalism: that it is too successful. Those liberals who feel satisfied with the belief-system are likely to maintain and perhaps exaggerate, but certainly transmit to their children, the liberal ethos, with its tolerance, its implicit universalism, and its faith in the social gospel and in vaguely moral behaviour. In the end, the extreme liberal has no reason to remain active in a liberal Protestant denomination. In the absence of a large increase in the support for conservative Protestantism, the decline of liberal Protestantism suggests that, far from having failed, it has done its job so well that those who accepted it feel no further need for it.

Although there are difficulties in measuring and comparing satisfaction with competing belief-systems, there are equally serious problems with the explanations of those, such as McGaw, who have followed Kanter's lead and attempted to discuss organizational strategies and social contexts as if they were independent of ideology. While there are obviously things which organizations can do to encourage their members to remain committed, the nature and success of such activities is strongly related to the ideology of the organization. Conservative Protestant churches can do things which liberal churches cannot do. What I have tried to do in this discussion is to pioneer an alternative level of analysis which takes ideology seriously but which does not attempt to evaluate customer satisfaction. I have suggested that we can compare certain features of belief-systems that are, in some sense, independent of believers' reactions to them. We can, by a combination of reasoning and observation, infer a series of organizational consequences of belief-systems. In contrast to conservativism, liberal Protestantism shares the organizational precariousness common to all diffuse belief-systems.

Chapter Seven

THE CONSERVATIVE RESPONSE
TO PLURALISM

CHURCH, SECT, AND DENOMINATION

Much of the modern debate about church growth and decline begins from Dean Kelley's *Why Conservative Churches Are Growing* (1972). In his answer to the question of the title, Kelley argues that conservative Protestant Churches grew because they offered 'strong' religion. Twelve characteristics are used to describe conservative and liberal varieties of Protestantism: six for each. Organizations with 'strong' religion (1) demanded considerable sacrifice, (2) disciplined their members, (3) possessed missionary zeal, (4) were ideologically absolutist, (5) made their members conform to common standards in matters peripheral as well as central, and (6) encouraged fanaticism. In contrast, 'weak' religion (1) was relativist, (2) permitted diversity, (3) encouraged dialogue with competing religions, (4) attracted only lukewarm support, (5) was individualist, and (6), rather than forcing members to 'witness' their faith, permitted supporters to remain reserved (Kelley 1972: 56–85).

I entirely accept the substance of Kelley's comparison, which has many parallels with Bryan Wilson's pioneering discussion of the sociological types of the sect and the denomination (Wilson 1959). My only reservation is the same as Wallis's reservation about Wilson's typology, which is that there seems to be an element of '*ad hoc*-ery' about the descriptions. While the main thrust of the comparison is correct, some of its value is lost because of a lack of explanatory economy (Wallis 1976). Even when they are laid out in tabular form, Kelley's comparative observations on strong and weak religion do not form matching pairs, nor is it clear how any of the six items in the two clusters are related to the others.

If one considers what single item in either cluster could generate the others, and what single item could serve as the most potent point of contrast between the two clusters, the best candidate must be that which is at the centre of the argument of this book: that which is concerned with epistemology. The main point of the last chapter was not that liberal Protestantism did not maintain its boundaries, recruit new members, socialize children into the faith, or maintain the commitment of existing members, although that is the case; it was that the epistemological premise of 'new light' prevented liberal Protestantism from doing these things. The conservative Protestant claim to have access to a single unchanging source of authoritative salvational knowledge is the key to an economical description of conservative Protestantism. To use Wallis's terms, the liberal or denominational form is 'pluralistically legitimate' (that is, does not claim unique access to the one truth), while the conservative variety is 'uniquely legitimate' (Wallis 1976: 11–18).

There seems little value in rehearsing or adding to the well-aired definitional discussions of church, sect, and denomination. The sociology of religion is amply provided with the products of such typologizing (Wilson 1959; Wallis 1975; Robertson 1972: ch. 5). However, Kelley's comparisons of strong and weak religion, and my criticisms, do draw on such debates, even if the borrowings have so far not been made explicit. As I have already described conservative and liberal Protestantism as being, respectively, sectarian and denominational, it is worth spelling out a little more clearly what I mean by these terms.

Although there are interesting and important differences between the sociological type of the church and the sect, for the point of this discussion the two can be conflated and contrasted with the denomination. The church/sect claims unique access to the one unchanging truth; the denomination allows that what it has is only a part of the truth. From this simple difference follow most of the others concerning membership, discipline, the interpretation of the truth, relations with competing organizations, and so on. In this view, the major difference between the church and the sect is not so much ambition as achievement. A church is a sect which has attained hegemony. Of course, there is

156

a price to be paid for success. No society could survive if even a large proportion of its members became religious virtuosi. Somebody has to mind the shop. Even in the most affluent societies only a small number of people can be released from productive labour to pursue rigorously ritual performance, moral rectitude, and asceticism. A church has to permit a division of religious labour in which the virtuosi are supported by the mass, while the mass live a much more relaxed religious life (Turner 1981: 109–41). The church then differs from the sect in having an inclusive rather than an exclusive attitude towards membership (Robertson 1972: 123). However, its inclusiveness comes from tolerating degrees of conformity to one set of doctrines and practices, rather than, as is the case with the denomination, from the lack of a single set of beliefs. The Church continues to hold an 'option' on the authoritarianism and discipline which is a feature of the sect.

There are two reasons for conflating what most sociologists of religion treat as two quite distinct types of religious organization. First, sectarianism is very often not so much chosen as thrust upon a religious organization by circumstances beyond its control. Second, the conservative variety of Protestant Christianity is misunderstood if treated solely as sectarian. As Chapters 3 and 4 should have made clear, many schismatic Protestant movements aspired to the status of churches or, indeed, once commanded the support of the majority of the population in particular areas and enjoyed the sort of cultural hegemony we associate with the sociological type of the church. Although some conservative Protestant movements eschewed hegemonic pretensions from their foundation, many either possessed or desired dominance, and only adopted the dog-in-the-manger attitude characteristic of introversionist and communitarian sects when it became clear that they had lost the battle for church status.

Many conservative Protestants retain their old attitude to the superiority of their beliefs and a corresponding desire to reimpose their standards on the rest of the world. They have become sectarian by trying to remain church-like in a pluralist environment; their sectarianism was produced by a change in power relative to other groups. The mainstream of conservative Protestantism has never been introversionist in intent. To the extent that conservatives have turned in on themselves, this is a

157

result of them failing to attain or retain cultural and political dominance rather than a direct result of their theology (although, as I suggested in the discussion of English dissent, the conservative Protestant stress on the conversion of individuals does create a tendency towards introversionism).

Although there are certain conservative Protestant organizations which are so thoroughly sectarian that they are normally called sects, conservative Protestants are to be found in large numbers in those major religious organizations which call themselves churches and which, confusingly, approximate to the sociological type of the denomination. It thus makes sense to see sect and denomination as appropriate terms for the polar ends of a continuum. Particular organizations will occupy places at various points on this scale. For example, the Southern Baptist Convention is mostly conservative Protestant or sectarian with a minority of more liberal or denominational Protestants. The United Methodist Church is predominantly denominational with only a small proportion of sectarians. This chapter, like the last, is concerned with the fortunes of a set of beliefs and not with discrete organizations.

IDEOLOGY AND CONTEXTS IN CONSERVATIVE SUCCESS

The stimulation of Kelley's work has led a number of researchers to detailed investigations of the causes of church growth and decline. Some of their work has been mentioned in the last chapter (and even more of their conclusions have been drawn on). Before going on to an explanation of the relative success of the conservative Protestant response to the pluralism of the modern world (the causes of which have already been implied in the discussion of liberal decline), one recent attempt to test Kelley's propositions will be introduced in order to clarify the logic of my argument.

Hoge (1979) surveys the membership patterns of the sixteen major American Protestant denominations for which reliable membership figures are available. He correlates their fortunes with measures designed to test Kelley's theories about the nature of 'strong religion' and to examine the influence of a number of 'contextual' variables, such as differential birth-rates in particular regions, migration, age profiles of particular constituencies, and the socio-economic status of church members. To summarize his conclusions, Hoge partly agrees with Kelley's basic claim that the difference in fortune between the growing conservative and the declining liberal churches can be explained by the consequences of their theologies. However, he stresses the importance of a number of contextual variables which Kelley had neglected and offers them as complementary causes of conservative success. In his conclusion, Hoge says:

> Kelley's own depictions of exemplary 'strong' churches should be carefully analyzed to discern the social contexts in which they flourished. Our impression is that they grew in distinctive social settings, usually involving some separateness from the mainline culture and main power structures. The committed members felt alienation from 'the world' – from social and political powers. They were not wealthy or cosmopolitan people, and they often had a sort of pariah status in society.
>
> (Hoge 1979: 195)

Initially, I would have no argument with this. Like Hoge, I have some problem in accepting the work of analysts such as Mol (1976), Kelley (1972), and Stark and Bainbridge (1985) which explains the relative strength of the conservative variety of Protestantism with the claim that it better satisfies its customers. The extent to which people think they are satisfied by a belief-system is not simply a consequence of internal features of that set of beliefs. However, in his desire to escape the dangers of circularity inherent in discussions of satisfaction, Hoge (like Kanter in her discussion of commitment) goes too far in the other direction when he says 'that contextual factors should be seen as causally prior, since they form the backdrop for institutional factors' (ibid.: 194). Consider a contextual factor such as possessing 'a sort of pariah status'. Hoge identifies it as a cause of church growth which can be regarded as causally distinct from the conservative theology of those churches which are growing by attracting slightly marginal people. This seems an artificial separation. As Wilson in his description of sectarianism, and Kelley in his definition of 'strong' religion suggest, a rejection of certain elements of worldliness is a corollary of the conservative Protestant absolutist belief-system and can hardly be meaningfully separated from it. Although the statistical analysis of the sort practised by

Hoge, Roozen, and others requires the artificial separation of 'variables', it is a serious mistake to allow an assumption made in order to facilitate statistical analysis to appear as an element of explanation.

Although it introduces such complexity that it prevents us from producing neat path models of causation, it is more accurate to suppose a constant interplay between the two sorts of factor which Hoge calls 'institutional' (that is, things internal to the churches) and 'contextual'. For the sake of completeness, one might add that there is also constant interplay between ideological and institutional factors. Understanding Protestantism requires an awareness of the interrelations of beliefs, religious organization, and the surrounding world. What people believe about this and the next world has profound consequences for the organization of their actions and their relationships with unbelievers. Similarly, relations with unbelievers and patterns of actions which have secular causes have consequences for theologies. In short, Hoge is guilty of the mistake made by McGaw and Kanter of artificially separating ideology, organization, and action, and then reversing the obvious causal sequence so that what believers themselves see as an expression of their belief and commitment becomes a cause of those things. It is in order to do justice to the complexity of the links, while remaining true to believers' own perceptions of their actions, that I have attempted to analyse those areas where the ideology of conservative Protestantism creates the social and organizational conditions for its maintenance.

At this point, it is worth revising the thesis of this book by recasting the point of the early historical chapters in the language now being used. The first half of the book described and explained Protestantism's loss of church status. Faced with a situation in which they can no longer be a church, Protestants have the choice of adopting either denominational or sectarian forms. The career of the denominational form has been discussed in the last two chapters. This chapter is concerned with the fortunes of conservative or sectarian Protestantism. As Kelley, Hoge, and others have framed the debate as an answer to the question of why conservative Protestantism has survived this century in better shape than the liberal alternative, this discussion will also be constructed as an explanation of relative conservative success. How my argument differs from that of Hoge can be characterized by saying that it concentrates on the organizational consequences of the core epistemological beliefs of conservative and liberal Protestantism.

THE STRENGTH OF CONSERVATIVE PROTESTANTISM

If it is the case that pluralism is a key cause of secularization, then any explanation of the survival of conservative Protestantism will be concerned with the ways in which it mutes pluralism. Although some people do convert to conservative Protestantism, their number is very small compared to the total number of conservative Protestants. As will be made clear in the final chapter, the last hundred years has seen very little by way of conversion of the heathen of the First World. For this reason, we need not be overly concerned with the belief-system's appeal (particularly in the sense of appeal to outsiders). We can concentrate instead on the resilience and preservation of the faith.

Before embarking on that examination, it is worth clarifying my position on an issue which has provoked some criticism of my writings on conservative Protestantism. Although I stress the survival and resilience of evangelicalism and fundamentalism, I do not wish to give the impression that conservative Protestantism is an anachronistic survival or that it had been untouched by modernity. Far from it; although conservatives insist that they have not changed – and in that myopia lies their strength – there has been considerable accommodation to the modern world. As I have recently argued in detail, American fundamentalism is a religion extremely comfortable with the economy and polity of an advanced capitalist democracy (Bruce 1988; forthcoming).

Regional sub-cultures

Although the second half of this book has been presented as an analysis of the two main Protestant responses to pluralism, it should, at the start, be noted that a good part of the recent success of conservative Protestantism results from the fact that the geographical isolation of its bases has weakened the impact of pluralism. There is really no need to dwell on the greater ability of conservative Protestantism to withstand secularizing influences in those cases where there were fewer such influences. In the

161

geographical peripheries of modern societies, the sectarianism of conservative Protestants is not so much a deliberately chosen response to the pluralism of the modern world as a continuation of the culture which was dominant in much of the society, but which has been eroded in the centre.

When the Free Church of Scotland was created it drew heavily on two quite different constituencies: the rising urban bourgeoisie and the highland peasantry. The rapid shift to a more liberal position, which permitted the Free Church to unite with first the liberal Presbyterian dissenters and later with the established Church of Scotland, was essentially a movement of the urban element. The highland peasantry remained committed to the evangelicalism to which it had been converted only relatively recently. This can be seen very clearly in the composition of the two 'rumps' left behind at each union. The remnant who walked out of the Free Church in 1898, when the Church's commitment to the Westminster Confession of Faith was modified, and took the name 'Free Presbyterian', was almost entirely confined to the Western Isles (McPherson 1972). Similarly, the larger remnant who refused to join the United Presbyterians in 1900 was overwhelmingly highland and had little presence in the lowlands and the major urban areas (Collins 1976). Where there were lowland Free Churches, for example, in Glasgow, these tended to be immigrant congregations whose appeal was largely derived from their ability to offer some sense of community to those who moved south in search of work. It was in recognition of this that they were often known as Highland or Gaelic congregations.

Two observations can be made about the areas which continued to support Calvinist evangelicalism. The first is that they were relatively homogeneous. Although the return of members who had worked in the lowland cities or fought in the two World Wars introduced some cosmopolitan elements, it was generally the case that those migrants who most absorbed parts of modern culture were those who did not return, or who returned only sporadically and briefly. Thus the Protestant parts of the Western Isles remained, until well into the 1960s, strongholds of the 'pure gospel': places where the social values of evangelicalism – temperance and sabbatarianism, for example – remained well-embedded in the general culture. As late as the 1970s, the Northern Lighthouse Board gave instructions to lowland keepers who were posted to the western highland lights not to offend the local sympathies by performing unnecessary work on the sabbath.

Similarly, the strength of conservative Protestantism in the Appalachian Mountains, and in other rural parts of the American South and Southern Atlantic coast, is not so much a successful reaction to modernity as evidence of regional cultural autonomy. In Scandinavia, revival and pietistic movements tended to be predominantly rural (Hunter 1965: 145–9).

A second point about the margins is well made by Martin (1978a). Where there is a clear difference in religious orthodoxy between the centre and the periphery, people in the the periphery may, as part of a general rejection of the centre, remain (or become) more traditional in their religiosity. The Haugean revival movement in Lutheran Norway drew heavily on the most rural areas, and part of its appeal was to those sections who felt both neglected and offended by the centre (Vogt 1972; Hale 1981). The notion of centre–periphery does, however, have to be used with a certain sensitivity. The centre is not always the political or cultural capital of the nation-state. Each potential unit of analysis has its own centre and periphery. For the British Isles, the centre is London and the 'Home Counties'. In the Scottish case, the centre is not so much London as Edinburgh, regarded by many Scots as an outpost of English power, culture, and manners. One of the two large Victorian railway hotels in Edinburgh was called the North British and, for many highlanders, the North Britishness of Edinburgh (and to a lesser extent Glasgow and the other lowland cities) was as foreign as the culture of London or Australia.

While the tension between centre and periphery, by increasing its additional resonances, enhances the appeal of the traditional religion, it localizes the faith and makes it vulnerable to changes in the general fortunes of the locality. Although the two Free Churches have remained strong in the Scottish highlands, they have made little impact outside the *laager*. The distinctive beliefs and social attitudes of the 'wee frees' are mocked by lowlanders who feel themselves generally superior to highlanders. Although the inability to convert lowlanders has had the unintended consequence of strengthening the hold of the Free Churches on the highlands by making Free Church support an important part of the identity of parts of the highlands, it has made them heavily dependent on the demography of the periphery, and they have been weakened by the gradual depopulation of their constituency.

Of course, being strongly associated with the culture of a periphery has advantages if the periphery is becoming more, rather than less, powerful. Some of this can be seen in the rise in respectability of American evangelicalism as the south and south-west, the strongest constituencies for evangelical Protestantism, has experienced something of an economic and political revival in the last twenty years. There is no doubt that the appearance of the new Christian right as a political force in America owes a great deal to an increase in the population, economic power, and hence confidence, of the south. This can be sensed in media reactions to southern evangelicalism. Twenty years ago the south was reported in much the same way as the Scottish highlands are regarded in Britain. The Bible Belters were stereotyped either as exotic figures of fun or as primitive survivals. While some of the Appalachian mountain people might still be described (in the title of one ethnography) as *Yesterday's People* (Weller 1965), the election of the Georgian Jimmy Carter as President and the impact of conservative southerners on the politics of the Reagan Republican party has led to a new respect for the south. It is no accident that the Southern Baptist Convention remains the fastest growing of the main Protestant denominations and that the Convention has unusually combined expansion with a shift to the theological and political right.

Naturally regional sub-cultures vary in the extent to which their region offers barriers to the encroachment of cosmopolitan culture. A good example of a religion which declined, because the region which provided its core constituency was easily penetrated, is Reformed or Covenanter Presbyterianism. Although the Covenanters remain viable, if not growing, in America and Ulster, the mother church in Scotland has shrunk to the point where two of its four full-time ministers are American, and where its synod could seriously debate seeking a merger with the Free Church (it was debated in 1985 but a decision was postponed). The four remaining congregations are very small and the average age of members is somewhere in the sixties. Although it survived in Ayrshire and the western lowlands of Scotland longer than late Victorian commentators expected, its sub-culture was far more vulnerable to erosion than that of the Free Churches because it was less geographically and socially isolated. Motherwell and

Wishaw were industrializing towns in the heart of an industrial area and the remaining Covenanters spoke the same lowland Scots dialect of English as their non-Covenanting neighbours.

Immigrant sub-cultures

Another social formation in which conservative Protestantism can remain strong is the migrant sub-culture, which in many cases can be seen as importing the periphery into the centre. Pockets of Free Church evangelicalism survived in 'Gaelic' congregations in Glasgow because they provided some sense of community, of social solidarity, to migrants from the highlands. A similar point can be made about the recent growth of the West Indian and 'African' Protestant churches in England. Recent research has shown that it is these almost entirely Black organizations which have been most successful in recruiting members in the last two decades (Brierley 1984: 111). As Calley's *God's People* (1965) details, much of the attraction of the Black congregations lay in their ability to provide strangers with a sense of belonging. But, as is the case with the regional sub-culture, additional or 'latent' attractions leave the religious organization vulnerable to changes – such as localized demographic trends and changes in 'ethnic' relations – which are outside the organization's control. Being publicly and strongly linked to a particular constituency means being affected by the size of that constituency and its degree of integration with the surrounding society. Most of the highlanders who moved to Glasgow quickly became assimilated into the mainstream and moved from the Free and Free Presbyterian Church to the Church of Scotland, or drifted away from the churches altogether. Unlike British Blacks, the children of first generation highlanders had few distinguishing marks to prevent them becoming thoroughly integrated if they so wished. British Blacks, even of the second and third generation, still find themselves in a disadvantaged position and may thus still be attracted to social institutions which offer a sense of community and social worth, and an environment in which their 'blackness' ceases to be their 'master status', to use Hughes's term. However, even where the immigrant population is not assimilated, its religious organizations may still be vulnerable as second and third generations seek alternative means to express their sense of oppression. Many young British Blacks of West Indian origin have abandoned the more traditional Pentecostal churches in favour of Rastafarianism, presumably because their experience of being in the land of Egypt is significantly different from that of their parents and grandparents (Barrett 1977; Cashmore 1979).

There is clearly an element of deliberate social construction even in the case of the regional sub-culture. Such cultures survive only as long as their carriers refuse to be seduced by cosmopolitanism. There is even more social construction involved in the migrant sub-culture in that its viability depends on the extent to which the immigrants wish to be assimilated, and on the extent to which the host culture is willing to accept the migrants.

Perhaps the most dramatic example of the successful immigrant sub-cultural religion is the introversionist conservative Protestantism of the Amish (Hostetler 1963), the Doukhobors (Woodcock and Avakumovic 1968), and the Hutterites (Peters 1965). The Hutterites have, with only some small breaks, maintained a communal way of life for more than four centuries. They have no distinctive church organization because the church and the community are 'used interchangeably in their articles of association' (Wilson 1970: 126). The followers of Jacob Hutter were sixteenth-century Tyrolean Anabaptists who wandered through Slovakia, Transylvania, and Russia in an attempt to escape persecution before moving, in 1874, to settle in Dakota. When they again faced hostility – for their pacifism during the First World War – they moved to Canada, where they flourished. Wilson estimates that by 1965 there were 12,500 in Canada and more than 5,000 in the United states. The Hutterites run large communal farms and make no attempt to convert outsiders. They survive and grow by a combination of a high fertility rate (so high that demographers use the Hutterites as the bench-mark of unrestricted fertility) and very successful socialization which keeps most of their children within the community. The ideological key to their survival is the importance which their theology places on membership of the community as the source of salvation. The central beliefs about the importance of the community are buttressed by a variety of social practices which keep the outside world at bay. One such device (which has relevance for the maintenance of all distinctive belief-systems) is the use of a distinctive language within the community; in this case it is a sixteenth-century Tyrolean dialect which acts as a source of shared identity and as a barrier between the Hutterites and the surrounding society. Distinctive language is also important in social cohesion in that languages are not just neutral media of communication. They not only denote; they also connote. They embody 'stocks of knowledge' so that every instance of their use reaffirms the particular world-view there embedded (Berger and Luckmann 1973: ch. 3).

The Old Order Amish are also heirs to European Anabaptism but they do not hold property in common. None the less, they form clearly identifiable communities with a high degree of residential segregation. As Wilson puts it:

> Perhaps because they lacked the rather closer confinement of Hutterian communitarian organization, the Amish have stressed more fully than Hutterians the importance of rigorously conservative attitudes to dress, speech, and material goods, as ways of marking themselves off from the wider society. They make no use of modern motor transport or tractors, but continue to use their 'high buggies', drawn by horses, and relatively rudimentary techniques of farming.
>
> (Wilson 1970: 131)

Like the Exclusive element of the Brethren, the Amish maintain internal discipline by 'shunning' members who reject their teachings. Banning deviants permits the community to maintain its religious purity.

Non-geographical sub-cultures

Consideration of evangelical Protestantism in geographical peripheries or in introversionist and communitarian sects, while interesting, does not take us to the heart of the strength of contemporary conservative Protestantism. The above remarks could have been made about any religion in a periphery, any religion which serves as a vehicle for immigrant or minority solidarity, or any belief-system which lays great stress on isolation from the world and the maintenance of purity by avoiding contact with the impure world. Although there are differences in the extent to which liberal and conservative Protestantism can function satisfactorily in these conditions, it is in their ability to function as skeletons for the construction of social enclaves based more on religious belief than on ethnic origin or social status, which is most relevant to our concerns. It is the ability of evangelical Protestantism to survive as pockets of deviant culture in the heartland of modernity which is of greatest interest. Naturally, conservative Protestants tend to be ethnically and socio-economically homogeneous, but it is not their sharing of ethnic or class characteristics which defines them as a sub-culture. It is their commitment to a set of minority religious beliefs which separates them from their fellow whites or others of their class, and which gives them a sense of shared identity.

What was implied in the pivotal discussion of the corrosive effects of pluralism was that the plausibility of any minority belief-system was related to its ability to neutralize pluralism; to create a micro-environment in which it was hegemonic. With what Lyons (1985: 124), in a review of an earlier account of the evangelical sub-culture, described as 'forgiveable hyperbole', we can construct the following life-world for committed evangelicals in any modern society. They will be married to others of the same faith. They will spend at least four hours on a Sunday in church. At least one evening a week will be spent in a church-related prayer meeting or Bible study. They will rarely watch television or go to the cinema. Instead they will seek entertainment in crusade meetings, evangelistic services with what Paisley's Free Presbyterian Church calls 'special singing', and gospel concerts. They will watch religious films and videos. While they may glance at the secular press, they will read a religious weekly paper or magazine. They will probably begin and end the day with some organized Bible study, followed either from printed notes or from cassettes. In their cars, they will have a cassette machine and a collection of gospel tapes or recorded sermons. If they are American, they will listen to an evangelical radio station and watch 'old time gospel' shows. By tuning in to the Christian Broadcasting Network, they will be able to watch 'born again' soap operas, evangelical chat shows, and news broadcasts which present a conservative Protestant view of world and domestic affairs. If they wish, they may even arrange their consumption and spending in a particularistic fashion by subscribing to 'Christian' Yellow Pages. They may send their children to Christian schools, Bible colleges, and fundamentalist universities.

They will give between a tenth and a fifth of their earnings to church-related work. When they are moved to take an interest in global issues, such as the famine in Ethiopia, they will channel their concern through evangelical charities and missionary societies. They will often sponsor a missionary family or take a personal interest in one particular mission field in the Third World.

At the centre of their subculture is the desire to interact primarily with fellow believers. As one of the fundamentalists in the congregation studied by Ammerman (1987: 109) put it:

> Having fellowship with believers is what really gives us the confidence in our salvation ... good fellowship, getting together with fellow Christians and sharing with them, sharing what the Lord is doing in your life, admitting problems, and the other person can give you some encouragement.... We try to fellowship with Christians as much as possible. We feel that is very essential.
>
> (Ammerman 1987: 109)

In an attempt to quantify the relationships within the social circles of various types of Protestant, Dynes asked respondents to say how many of their 'five closest friends' shared their affiliation. The mean score for liberal Protestants was 1.3 out of a possible maximum of 5. For conservative Protestants, the mean score was 3.1 (Dynes 1957: 333). Socializing and maintaining the faith are, for many, inseparable activities. Evangelicals go to crusade meetings because they wish to hear the preaching and to demonstrate religious commitment. But they also go because they enjoy the company of believers and because they derive considerable satisfaction from working with others in the pursuit of their calling. It need hardly be said that conservative Protestants marry like-minded people and seek to ensure that their children are not yoked in marriage with unbelievers. Peshkin's excellent study of an American fundamentalist school notes that 'its students are encapsulated in a social network that essentially endorses its doctrinal standards' (Peshkin 1985: 169). Sixty-nine per cent of the students said that most of their non-home activities were sponsored by the school or its associated fundamentalist church.

In short, the committed evangelical will spend a considerable amount of time and devote a considerable amount of energy to doing things which are both expression and cause of their religious commitment. The sociologically important point is that we cannot assume that the religious pluralism of a society impinges equally even on those members of the society who are not geographically marginal. The distribution of beliefs, values, and attitudes cannot be reduced to social geography. There remains the vital question of the varying degrees to which people internalize what is objectively present in their culture. The above sketch of the evangelical world might suggest that the amount of time spent in sub-cultural activities is central in explaining resilience. It is, but there is no straightforward connection between time and attention. Some people can remain committed to deviant world-views while spending little time in activities related to that world-view. At the other extreme, some people who are immersed in such activities can, none the less, become seduced by alternatives and defect from the true faith. However, it seems sensible to suppose that, in most cases, commitment is correlated with activity.

Kanter (1972a, 1972b) and McGaw (1979) have already been criticized for assuming a unidirectional (and in the wrong direction) causal connection between ideology and commitment mechanisms. Some sociologists regard it as axiomatic that the business of sociology is to explain all beliefs, ideas, and actions as resulting directly from position in the social structure. Often (and certainly in this case) that would be a case of cart preceding horse. If one considers why evangelicals are willing to engage in such activities (or to use Kanter's language, to respond to commitment mechanisms and organizational strategies), the answer must be because they believe such things to be either necessary or good for salvation, or necessary or good as an indicator of already having been saved. Either way, the shared beliefs are logically and temporally primary.

Of course, although not themselves causes of belief, many shared activities through which one can 'grow in the faith' are important in sustaining that faith. Such activities are also vital in socializing the next generation in the faith. The existence of a viable and almost all-embracing sub-culture allows the children of evangelicals to grow up in an evangelical world. They need not live in a multi-cultural society. In most parts of Britain, the children of evangelicals would have to interact with non-evangelicals'at school but this can be compensated for by intensive socialization at home so that the evangelical child reacts negatively to elements of alternative belief-systems. The success of such socialization can be illustrated with the example of the children of one Ulster evangelical family who were so thoroughly socialized that when their school used a book of carols produced by the BBC, the children alerted their father to the presence of a carol to Mary. The father asked the school to either drop the song or excuse his children from carol-singing. The offending song was dropped.

The problem for evangelicals in Britain is that they are far less free than their American counterparts to create an alternative sub-culture. This will be pursued in the next chapter but the example of broadcasting can be mentioned here. The structure of American broadcasting permits both the airing of avowedly evangelical programmes on 'mainstream' stations and the licensing of entirely evangelical stations. The American evangelical can thus consume subcultural products in a mainstream fashion. The British evangelical has to boycott conventional broadcasting and to rely on cassettes and videotapes for suitable material. The structure of American education similarly permits a greater variety of schools and colleges, and allows evangelicals to be educated in avowedly evangelical institutions from kindergarten.

This introduces the important point of cost. Living in a deviant sub-culture involves two kinds of cost: those of maintaining the sub-culture and the losses that are incurred by opting out of the mainstream. In addition there are sometimes costs which the mainstream inflicts on the deviant for opting out. Costs of the first kind are not particularly significant in that they are comparable to the price most of us pay for maintaining our participation in whatever voluntary associations we may wish to join and in pursuing our hobbies. They are, of course, higher than those incurred by liberal Protestants but hardly different from those incurred by, for example, enthusiastic participants in political parties.

What are much more important are the second and third types of cost. A good example of the losses resulting from opting out can be found in the biographies of members of the Exclusive Brethren. The Exclusive or 'Closed' Brethren differ from the Plymouth Brethren in taking much more seriously the Pauline injunction to 'Be ye not yoked with unbelievers'. While most other evangelicals take this only to mean that one should not marry an unbeliever, the Exclusives, like the Old Order Amish, take it as a general principle for social interaction and go to considerable lengths to avoid being so yoked. Since the mid 1960s, this has been rigorously interpreted to mean that they cannot join any organization which is also open to unbelievers. As a result, they no longer go to university because being a student at a British university brings with it automatic membership of the students' union. The necessity to belong to a secular organization also closes off certain prestigious and lucrative occupations. A compromise was negotiated with the Pharmaceutical Society: Brethren who wished to become pharmacists would take the Society's examinations but would not actually be required to join. However, an Act of Parliament was needed to permit this and, although it was passed by the Commons, the bill was rejected by the House of Lords. Twenty-six practising Brethren pharmacists gave up their jobs (Wilson 1964).

Even those evangelicals who do not have hard-and-fast rules about interacting with outsiders will suffer general costs of restricted interaction. Or to be more precise, their standard of living will be restricted to that which can be supported or promoted by the community of believers. A freemasonry principle of favouring co-religionists may be an advantage if, as in the case of London and Glasgow Jewry, the standard of living of the believing community is higher than that of the population at large. If, however, the community is of relatively low social status (and in the case of evangelical Protestantism, it usually is) then confining one's interaction to other believers means restricting opportunities for upward social mobility. Naturally, the committed believer will see this as no great sacrifice. An excellent ethnographic study of an American fundamentalist school documents the 'poor' conditions of service for the teachers, who work considerably longer hours than their secular colleagues for far less money (Peshkin 1985). The same can be said of the staff of the schools run by the Free Presbyterian Church of Ulster (Bruce 1986: 171–8). But neither group feels hard done by and each has considerably better morale than the mainstream teaching profession in either country. They are making sacrifices for the Lord. However, the less committed faithful cannot help but be aware of what is available outside the evangelical community.

As an example of the third cost, one could offer the example of those Protestant sects which maintain a conscientious objection to war. The state may refuse to permit certain kinds of deviation or exact a high price for permitting them. As the state became increasingly secular, the range of religious deviation which was punished was drastically reduced. As was described in Chapter 4, the nineteenth century saw the removal of most dissenting disabilities, but the most rigorous dissenters are still faced with certain choices. Those Christians who refuse to send their children to state schools, or to make what the state accepts as adequate alternative provision, will be fined and, in the last resort, imprisoned.

ACCOMMODATION AND REJECTION

The issue of the cost of sectarian withdrawal is perhaps not a pressing one for most conservative Protestants because they are not actually separated from the world. In part this follows from their need to maintain some sort of contact with unbelievers in order to remain 'evangelical'. The introversion of the communitarian sects involves two kinds of rejection: the rejection of the culture and values of the surrounding society, and the rejection of the carriers of that culture. The communitarians can be seen as models of the sort of social organization which gives enormous plausibility to minority beliefs by creating an insulated world in which such beliefs are not only dominant but enjoy a monopoly. But their method of social organization can only be followed by those people who place the preservation of their distinctive beliefs before their dissemination. Although introversion and isolation provide the best strategies for maintaining deviant beliefs, they preclude contacts with outsiders, and thus make it almost impossible to recruit others to the deviant perspective. Although in practice many conservative Protestants do live their lives as though the maintenance of their own purity was more important than converting the heathen, they nevertheless wish to maintain a rhetoric of conversionism and thus cannot completely isolate themselves.

Contemporary conservative Protestants are torn between retreat from unbelievers and missionary involvement with them. The same tension can be seen in their response to the culture and values of the secular world. For all their denunciations of

173

worldliness, most conservative Protestants are not greatly world-rejecting. The vast majority of them are not like the Amish or the Hutterites. On most major policy issues they are happy to conform to the standards of capitalist democracy. Even those who once stood against the modern world have reduced their areas of protest to small symbols which the state can happily ignore. For example, the Covenanters still maintain that they will not support the state until it accepts its God-given responsibilities to maintain the true religion. But in practice this rejection of the world consists only of not voting, not standing for political office, and not sitting on juries. Taxes are paid to 'the civil magistrate', and even the provision against voting is exercised only in the most feeble way. Orthodox Covenanters do not vote, but rather than break the law, they register their names on the electoral roll. Ironically, it is liberal and radical Christians who now engage in acts of dissent such as withholding that proportion of their taxes which they calculate goes to military spending.

One has to search hard among evangelical and fundamentalist sources to find much about the core practices and values of the modern world which they reject, which is perhaps not surprising given the important role that conservative Protestantism played in bringing such a world into being. Sir Frederick Catherwood's *A Better Way: the Case for a Christian Social Order* (1975), which is published by the Inter-Varsity Press (until recently a press representative of Anglican and English Free Church evangelicals), for example, contains little that a secular moderately conservative capitalist could disagree with. Rapacious capitalists are condemned but so are shop stewards who use their industrial muscle to achieve 'unfair' wage increases. Slightly more radical evangelicals such as Alan Storkey (1983) have attempted to discover biblical foundations for criticism of some of the less attractive features of capitalism, but in general evangelicals and even fundamentalists have confined their rejection of the world to what are widely regarded as matters of private judgement and individual behavioural choices. They do not drink alcohol, smoke, dance, countenance or consume pornography, swear, wear their hair long, or engage in pre- or extra-marital sexual activities. But, precisely because these are private matters, this does not cause great friction with their unbelieving neighbours and does not invite the wrath of the state. In fact, given that many other people,

174

for their numerous and varied reasons, share evangelical dislike of some of these activities, their renunciation may go unnoticed and unremarked.

This is an important point because, if it is overlooked, we may build a quite false impression of the sectarian response to the world. Conservative Protestants are not monks. They are people who to most appearances live normal lives. Unless one is invited into their homes, or works closely with them, one may be quite unaware that, while their bodies inhabit the same world as unbelievers, their thoughts are elsewhere. This is possible because of the compartmentalization which characterizes the modern world. We separate the worlds of work and the home. We permit people to play their work roles with a certain amount of 'role-distance' and to save their 'real' selves for the home and leisure sphere. While conservative Protestants resent differen- tiation and frequently assert their superiority over those they deride as 'Sunday Christians', they are incapable of reintegrating the world.

A few conservative Protestants refuse to accept compartmental- zation and abandon the normal world to build their own private environment in which they can reintegrate the private sacred world with the mundane realm of work. Often allied to some form of social service, such as care for the mentally handicapped, small counter-cultural groups of committed Christians can be found here and there. But the vast majority tacitly accept the licence to live their private lives as they please, provided their private beliefs do not interfere with the performance of their public roles.

Some conservative Protestants seek a pale shadow of re- integration on their own terms. As they cannot force the secular world back to Jesus, they fight to neutralize the most offensive elements of an unchristian culture with campaigns to clean up television or to bring morality back to public life, but, even in these, compromise is required. In the first place, the actual motive for involvement has to be played down. Such movements of cultural defence cannot be presented as attempts to restore the world to the shape that God gave it. Instead, they offer justi- fications which are more nebulous but which might attract wide- spread support, such as the claim that pornography is bad for our society.[1] Campaigning in the secular world requires that at least some of the methods and attitudes of that world be adopted. The danger is always that such involvement will end with the evangelical moving towards the world rather than the intended other way round.

By and large, conservative Protestants respond to the modern world by accepting what cannot be changed. Their energies are devoted to the creation and maintenance of sub-cultures which are sub-cultures, rather than sub-societies or sub-economies. For all the differences between liberal and conservative Protestantism, they have in common a lack of challenge to the economic and political status quo. Both respect the autonomy of these spheres and offer little or no challenge to the values which dominate them, liberalism because it has relativized to the extent of having no solid core of shared values from which to challenge anything else, and conservative Protestantism because it has, by and large, come to endorse the modern economy and its attendant values. In their different ways both liberal and conservative Protestantism have become privatized. Conservatives create alternative leisure zones which lay the foundation for alternative inner mental worlds; alternatives of consciousness rather than action. While such sub-cultures may seem trivial when compared with the world-rejection of the Amish or the Hutterites, they are enough to deflect the most damaging thrusts of secularization. In particular, they inoculate against pluralism. In the conservative Protestant sub-culture, people believe that there can be one truth and act as if they have it. Relations with representatives of other theologies are not entirely absent but they are rare and, when they do take place, they pose no threat to the security of the evangelical's world-view. The evangelical is so thoroughly socialized into the one true faith that unbelievers are devalued into implausibility.

In conclusion, one point must be repeated because it is overlooked by some analysts and flatly contradicted by others. It is no accident that conservative Protestants create sub-cultures and display considerable organizational resilience. It is no accident that they are good at raising their children within the faith. Nor is the contrast between conservative and liberal Protestant exhausted by noting that the former *wishes* to create his own world and indoctrinate his children while the latter does not, although that point is worth noting. The argument which has informed'this and the previous chapter can be succintly summarized. Even if (and when) liberal Protestants want to create organizations and social institutions which can preserve and promote their beliefs, they will (and did) find this very difficult because the nature of their core beliefs – their faith in 'new light', their commitment to diversity, their denominationalism – makes such activities difficult. It is the very nature of conservative Protestant ideology, with its repeated assertion that there is but one unchanging truth, which explains its successful reproduction.

Chapter Eight

AMERICAN PROTESTANTISM

THE PROBLEM

At first sight, the strength of the churches in America poses a major problem for most secularization accounts. Before considering how the case of America can be reconciled to the general account of this book, some of the evidence of American religious vitality will be presented.

According to the Princeton Religious Research Center (PRRC), 69 per cent of a recent sample of Americans claimed to be church or synagogue members; a figure only slightly higher than that produced by adding together the totals claimed by the denominations, and one which has only fluctuated by four points in thirty years. If one considers church attendance, 40 per cent of a representative sample claimed, in 1980, to have attended church (or synagogue) in the previous seven days (PRRC 1981: 32). To consider only the Protestant churches, which, after all, are the concern of this essay, 39 per cent of American Protestants claimed to have attended in a previous week in 1984 (Gallup 1985: 43). In contrast, for Canada the comparable figure is 27 per cent (Bibby 1985), for Australia it is less than 20 per cent (Barrett 1982: 152), and for England it is no more than 11 per cent (Barrett 1982; Brierley 1980). This sort of survey data has been produced sufficiently often for us to suppose it generally reliable. It is also supported by a number of community studies (Anderson 1978). The 1970s re-study of the Lynd's Middletown, for example, shows considerable stability in church membership, attendance, and support (Caplow *et al.* 1983: ch. 3).

Explanations for the American anomaly will be discussed in detail below, but a theme common to a number of accounts is 'internal' secularization. Whereas Europe became secular by people leaving the churches, American churches retained members while themselves becoming secular (Wilson 1966). In such an account, it is supposed that people's reasons for being active in religious organizations have changed so that what were once secondary consequences of church membership (such as a sense of belonging) are now primary motives. Were this the case, one might expect that continued high church involvement would be accompanied by a decline in the significance of religious beliefs. But here too Americans seem determined to confound secularization theories. Surveys of American religious attitudes and beliefs consistently produce what appears to be evidence of continued orthodox religiosity. Fifty-five per cent of a representative sample claimed that religion was very important in their lives (PRRC 1981: 39). Only 21 per cent of Britons made the same claim (Gallup 1976: 6). Forty-two per cent of Americans believe that 'the Bible is the Word of God and is NOT mistaken in its statements and teachings', and a further 30 per cent agreed that 'the Bible is the Word of God but is sometimes mistaken in its statements and teachings' (Gallup 1985: 47). In Middletown, 53 per cent of high school students believed that 'the Bible is a sufficient guide to all the problems of modern life' (Caplow *et al.* 1983: 334).

One may reasonably enter a number of reservations about these data. There may be an element of exaggeration, reflecting the respondents' assumption about what surveyors want to hear. They may wish to appear to be respectable. But even if this is what the figures represent, it is still an interesting piece of data. After all, in a secular society, people would not assume that assenting to religious beliefs is a mark of respectability and would feel no pressure to do so. But we should be cautious of reading what may be an index of generally held views about the social value of being seen to be religious as evidence about actual beliefs and practices.

A more important objection to the simple acceptance of these and other survey data is that formal assent to doctrinal or attitudinal statements may remain high while actual behavioural consequences decline. Caplow's Middletown respondents may, with the same frequency as their parents, say that the Bible is important but pay little attention to those behavioural standards which were thought by their parents to be biblical.

179

It is worth adding what may at first sight appear to be a methodological quibble but which has important consequences. It should be remembered that many surveys offer their respondents statements and ask them to agree or disagree. By asking what are in effect leading questions, they make it easy for people who have little acquaintance with a body of doctrines to appear knowledgeable. The unwillingness of respondents to admit that they do not understand a question, let alone have no opinion about it, is so strong that people will frequently express strong opinions for and against entirely fictional issues (Bishop *et al.* 1986). When such surveys attempt to test the religious knowledge of respondents without giving them assistance, they produce evidence of massive ignorance of even the most basic elements of the Christian faith. When probed, more than half the respondents in a 1950 survey could not name any of the first four books of the New Testament, and that in a nation where Matthew, Mark, Luke, and John are common 'Christian' names! (Gallup 1985: 6.) The vast majority have no idea who preached the Sermon on the Mount. We thus have to be wary of taking survey professions of agreement with orthodox Christian attitudes and beliefs as indices of personal faith.

A decline in church participation and a decline in the popularity of religious beliefs are two indicators of secularization. The third element – the reduction of the political power of organized religion and the differentiation of the religious from the political – is possibly the most difficult to assess. Church members can be counted. People can be asked what they believe, and even if the responses cannot be taken as reliable in an absolute sense, trends can be identified. But how does one 'measure' the degree of differentiation of the religious and the political? Hadden (1986) has suggested that the formal separation of church and state be taken as the mark of secularization. By his definition, America is a secular country, while England and Scotland, because they have state churches of which the monarch is the head, are religious. The legal status of religious institutions is not without interest, but to take formal establishment as an index of secularization is perverse, given the apparently inverted relationship between establishment and religious participation. A more realistic picture is painted if one takes a broader view of political influence, and notes that American public life is permeated by religious beliefs and symbols. One does not have to endorse Bellah's civil religion thesis (McLoughlin and Bellah 1968: ch.1) to be aware that much of American public life, if it is not still informed by an image of America as a nation 'under God', is certainly decorated with such rhetoric. It is the residual strength of that image which has made possible some of the successes of the new Christian right. Although by no means all the motivation of those people involved in the new Christian right comes solely from theological considerations, there can be no doubt that the high correlation between fundamentalist theology and support for the conservative social, political, and moral agenda of the NCR, shows it to be a primarily religious movement which has politicized believers, and influenced 'non-believers' such as President Reagan, by playing on the religious elements which persist in American political imagery (Bruce 1988). To put it simply, while no American church is legally established, religion plays a greater part in American politics than it does in the political life of Britain or any of the Scandinavian countries.

Assuming, for the sake of argument, that religion remains more popular in America than in other predominantly Protestant cultures, there are a number of possible explanations. It is worth saying that some of these accounts get into difficulty by attempting to explain the success of 'religion', or a variety of religions, with a single cause. Because I believe that the conditions in which they flourish are likely to be quite different, I will treat conservative and liberal Protestantism separately.

Cultural pluralism

The central thesis of this book is that pluralism has a de-legitimating and hence corrosive effect on religion. Conservative or sectarian Protestants react to the pluralism of the modern world by trying to create sub-cultures which are relatively homogeneous. At the start of the last chapter, it was noted that some of what appear to be successful conservative reactions to modernity are actually cases where there has been relatively little pressure from the modern world. Protestants in certain areas have remained conservative and orthodox because those areas have not been heavily penetrated by pluralism. It is less a matter of successful response and more a case of less of a problem.

No one would challenge the description of America as culturally pluralistic, but it is important to be careful of imputing the gross characteristics of the abstract society to all sections of the population. Many observers of American religion take for granted de Tocqueville's description of America as the land of a large number of competing churches (Tocqueville 1969). But de Tocqueville built up his impression while *travelling*. His observations of place after place were used to paint a composite image of America. What was overlooked by the peripatetic Frenchman, and has been ignored by many contemporary commentators, is that many areas were until recently, or still continue to be, dominated by one denomination or by a small group of very similar denominations.

The south, a key constituency for conservative Protestantism, does not possess a pluralistic religious culture. While only six of every ten Americans in non-southern states are Protestant, the figure for the south is nine out of ten (Hill 1966: 34–9). Almost all of these people are Baptist or Methodist and, as Hill argues, in the south, the two denominations are almost identical. The religious life of the region is thus dominated by evangelical Arminian conservative Protestantism. As Reed adds: 'If anything, the religious homogeneity of most Southern communities is understated by these data, since Southerners not in the religious mainstream are geographically concentrated within the South' (Hill 1972: 58). To a lesser extent a similar point could be made about most rural areas of the United states; only in the cities does one find what one normally thinks of as religious pluralism. It is also worth noting that the fastest growing of the major religious organizations is that which has the most homogeneous constituency as its home base: the Mormons or, to give them their proper name, the Church of Jesus Christ of Latter-Day Saints. Utah is Mormon in the same way that Spain is Catholic.

The general point here is that a comparison of the degree of pluralism requires the use of comparable social units. The smallness of Britain and the centralized nature of its media and public life means that the pluralism impinges much more directly on the lives of the average inhabitant. Or, to put it another way, what is important in understanding the beliefs and actions of people is the world they actually inhabit and not the world we impute to them on the basis of characteristics of the largest social unit to which they can be regarded as belonging. What is important is not the social or cultural system of America, but the composition of the reference groups of actual Americans. While America taken as a whole might approximate to the social type of a society lying at the pluralistic end of the continuum, many Americans actually live in worlds which are characterized by considerable cultural hegemony.

It is also worth adding, for those theories of secularization which stress urbanization and industrialization, that, while America may now be described as a largely urbanized industrial economy, this is a recently attained state. In 1851 only 22 per cent of the British working population worked in agriculture. By 1881 it was less than 8 per cent. In contrast, as late as the 1870s half the working population of America were employed on the land. If one considers the extent of urbanization, Britain reached the point where more than half the population lived in towns and cities some time before 1851. It was not until the end of the First World War that America became similarly urbanized (Hobsbawm 1977: 157–8; Nugent 1977: 145). The images we have of late nineteenth-century Chicago, New York, or Philadelphia should not be generalized to the vast rural areas of the west, mid-west, and south.

Constructing sub-cultures

Having suggested that America is, for the lives of many of its inhabitants, less pluralistic than the gross comparisons between Europe and the New World assume, I would now like to go even further in inverting the conventional wisdom and argue that the pluralism which does exist has consequences almost diametrically opposed to those normally supposed. To state the case starkly, where considerable cultural pluralism is accompanied by a relatively open and decentralized polity, sectarians may successfully use their freedom to re-create an homogeneous world.

Most conservative Protestants have reacted to the modern world by trying to create social institutions which maintain the plausibility of their deviant world-view by denying its deviant status. As I suggested in the last chapter, American conservative Protestants are better able to do this than their British and European counterparts because the political structure is far less centralized. The way in which broadcasting is organized offers a good example. Until

183

four years ago, Britain had only three television channels, two of them run by the British Broadcasting Corporation. Although the Corporation has regional outposts which periodically 'opt out' of the national network broadcasts to air their own productions, the vast majority of programmes are made in London. Although regional offices are supposed to respond to local needs and interests, they are staffed by people whose loyalty is normally to the cosmopolitan centre in London, and who see their stretch in the provinces as a step in a career which will take them back to the centre. The commercial companies which broadcast in various regions on the third channel are required, as a condition of their licences, to broadcast programmes of local interest, but they too are staffed by mobile cosmopolites and fill most of their air-time with nationally produced products. Until recently radio broadcasting was dominated by the BBC and was similarly centralized. Although the last decade has seen the expansion of local radio stations, these are prevented by commercial considerations, and by the conditions of their government-granted licences, from directing their product at one particular ethnic or religious sub-culture.

The British government's parsimonious allocation of licences restricts broadcasting to basically four national television channels and, in addition to the four BBC national radio channels, to normally only two competing radio stations in any locality. In the absence of the American system of cable television and easily granted radio licences, British audiences are severely limited in what they can see and hear. Most of that product reflects the 'moderate', secular, and cosmopolitan culture of London.

Not only can one not establish a television channel or a radio station in Britain but, except for the short slots reserved for advertising on the commercial channels, British television and radio air-time is not for sale. The BBC does not air advertisements, and even the independent companies are prevented from selling time for political or religious advertising. Time is allocated to political parties roughly in proportion to their popular electoral support: it cannot be bought. Rather than being shown as short commercial breaks in popular programmes, party political broadcasts are announced as programmes in their own right and are thus easily ignored by the audience.

To concentrate on religious broadcasting and cultural minorities, there is thus no possibility in Britain of distinct religious groups setting up their own stations or buying time on the main channels to air programmes which celebrate and reinforce their culture. The BBC and the independent companies are obliged, by their charters, to devote some time to religious broadcasting, but their worship services are always of a vaguely ecumenical 'highest common factor' kind, designed to offend as few people as possible, and much of their 'religious' output consists of programmes about, rather than on behalf of, particular theologies.[1]

The openness of American broadcasting has two important features for the maintenance of sub-cultures. First, it allows much greater localism. Radio stations especially can direct themselves at their own small home market which will often display considerable cultural homogeneity. Even if they operate in a pluralistic environment, they are permitted – and find it commercially viable – to serve a particular ethnic or religious minority, or special interest group. Even small towns may have a black music station, a fundamentalist station, a middle of the road secular station, a rock music channel, and so on. If fundamentalists want fundamentalism, they do not have to watch CBS or NBC show balanced documentaries about fundamentalism. They can tune to Pat Robertson's Christian Broadcasting Network. And the selling of air-time means that, where there are sufficient conservative Protestants to convince an evangelist that donations will exceed costs, air-time will be purchased for 'old time gospel' shows.

The structure of American broadcasting permits the audience to respond by choosing a channel or a regular broadcast which suits their interests. This is the important point about pluralism as choice. While the availability of a wide variety of cultural products suggests that the society as a whole is culturally plural, it also means that the structure is conducive to the maintenance of sub-cultures because choice permits people consistently to choose the product which best suits their needs. To state it like this is to allow us to draw a quite different conclusion from Caplow's observation about pluralism and the survival of religion (Caplow 1985). A high degree of pluralism, provided it is reflected in an open-market, de-centralized system of communications, allows those who wish to do so to create an artificial world with a very high degree of cultural homogeneity. They will know that other products are on offer and that the infidel are out there somewhere, but they need not share

185

the same world with such people because they are able to opt for a staple diet of their own cultural products.

The same contrast between America and most European societies can be made about the 'local option' control of alcohol consumption, gambling, and other morally contentious areas. More importantly, it can be made for the control of education. Although the trend has been towards greater centralization, education in America is still considerably less centralized than British education. Locally elected school boards and state legislatures have considerable influence over curriculum. As some recent and highly charged debates about evolution, sex education, and 'secular humanism' have demonstrated, not only can Americans readily create private Christian schools but they can also prevent professional educators from imposing their standards on local public schools.[2]

To summarize the three main points of this discussion: (a) there may be far less pluralism in the everyday-life-world that many ordinary Americans inhabit than there is in Britain; (b) the nature of American civic life permits a considerable degree of regional and local autonomy; and (c) the *laissez-faire* nature of American broadcasting (and to a lesser degree, American education), by providing people with a wide range of alternatives, allows them to select just the one they prefer. Americans are able to create their own private culturally homogeneous world.

LIBERAL PROTESTANTISM IN AMERICA

The above observations explain why the problems of pluralism are either (a) less pressing than one would suppose if it were the case that Americans actually lived in the America of the sociologist, or (b) more easily solved in America than they are in Britain and other European countries. They explain why the challenge to orthodox Protestantism was weaker in America than in Britain and why, when it came, the sectarian response of American conservative Protestants was more successful than that of their British counterparts. But this leaves unanswered the more commonly addressed question of why it is that the broad mainstream or liberal American churches – Protestantism in its denominational mode – seem to have been more attractive than the British denominations. After all, the vitality of the conservative Churches accounts for only part of the difference between American and British religiosity. To consider the appeal of the liberal churches, we must consider the appeal of religion in general.

Popularity and the market

Martin (1978a) and Caplow (1985) present explanations which rest the present popularity of religion in America on its having avoided a collapse of public support in the early nineteenth century. In their view, the strength of religion in modern societies is directly, rather than inversely, correlated with pluralism. The largely unchallenged Scandinavian Lutheran churches retained a formal monopoly until well into this century, but lost most of their popular support. For Martin, the contrasting situation of religious *laissez-faire*, which obtained in most parts of America from shortly after the War of Independence, meant that free competition ensured there was a set of beliefs and practices to suit every social and regional group. The greater variety of religion caused fewer sections of the population to become alienated from the churches; there was something for everyone. Caplow makes a related point by reviving the de Tocquevillian thesis that the vitality of American religion has been due to its fragmentation. No church or sect was powerful enough to become associated with the state and hence religion was not compromised by its political associations. No major part of the population was alienated from religious institutions by their close ties to the ruling class. In contrast, Protestantism in Scandiniavia and Britain has suffered from its close links with the state.

There is some considerable merit in these observations. There is no doubt that the established churches of England and Scotland were slow to adapt to the movement of population from the country to the city. It is also certainly the case that many people were alienated by the class associations of the churches. However, there are limits to how much of the variation between Europe and America can be explained by the competitive market situation which the churches faced in the New World. After all, as chapters 3 and 4 should have amply demonstrated, European countries were not without large dissenting movements. Even at the time of its strongest hegemony, the national Kirk in Scotland faced competition from recusant Catholicism and Episcopalianism on the right, and from the Covenanters, the Seceders, and then the Free Church on the left. Similarly, from the moment the Henrican Reformation freed the Anglican Church from Rome, it faced competition from Baptist, Independents, Quakers, and Presbyterians. When old dissent faded, its place was taken by the new dissent of Methodism and a revitalized Baptist movement. It is simply not the case that the majority of Britons were denied the possibility of alternative religious activity. Although there were costs in dissenting, the price of nonconformity was low for most people. By the end of the eighteenth century, dissent was well established. Additionally, the growth and survival of the most persecuted of the dissenters – the Quakers – shows that even an aggressively intolerant establishment did not dissuade those people who wished to engage in alternative forms of religious activity from so doing.

If the monopoly–competition axis is to be used to explain behaviour, then the principle for comparison must be the actual availability of alternatives. As a corrective to those who stress the open market of American religion, I would suggest that most inhabitants of most parts of the British Isles have, for the last 150 years, had available to them, within walking or riding distance, alternatives to the national churches.

On the second element of the de Tocquevillian thesis – the alienating effects of the political associations of Erastian church establishments – a similar degree of scepticism seems appropriate. Although there are cases where the association of the dominant religious tradition with the ruling elite has provoked a rejection of religion, this seems to be more the case for the Catholic Church where, as in France and Italy, the Church's support for the *ancien régime* lead progressive social forces to become anti-clerical. But, as Wallis (1986) has argued, even for the Catholic Church, there is no necessary connection between hegemony and political involvement, on the one hand, and a decline in popular support on the other. After all, the Catholic Church remains extremely strong in Ireland and in Poland: countries where it has a near monopoly. In the former it supports the state, while in the latter it acts as a semi-official opposition, but in neither case is there evidence that any significant number of people feel alienated from such 'compromised' monopolies.

The Caplow–de Tocqueville thesis is even less convincing for Protestant countries. The ability of Protestants to shape their religion to suit their political, social, and economic needs allows an alternative to anti-clericalism. Rising classes may reject the religion of the establishment by adopting an even stricter 'virtuoso' form of the dominant religious tradition. The new bourgeoisie of Scotland supported the Seceders and the Free Church (MacLaren 1974). The highland peasants rejected the moderate Presbyterianism endorsed by their landlords and adopted, instead, an enthusiastic Calvinist evangelicalism. The rising English urban bourgeoisie did not become socialists, they became Methodists. It is certainly true that the strong association between the Anglican Church in Wales and the anglicized upper classes alienated a majority of the Welsh from the Church, but they remained available for recruitment to Calvinistic Methodism. This suggests that the continued vitality of American religion cannot be explained simply by pointing to the contrast between the 'institutionalized' dissent position of American churches and the religious establishments of many European Protestant countries.

Migrant religion

The examples just given, of opposition to the ruling elite taking the form of religious revitalization movements, suggest a more fruitful general proposition. In his recent discussions of American and European religion, Wallis (1986, 1987) draws on a sensible general assumption about the circumstances in which religion may decline. We may begin by accepting Weber's view that some of the appeal of religion comes from its ability to provide theodicies of success and failure. Religions may explain why good men suffer and bad men prosper. Modern industrial societies have a variety of secular theodicies which acquire legitimation from their resonance with modern ideologies and the more abstract elements of rationality, and with what Berger *et al.* (1974) call 'technological consciousness'. We may thus expect religion to decline in the modern world. However, it will remain popular if it plays an important part in social integration or in the preservation of ethnic identity.

In most discussions of American religion, it is the integrative function which is emphasized. American churches are attractive, not because they explain suffering and reconcile people to the nasty, short, and brutish nature of their existence, but because they provide a sense of community. With their own distinctive emphases, Berger (1961), Wilson (1968), and Herberg (1960) all argue that, whereas Britain became secular by people abandoning the churches, church affiliation in America remained high while the churches themselves became fairly secular institutions.

> American churches have for a long time operated more as distinctly social and charitable institutions than have churches in Europe, but they have always seemed to be – except in periods of evangelistic fervor – only mildly spiritual. In contrast with England, where so few remain in the churches, but where those who do appear to be highly committed, American churches seem almost casual – affirming a vague ideological orientation, rather than a deep spirituality, and affirming it largely through social activities which have little specifically to do with spiritual values as such.
>
> (Wilson 1968: 79)

If, as Herberg (1960: 3) puts it, 'the religion which actually prevails among Americans today has lost much of its authentic Christian (and Jewish) content', then it seems sensible to assume that the reasons for commitment to it are similarly less concerned directly with religious belief and practice, and more concerned with the secondary benefits or 'latent functions' of membership and attendance. For Wilson, a major latent function is the provision of a substitute for community. Church-based social activities provide 'a sense of belonging to a community in a society in which high mobility (of all kinds) makes a deep community attachment difficult to achieve as a purely spontaneous, unorganized growth of the sustained life of the people of a neighbourhood' (Wilson 1968: 79).

Although he does not make it explicit, the desire for a sense of community seems to be central to Wallis's explanation of the apparently significant difference in the average indices of religiosity for the old 'exporting' Protestant countries of Europe and those of the newer settler societies of America, Canada, New Zealand, and Australia (Wallis 1987). Herberg offers a more detailed version of the same reasoning. His essay is so well-written and argued that it deserves better than to be presented in a few sentences, but his thesis is that the importance of religion in American life can be appreciated if one considers the differences between generations of immigrants. The first generation becomes enthusiastically committed to its ethnic culture; something which in a real sense it discovers in America. Prior to migration, the identity of the settlers was based on their village and locale rather than on their nationality. In the new environment, language group became a source of identification and identity. The second generation rejects much of the ethnic culture of the first, prefer- ring to see itself as 'American' and allowing itself to be assimilated. However, the third generation, confident in its Americanism, but still being identified by others in terms of its ethnic origins, is willing to return to its ethnic roots:

> the old family religion, the old ethnic religion could serve where language and culture could not; the religion of the immigrants – with certain modifications, such as the replace- ment of the ethnic language by English – was accorded a place in the American scheme of things that made it at once both genuinely American and a familiar principle of group identification.
>
> (Herberg 1960: 31)

With some minor modifications, a similar explanation of the place of the churches could – as Wallis suggests – be presented for other settler societies. Participation in organized religion is higher in migrant-based societies than in those which have been net exporters of population, because churches in the former types of societies can service a felt need for community and social integration.

Any sort of voluntary association may be socially functional in encouraging people to come together to form a community, but religious associations have a number of advantages over secular ones. They were often the first such institutions in place. Although the migrant-based societies did develop class structures, status groupings, and political interests, and the organizations which went with such differentiation, churches already existed and were thus able to act as locations for the development of community. Although different classes and waves of settlers later developed an array of occupational and fraternal associations, churches were initially good places to meet like-minded and like-situated people.

Religious associations have a second advantage over secular alternatives in being relatively undiscriminating. Within the limits of whatever class or ethnic identity was established, the churches would welcome the poor, the sick, and the needy. Very often the only test for admission was a declared willingness to try to change one's life, often in a direction which was already appropriate to the social and economic situation of its potential members. The Elks, the Buffaloes, and the Rotarians are selective, but the Lord loves a sinner. Finally, although modern societies possess a range of secular theodices, the ability of religious organizations to provide, in addition to company and social integration, comfort for the lost, the lonely and the frightened, remains important in understanding their attraction.

To summarize, organized religion is important in migrant societies because it offers, at least, a partial solution to the anomie which results from the abandonment of a stable world with its known class structure, language, and social institutions. America is a settler society which still has a high degree of geographical and social mobility. Hence there is a greater need in America than in Europe for the integrative functions of the churches.

While initially plausible, there are problems with this explanation of the differential religiosity of Europe and America. Taking evidential weakness first, the point has already been made that general Old World–New World comparisons may suffer from exaggeration and the ecological fallacy. There is also a need to distinguish time periods in the development of migrant-based societies. The Herberg account seems well sustained by his own data, and we may wish to accept the application of the argument to the early settlement periods of other societies such as Canada and New Zealand, but still reject the view that it is the anomie of *present-day* America which explains the enduring appeal of church participation.

The notion that the anomie of initial settlement explained the appeal of the churches in some earlier period will be considered again later. First, the claim that present American religiosity is explained by some version of anomie or social disorganization will be considered.

192

Mobility and religion

Any attempt to characterize a society as vast and as complex as modern America will clearly run into evidential problems. For example, Wilson offers the high divorce and crime rates of America as part of a contrast with a Europe in which 'community breakdown has proceeded less far and [in which] community functions still appear to be performed in stable social groups' (Wilson 1968: 87). We are now sufficiently well informed of the many elements that go into the construction of indices of crime and deviance to be less willing than Wilson was twenty years ago to accept the higher crime rates of America as proof that it is a more anomic society than Britain. More recent studies have also called into question the notion that America departs radically from European societies in having a much higher degree of social mobility. Erikson and Goldthorpe conclude their survey of comparative social mobility rates by saying:

> there is no basis for claiming, for the twentieth century at least, that American society has been distinctively open in the Tocquevillian sense . . . . Likewise there is no basis for claiming that American society is unique in the extent to which it has provided opportunities for upward mobility in consequence of the rapidity of its structural transformation . . . . [From] the English-American and Swedish-American comparisons that we have carried out, it is already apparent that the USA does not, or at least does no longer, stand apart from all other nations in the amount of its social mobility . . .
>
> (Erikson and Goldthorpe 1985: 19)

But even if one were to accept the broad contrasts of New and Old World, the problem which dogged Durkheim's celebrated attempt to explain suicide rates in a similar manner would remain. However much we may disguise it behind talk of social facts and social forces, the correlation of any two rates or sets of rates must, if correlation is to become explanation, be 'unpackable' to a story about motives and actions (Wallis and Bruce 1986: ch. 1). If anomie, or something like it, is to explain religious participation, we must be able to connect anomie and religiosity in identifiable people. This leads to two problems: one evidential, the other analytical.

If it is the case that geographical mobility prevents the development of naturally occurring communities, and hence creates a market for the artificially constructed versions offered by the churches, it seems sensible to consider what is actually known about the relationship between movement and church participation. The study of highly mobile individuals does not exhaust the topic, but it should still have some bearing on the case. Although it is thin, the available evidence suggests that American migrants do *less*, rather than *more*, religion than 'non-movers'. Dynes, Killian, and Beers and Heflin (in Nelson and Whitt 1972) all conclude that migration is associated with the abandonment of church associations. Giffin (1962) and Powles (1964) both report that Appalachian Mountainers who moved to Cincinatti tended to reduce their levels of religious activity.

Nelson and Whitt's own work compared the religious beliefs of Appalachians who stayed in rural Appalachia, who moved to an Appalachian town, and who moved to Detroit. They found no evidence to support Holt's 'cultural shock' thesis that the transition from country to big city would drive migrants to more sectarian forms of religion in their search for solace and security. While those people who migrated only as far as the Appalachian towns were more sectarian than those who remained behind, those who migrated to Detroit were less so.

Of course, this may mean very little because the research has no longitudinal element. We only know what these three groups were doing and believing at the time of the research. We have no knowledge of how the people who migrated to Detroit compared with their Appalachian neighbours before they moved. Perhaps they moved because they were less well integrated and less traditional in the first place. However, Lenski's Detroit survey does have something of a longitudinal element, in that it reports people's recollections of how their church attendance has changed since coming to the city. Lenski reports that 'Among first generation immigrants from abroad and first-generation migrants from the South, there was a net loss to the churches of 24 per cent' (Lenski 1963: 46). However, and this seems to support Herberg's generations thesis, the loss among second- and third-generation immigrants was a mere 3 or 4 per cent.

Using national survey samples, Lazerwitz was able to compare the percentages of various types and generations of immigrants who are active in churches. While about 50 per cent of all Americans went to church, only 30 per cent of white Protestant migrants were similarly involved. Like Lenski, Lazerwitz reports an increase in church participation with length of residence. Thirty-five per cent of the second generation and 39 per cent of the third are active (in Lenski 1963: 48).

If one approaches the problem from the other end and asks what circumstances are associated with disaffiliation, one discovers that many people who ceased to attend church give migration as the circumstance (if not the reason) for their defection (Gallup and Poling 1980). It also seems, from social histories of early American revivalism, that areas populated by recently arrived isolated individuals and families were not highly conducive to the spread of enthusiastic religion. Although it was the 'frontiers' which were most influenced by the evangelical revivals of the late eighteenth and nineteenth centuries, they were only so influenced ten or twenty years after settlement. Cross's excellent history of the 'burned-over district' of western New York state shows clearly that it was the older, more settled, areas which produced the strongest support for evangelicalism, revivalism, anti-slavery campaigns, and temperance reform. Heightened religiosity seems to have been characteristic of a maturing rather than an entirely new society. A certain degree of stability and social integration was required before people could be mobilized (Cross 1982).

The difficulty in collecting and assessing evidence comes from the vastly complex nature of what is at issue. There is good reason to expect that mobility creates a socio-psychological need for community (which can be serviced by churches). But we also know that urbanization is associated with secularization. The modern city, and the industrial work usually found there, undermine the social relations which sustain religion and reduce the plausibility of religious beliefs, as well as providing many seductve alternatives. Any gains in terms of individuals' felt need for solace and social support are more than cancelled out by the difficulties of creating sustainable communities. While it may be the case that anomie and social disorganization create the circumstances in which more people might become conscious of the value of a sacred canopy and a shared moral universe, desire may not be enough. If the environment is not conducive, the presence of some people who feel a heightened need for religion will not produce a world in which religion regains plausibility.

Many functionalist accounts of action can be reconstructed (along Herberg lines) so that it is the ability of a particular institution or pattern of behaviour to produce desired results at some time in the past, rather than its continued ability to do so, which explains the persistence of the institution or pattern. Thus the absence of evidence that contemporary migrants are unusually drawn to organized religion need not cause us to abandon some sort of anomie account. We could argue that organized religion in migrant-based societies once had added appeal because it performed certain desired social functions. In so doing, it acquired an importance and a respect which continues to this day, even though the social needs which the churches served are no longer as pressing, or are now also served by a variety of secular institutions. This is the essence of the view of sociologists such as Herberg and Lenski who see much of the appeal of the American churches as resulting from the now well-established view that being a church member was part and parcel of being American.

A nativist addition

If the above suggests a solution to the evidential problem, there is still an analytical difficulty. Holt's (1940) cultural shock thesis and others like it have supposed that, if anomie is the cause of certain types of behaviour, it acts by affecting those people whose position is most anomic: migrants, for example. However, there is another possibility. It could well be that evidence of social disorganization (such as a rise in indices of criminal, deviant, and socially unacceptable behaviour) has its greatest impact on members of stable, 'socially organized' communities who feel that their way of life is being threatened by the alien and heathen hordes on their doorstep. It is certainly possible to interpret those kinds of social movement which are concerned with defending the status of threatened cultures in this light: temperance crusaders were not ex-alcoholics but non-drinkers who were worried about the consequences of other people's drinking! It may well be that some of the apparent association between mobility and religiosity is produced by reactions to migrants rather than by migrants. This possibility is really just a logical extension of the more conventional integrative function view of religion in migrant-based societies. Unless the migrants are culturally homogeneous, there is bound to be a double-edged quality to the community building of the churches. The evangelical Protestant churches which did so much to provide a sense of belonging for one generation of settlers in America also provided the ideological and associational base for the rejection of the later waves of non-Protestant immigrants. It is in appreciation of this that Herberg replaces the idea of America as a giant melting-pot with a three-pot analogy. Although there was considerable mixing, through marriage, for example, it was confined within the limits of the three major divisions of Protestant, Catholic, and Jew.

Nativist religious revivals are most extensively documented in the American literature but there were similar (although less successful) movements in New Zealand and Australia where the growth in size and confidence of the Irish Catholic populations produced the reactive formation of political and fraternal Protestant associations.[3]

This discussion of the effects of migration and mobility can now be summarized. I have argued that some of the elements of the explanation of American religiosity should be regarded with a degree of scepticism, because they are based on a comparison of Europe and America which exaggerates the differences between the Old and the New World. I have also suggested that such exaggeration is accompanied by an insensitivity to the problem of generalizing from the society as a whole to any particular part of that society's population. The argument that present American religiosity is to be explained by America's relatively high rates of social and geographical mobility, while intuitively plausible, is made extremely difficult to evaluate because, as its advocates recognize, there is a counter-tendency which cancels out its effects. On the one hand there is the desire of members of a highly mobile society for community. On the other, there is the secularizing impact of the modern industrial city.

There is another explanation for the lack of survey evidence for a strong link between mobility and heightened religiosity which argues that studies, such as that of Nelson and Whitt, are looking for too simple and direct a causal connection. We can sensibly argue that the dual roles which religious associations played in the early period of settlement – initially integrating one wave of settlers and then acting as a base for the assertion of superiority over a later wave of migrants – gave the American churches a social and cultural importance which has remained with them. This version of the argument adds the element that is missing from the more socio-psychological attempts to link anomie and religion: tradition.

While this may seem like a trivial observation to make in concluding a discussion of essays as rich and sensitive to historical nuance as those of Herberg and Wilson, it is important because it allows us to consider the future of American religion. Shifting the location of the secondary appeals of religion from the present to some historically specific past allows the possibility of a decline in religiosity. The church involvement of Herberg's third generation may have been a way of expressing their dual identity – Polish and American, German and American, and so on – but there are a large number of secular class, occupational, and political associations to which people can belong. These may lack some of the elements which make churches attractive but there seems nothing in the explanations of the popularity of American churches which makes them irreplaceable. If an element in their success was their head start, there should be some signs that the churches are losing ground.

Furthermore, if the Herberg and Wilson claim that American churches have become secular is to be sustained, there should be some evidence that, while church participation may remain high, orthodoxy is fading.

Changes in religiosity

There is evidence of decline in American church adherence. It has not been on the scale of defection in Britain but, none the less, it has been real. According to Gallup, the high point for American church membership was 1947, when it was estimated that 76 per cent of the population were church members. It now stands at 68 per cent. Taking only Protestants, the comparable figures show a proportionately slightly greater fall: from 69 per cent to 61 per cent in 1980 (PRRC 1981). The turning-point for most churches was 1965. If one compares the decades before and after that year, one finds that the large mainstream denominations had shifted from membership growth rates of 22 per cent (Lutheran Church

in America), 20 per cent (Episcopal Church), 17 per cent
(Presbyterians), and 10 per cent (United Methodist) to *declines* of
5, 17, 8, and 10 per cent respectively (Carroll *et al.* 1979).

Church attendance has also shown a decline. Whereas 47 per
cent of Protestants claimed to attend church in an average week in
1954, by 1980 the number making such a claim had fallen to 39 per
cent (PRRC 1981: 33).

There has also been a noticeable decline in the numbers
assenting to particular doctrinal propositions. While vague and
general belief in the supernatural seems common, there has been
a fall in the popularity of traditional orthodox Christian beliefs.
Gallup reports that the proportion of Americans believing the
Bible to be the literal Word of God has fallen from 65 per cent in
1963 to just 37 per cent in 1984.

Of greater long-term importance than what Americans believe
is the way in which those beliefs are held. There is considerable
support for Berger's view that American religion has become
privatized. Although Caplow *et al.* begin their discussion of
secularization with the assertion that religion in Middletown shows
massive stability, they go on to document a crucial change. In 1924
the Lynds asked for responses to the statement that 'Christianity is
the one true religion and all people should be converted to it'.
Nintey-four per cent of those asked (that is, almost everybody)
agreed. When responses to the same proposition were solicited in
1977, less than half of those asked – 41 per cent – agreed. More
than half the sample had accepted the denominational position of
supposing that what was true for them need not be true for other
people. Putting it starkly, Caplow *et al.* report that:

> half of Middletown's adolescents who belong to and attend
> church and who believe in Jesus, the Bible, and the here-after
> do not claim any universal validity for the Christian beliefs they
> hold and have no zeal for the conversion of non-Christians.
> Such a situation may never before have existed in the long
> history of Christianity.
>
> (Caplow *et al.* 1983: 98)

It may never before have existed in the short history of American
Christianity, but it was the position of those turn of the century
British evangelicals who later became liberals. It is religious belief

as a matter of preference and not necessity. Once taken, this step opens up the possibility of deciding that one does not prefer religious belief. As Gallup and Poling conclude from their review of recent surveys:

> Many young people seem quite comfortable with a solitary, personal approach to matters of faith – so much so that three out of every four state that they believe a person can be a good Christian even if he or she does not attend church. Should that attitude prevail for long, it means an absolute goodbye to the present religious arrangement in North America.
>
> (Gallup and Poling 1980: 17)

The Middletown re-study also provides good illustration for Wilson's point about the attenuation of the religious in many American churches. Between the Lynd's study in 1924 and the 1977 return, the reasons given by Middletown women for church attendance and involvement had shifted from obedience to pleasure. Naturally, all of the 1924 sample would have described their church involvement as pleasurable, but in traditional and orthodox Christianity the pleasure comes from obeying God and doing what is right in his eyes. As Gallup and Poling rightly observe, the privatization of religion from necessity to personal preference is likely to have considerable consequence.

Change among evangelicals

The shift towards denominationalism is not confined to mainstream Protestants. Although conservative Protestants are cushioned against modernity either by their geographical isolation or their sub-cultural institutions, they are not immune.

James D. Hunter's recent and detailed study shows a decline of orthodoxy among young evangelicals (1987). The inerrancy of scripture, the historicity of the Bible's miracle stories, the need to separate from apostasy, and the reality of eternal punishment for unbelievers; these are all issues on which students in evangelical colleges and seminaries are considerably less orthodox than their parents.

Although it is more difficult to quantify, it is also important that there has been a major change in the behavioural consequences of religious beliefs. Much has recently been made of the evangelical revival which has given a new presence and popularity to the claim to be 'born again'. What has less often been observed, except by Quebedeaux (1978), is that, as the popularity of being born again has increased, so the amount of renunciation involved in the notion has fallen dramatically. It is now common for young women in evangelical gospel choirs to wear expensive coiffures and heavy make-up, and to display an amount of cleavage which would have horrified evangelicals of the pre-war period. Statistical support for the impression that young evangelicals are becoming more and more worldly is provided by Hunter. Young evangelicals are far more willing than their parents to go to the secular cinema, dance, wear make-up and engage in 'light' petting (Hunter 1987: 59). The new Christian right's use of the AIDS epidemic to attack the rights of homosexuals has received considerable publicity, but Hunter identifies a noticeable softening of the attitudes of mainstream evangelicals to homosexuals (ibid.: 62).

To date, these changes are restricted to the less conservative sections of American evangelicalism: the Wheaton College evangelicals and members of churches in the National Association of Evangelicals, rather than the Bob Jones University fundamentalists. But even leaders with solid fundamentalist credentials have moderated their views on significant areas of social and moral behaviour. A fascinating analysis of evangelical and fundamentalist sex manuals shows a clear shift from regarding sex as a necessary evil to seeing it as a gift from God, to be enjoyed in its own right (within marriage, of course), and not merely as a means to procreation (Lewis and Brisset 1986). For example, a book by Tim and Beverley LaHaye, two prominent leaders of a variety of new Christian right organizations, allows that oral sex and masturbation are acceptable forms of sexual activity for born-again Christians. Marabel Morgan's *The Total Woman*, although extremely conservative in its view that women should be husband-obeying home-makers, devoted three chapters to ways in which women could sexually please their husbands, and suggested such elegant variations as coupling under the dining table.

For the interests of this book, perhaps the most significant documented change concerns the claims which conservative evangelicals make for the status of their religious beliefs. Hunter's study shows the first signs of a shift from sectarianism to denominationalism in attitudes towards those who do not share

201

the faith. Evangelicals still insist that one must be born again to enter the kingdom of heaven, but their view on what will happen to the unconverted has moved from blanket condemnation to eternal hell-fire, to a more agnostic view which permits that (perhaps) some of the more 'godly' heathen will be allowed to escape this fate.

The above suggests that evangelical socialization is not entirely successful. Although evangelical sub-cultures in America are more viable than their British counterparts, ideological drift still occurs. In addition to the 'social sources of denominationalism' made well known by Niebuhr (1962), there are external pressures on their sub-cultures and stresses generated by internal competition.

There are good reasons for supposing that the direction of social development in the United states is raising the costs of the sectarian response. To pursue the example of education, most states now have regulations concerning minimum standards of curriculum development and teacher training. Recent court decisions have upheld the application of these regulations to independent Christian schools. Those fundamentalists who have taken the extreme position of refusing to recognize school administration as part of what is due to Caesar have paid the price of fines and imprisonment. For their refusal to accept government policy on the promotion of racial integration, the Bob Jones University and a number of Christian schools have lost their tax-exempt status. In the short term this has actually increased their income as sympathizers have responded to what they see as secularist attacks, but it has considerably increased the cost of opting out of the secular world. Most evangelical parents who desire a Christian education for their children choose to send them to more moderate evangelical establishments.[4]

It is in these establishments that the gradual acculturation process described in detail by Hunter is most visible. Forced to compete with each other and with secular schools and colleges, many evangelical institutions have put pressure on their faculty to acquire good secular credentials. Although piety is still desirable, it is no longer enough, and staff are expected to publish their research in secular journals, to be invited to address secular conferences, to acquire higher degrees, and so on. As Quebedeaux puts it:

with the proliferation of faculty with the best doctorates in every academic discipline teaching at evangelical seminaries and colleges, it is small wonder that these same institutions have been profoundly influenced by the scholarship produced and taught at the most prestigious secular universities.

(Quebedeaux 1978: 15)

One does not have to assume that the secular institutions are superior to sustain this argument. Secular institutions produce more scholars than evangelical colleges. If evangelical colleges hire the best staff, the evangelical element will steadily decline.

Jerry Falwell's Liberty University (previously Liberty Baptist Bible College) is proud of its academic record and anxious to do more than train potential ministers. For this reason, it is keen to seek formal accreditation from secular professional bodies. Perhaps a majority of America's colleges were initially religious foundations. Princeton, Yale, and Harvard in the first wave, Southern Methodist in the second, Wheaton in the third; these are all colleges which were founded to teach theology, train ministers, and promote a particular religious tradition. The first two waves are now thoroughly secularized. Hunter and Quebedeaux suggest that the third wave are moving in the same direction. It is difficult to resist the temptation of supposing that Liberty University will evolve to resemble Southern Methodist or the many American Catholic universities, which offer an essentially secular education with some Catholic overlay and strong Catholic input only in the theology faculty. To return to the major differences between the elements of the Christian tradition discussed in Chapter 2, the problem for Protestant religious colleges is that such a drift towards secular standards and content in education is less easily stemmed than the similar process in Catholic colleges. The Catholic authorities in the Vatican decide which teachers and which colleges are recognized as 'Catholic'. There is no such central authority for conservative Protestants and thus accommodation to the surrounding culture is more difficult to control.

External pressures to accommodate are accelerated by the competition within the evangelical sub-culture. While a small number of colleges can thrive by being ultra-orthodox (and by making teaching in such colleges 'missionary' work for which good staff will accept low salaries), the majority cannot: the market is not yet there. For the majority of bigger colleges there is a strong temptation to reduce their evangelical ethos in order to make themselves attractive to a larger market. The successfully socialized evangelical will not be seduced by the more relaxed atmosphere, the greater intellectual freedom, and the better facilities of the larger 'accommodating' colleges. But a lot of those closer to the edges of the sub-culture will be.

Fighting back

Increasing pressure from the cultural and political centre produces either acquiescence or resistance. If they choose to resist, American conservative Protestants have two options: they can either continue to maintain their sub-cultural *laagers* at increasing personal costs, or they can try to reduce personal costs, either by gaining more social space for themselves or by changing the content of cosmopolitan culture so that its incursions are less damaging. The problem of active resistance is that it places those who engage in it in a position similar to that of the liberalizing evangelicals: one of considerable temptation to accommodate to the prevailing culture.

In order to resist modernization, fundamentalists have been forced to engage in political action at the national level. Although they may be dominant in particular regions, success at national level requires the cultivation of alliances with non-fundamentalist conservatives. This in turn has given fundamentalist leaders good reason to temper their public criticism of competing religious groups who may be needed as cooperating political allies. Between the foundation of the Moral Majority (later renamed Liberty Federation) and his retirement from politics in 1986, Jerry Falwell considerably moderated his public image. Local chapters have been censured, and even expelled, for 'extremist' positions and protests. Whereas in 1980, Falwell was a vociferous critic of George Bush, who was widely regarded by the new Christian right as being too liberal, in 1986 he endorsed Bush's campaign to succeed Reagan as the Republican Party's presidential candidate.

Pat Robertson, who runs his own Christian Broadcasting Network on which he presents a 'born-again' chat show, in 1986 entered the running for the 1988 Republican nomination. As his

CBN organization has grown, and as his chances of political office have increased, so has he downplayed a number of activities, such as speaking in tongues and claiming miraculous spirit healing on television, which might have alienated potential viewers or voters. If Robertson is himself in any doubt about the need to make such changes, his critics are quick to remind him, as they did when making fun of his claim that God diverted a hurricane at his request.

The general point is this: while America offers a more fertile environment for building and maintaining sectarian sub-cultures, there are still considerable and increasing pressures towards cultural homogenization. It is precisely because such pressures have been increasing that fundamentalists have been forced on to the offensive in such movements as the new Christian right. They appreciate that their sub-cultures are under threat. However, to fight back involves them in competing on the national political and cultural stage. When evolutionary theories in biology are invading their world through the medium of textbooks written, edited, published, and distributed by people whose reference group is not rural Tennessee, the fundamentalists must take the fight to a plane higher than that of local influence. In practice, that has meant the passing of laws which require that schools give 'equal time' to evolution and creation as plausible theories of the origins of the species. In order to have such laws passed, fundamentalists have to change the grounds on which they advocate evolutionism. They can no longer assert, as William Jennings Bryan did, that if the Bible is contradicted by science, then they are for the Bible (Russell 1976). Instead, they must adopt the rhetoric of science. Creationism becomes Creation Science. This in turn means that it will be evaluated by the dominant criteria for judging scientific knowledge.[5] Furthermore, such laws will be struck down (as they have been already) until fundamentalists can convince the national legal, political, and intellectual elites to support them.

The alternative to engaging in combat with the carriers of modern secular culture is to campaign for greater regional and personal autonomy. Thus while some new Christian rightists are campaigning for the return of public prayer in schools, others are trying to have the issue taken out of the national arena and returned to individual states (or even smaller units) for legislation.

However, there seems very little sign that America will reverse the trend of two centuries towards greater centralization. In addition, there is little reason to suppose that the campaign for less government regulation and intervention will succeed. In the first place, conservative Protestants are themselves divided, with many fundamentalists being unhappy about the libertarianism of some elements of the new right. While they wish less 'government meddling' in some parts of their lives, they advocate greater restriction in others. In the second place, the south – one of the main bases for conservative Protestantism – has long had a tradition of 'big government' interference in its economic affairs. While some lip-service is paid to free-market entrepreneurial capitalism, generations of southern businessmen and politicians have been raised on government subsidies and 'pork barrel' politics (Phillips 1982: 94–8). For all these reasons, it seems very unlikely that the trend towards greater central regulation will be reversed. Hence the costs of sectarian retreat from the world will continue to rise.

Finally, there is no chance of the majority of Protestant fundamentalists becoming communitarian sectarians. They are not about to abandon their rather comfortable places in the modern material world to engage in the sort of renunciation of worldliness which would make them, like the Amish and the Hutterites, relatively immune to what goes on around them. Modern conservative Protestantism is far too individualistic, and even when conservative Protestants create a viable sub-culture, it only involves them interacting in a fragmented and segmental fashion. Although 'televangelism', with its feedback devices, such as telephone lines for personal counselling and computers which produce the impression of a personal response to the problems of members of the audience who write in, has created some sense of community to overlay the individual congregational associations into which conservative Protestants are divided, this is hardly likely to evolve in the strong sense of community required to sustain an introversionist communitarian sect. Anyway, the communitarian movements which have survived are ones which began centuries ago, and which were aided in their desire to be left alone by considerable public hostility and wide open spaces. Persecution only reinforces internal strength if there is considerable commitment there in the first place. Most attempts to start communitarian movements *de novo* in modern societies have not been successful.

CONCLUSION

This chapter has been concerned to explain why religion has not followed the same career in America and Protestant Europe. It is possible to argue that secularization is proceeding in the same way in both settings, and that the apparent difference is due simply to the relative youth of the New World. It is possible but unsatisfactory. It smacks too much of the unreformed Marxist's response to the failure of Marx's predictions: class struggle will intensify and produce revolution sometime. It may well be that in the long run (that last refuge of the feeble-minded) the American Protestant churches will become as unpopular as their European relatives. At the moment they are a long way from that fate. I have suggested two explanations for the resilience of religion in America. For religion in general, there is the Herberg thesis concerning the role of churches in the development of immigrant responses to the New World. But for all the 'added value' which the situation of the settler gave to the churches in America, there is still evidence of a decline in the fortunes of the mainstream liberal Protestant churches. A similar process is discernible among Catholics and Jews. The more liberal element is absorbed into the wider cosmopolitan culture and the 'centre' of the faith moves towards the conservative end of the spectrum. Liberal Catholics and Jews are losing their Catholicism and Jewishness. Those people who wish to remain Protestant, Catholic, or Jewish have to become more conservative, more sectarian, in their faith.

The second explanation for the vitality of American religion lies in the relative openness and decentralization of the American polity. American regional cultures and sub-cultures have been freer, than their European counterparts, to create and maintain institutions which preserve their distinct identity, and which protect them against modernization. Although this discussion is not intended as an essay in prediction, it seems likely that American conservative Protestantism will gradually be eroded by a combination of increased personal costs for those who persist in maintaining their isolation and, for those who engage with the wider society, considerable incentives to accommodate to the prevailing culture. There is nothing new in this. Although conservative Protestants pride themselves on following the 'old paths', they have changed in response to the changes around them, and will continue to so do.

Chapter Nine

THE SPIRAL OF DECLINE

There are many aspects of reformed Christianity which could usefully have found a place in this study, but I have been guided by a desire to present a coherent sociological explanation of three complex and interrelated features of Protestantism in the modern world: its fragmentation and the part this played in the advent of religious pluralism and tolerance; the rise and decline of liberal Protestantism; and the more recent relative success of conservative varieties of reformed Christianity. This final chapter will use the example of religious revivals to bring together a number of the central themes, and to present a concluding sketch of the career of Protestantism in the modern world.

RELIGIOUS REVIVALS: CAUSES AND CONSEQUENCES

In the opening discussion of secularization, the point was made that no sensitive analysis of the decline of religiosity would depict that process as regular, uniform, or constant. Although the last 200 years can reasonably be described as a period of decline in the importance of religion in most Protestant countries, the actual pattern has been one of alternation between periods of stagnation, decline, and growth. The periods of growth have often been characterized as awakenings or revivals.

America saw the first 'great awakening' led by Jonathan Edwards in the middle of the eighteenth century, Charles Finney's revival in the first quarter of the nineteenth century, and a third period of revivalism at the end of the Victorian era (Weisberger 1958). Some scholars add two more 'awakenings': one in the 1950s, when Billy Graham and others modernized the techniques of mass evangelism (McLoughlin 1957, 1959), and one in the early 1970s which laid the foundation for the present 'new Christian right' movement in American politics. There were revival movements in Scotland: in the lowlands around the town of Cambuslang in 1742 (Gillies 1981) and in the highlands in the late eighteenth century (MacInnes 1951). England saw the Methodist movement and the late nineteenth-century revival inspired by the visit of Moody and Sankey, which produced, among other things, the Keswick Convention meetings (Pollock 1964). Methodism had considerable impact on Wales, and there were revivals in 1859 and 1904 (Williams 1952). Like England and Wales, Ulster was affected by the 1859 revival, and witnessed another revival in 1922 and 1923 (Gamble 1976). Although Lutheran cultures were less prone to evangelical enthusiasm, even Sweden had its revival movements, of which Haugeanism was the most prominent (Hunter 1965).

Recently some historians and sociologists of religion have come to question both the reality and the causes of religious revivals. Timothy L. Smith was one of the main promoters of the notion that American Protestantism had been characterized by cycles of stagnation and enthusiastic revival. He now argues that the notion of a revival is only an observer's construct (Smith 1983). Drawing on detailed studies of small towns, the critics of the awakenings model argue that religious life, when examined in detail, shows stability more than it does spurts of growth or decline, and that, where there were 'revivals', these were local affairs which were not part of any wider movement. Smith and others believe that the view of the religious life of previous centuries, as being characterized by waves of stagnation and revival, tells us more about the partial and uneven attention of secular observers than it does about life in (or outside) the churches.

There is an element of truth in this criticism. There is no doubt that outsiders suffer from lapses of attention and then explain the fact that their interest has been aroused by some episode of religious activity, by assuming that the activity is in marked contrast to what was occurring in the earlier period when they were not paying attention. This is especially the case with journalists where the process is exaggerated by the profession's need to represent events as 'news'. The desire for an audience causes the journalist to construct the world as a series of sharply contrasting states: the old and the new; the before and the after. It is certainly

possible for us to read Jonathan Edwards's account of the revival
in Northampton between 1740 and 1742 and pass over his references to previous outbursts of enthusiasm in 1735 and 1736
(Edwards 1984: 158). But Smith and others have exaggerated this
useful truth in their criticism of the previous orthodoxy of revivals.
After all, it was not just outsiders who reported the first great
awakening as if it was precisely that. Edwards himself lists details of
numbers of souls saved in a way which makes it clear that he, at
least, was surprised. His references to previous revivals suggest that
they were less far-reaching and less profound in their implications
for individual conduct. Ministers involved in preaching to crowds
in Cambuslang and adjoining districts had no doubt that they were
witnessing something which was novel in their ministerial careers,
and like Edwards and those involved with him, they felt moved to
record their experiences and communicate them to others: hardly
something they would have done had these fruits of their labours
been commonplace (Gillies 1981). Such contemporary testimony
is supported by the detailed studies of John Hammond, who,
speaking of America in the period 1825–35, concluded:

> The quantitative data that I gathered, while dealing with only
> one period of revivalism, certainly shows that that period's
> revivals did occur and were perceived as uniquely widespread
> and renewing . . . . The church in the United states has
> experienced cycles of stagnation and renewal, and the renewal
> has come about through periodic intensifications of
> enthusiasm.
>   (Quoted in Gordon-McCutchan 1983: 87)

It is even more difficult to doubt the reality of the Methodist revival
in England or the highland revival in Scotland. The results, in
terms of the recruitment of very large numbers of people to a new
enthusiastic religion, were only too obvious. In Wales, the
Methodist movement and the 1859 and 1904 revivals all produced
easily identifiable increases in church membership. However, an
element of the criticism can be accepted; the episodes identified
as revivals were the most dramatic, rather than the only, episodes
of heightened religiosity. In between the best-known revivals, there
were minor increases (and decreases) in church membership and
attendance.

Those who contest the validity of the cycles model naturally also challenge the most common explanation of the periodic waves of enthusiasm. Smith (before his change of mind), Gordon-McCutchan, and McLoughlin, among others, see revivals as responses to rapid social change and upheaval, especially when such upheaval involves the disintegration of a community.

> When traditional communal bonds break down, new religious forms arise to meet the needs of people faced with anomie. These new forms, it seems, often emphasize 'inner-directedness': no longer able to rely on traditional behavior patterns, victims of social dislocation develop inner determinants of action. In the West, such inner determinants have often been provided by evangelical Christianity. Revival preachers have sought to stem the tide of social chaos by providing people with an inner religious 'gyroscope' ... thus making the masterless their own masters. Guided by the inner gyroscope of the Holy Spirit, evangelicals have been enabled to steer through the anomie of rapid transformation.
>
> (Gordon-McCutchan 1983: 90)

While the basic outline of this model can be accepted, there are a number of implied points which should be examined. In the first place, it is misleading to suggest that revival preachers deliberately sought to stem the tide of social chaos. If they did offer their gospel as a solution to anomie and uncertainty, they did so simply to take advantage of the opportunity which social needs had presented to them. Their purpose – as it was in earlier and later periods – was to see souls saved.

Another minor criticism of Gordon-McCutchan's explanation is that its stress on the attempts of the newly 'masterless' to solve their problems by adopting evangelicalism may cause us to miss those occasions on which the new masters promoted evangelicalism as a solution to the problems of others. Johnson's excellent *A Shopkeeper's Millennium*, an account of the 1820s revival in Rochester, New York, argues, with good evidence, that Finney's evangelicalism 'was a middle class solution to problems of class, legitimacy and order generated in the early stages of manufacturing' (Johnson 1978: 138). Although it would be shallow to reduce the Rochester revival to an example of the deliberate promotion of Marxian 'false consciousness' among an otherwise potentially disruptive workforce, it does seem to have been the case that the initial promotion of evangelicalism was considerably aided by the new economic and social leadership of Rochester. However, whether the initial impetus comes from an emerging elite anxious to legitimate its own position, or from a dislocated subordinate class trying to make sense of its anomie, there does seem considerable value in the general proposition that religious revivals follow periods of rapid social change.

This can perhaps be most clearly seen in the twentieth-century revivals which, for reasons considered in a moment, have been more localized in their impact. A good example is provided by the outbreak of enthusiastic religion which affected the Aberdeenshire fishing fleets of Fraserburgh, Buckie, and Peterhead (Duthie 1983). Until 1914 herring fishing and processing provided the economic base for the relatively isolated communities of the north-eastern coast of Scotland. The success of the fisheries meant considerable prosperity. However, the trade was dependent on European markets. The depression in the post-First World War German economy, and the severing of trade links with Russia after the 1917 revolution, dealt a serious blow to the prosperity of the area. In 1919 and 1920 the government supported the industry with a guaranteed price but this was not renewed in 1921 and standards of living collapsed. The problem was compounded by a poor summer's fishing off East Anglia, and many of the fishermen and allied fishworkers returned to Aberdeenshire after the summer with no profit and mounting debts.

As the fishing community was losing its economic prosperity and security, it was experiencing a religious revival. Half of the revival began in East Anglia and was led by Jock Troup, a cooper turned evangelist. At the same time, those people who had stayed behind were responding to the work of two itinerant evangelists. When the fleet returned north, Troup went with it, and that winter saw a wave of enthusiastic evangelical Protestantism washing over the fishing villages. Within four weeks, Troup could claim more than 400 converts in Fraserburgh. Ninety were claimed for the small village of Cairnburg (Duthie 1983).

That the roots of the revival were in some way related to the problems of the fishing industry seems clear from the very limited range of the awakening: only those villages which were dependent on fishing were involved. Other villages, only three or four miles

213

further inland, experienced nothing comparable. Although Troup and others saw the revival as the prelude to better things, the awakening did not spread. Duthie suggests that the causes lay, not only in economic depression of the fishermen but also in their attendant loss of power. Where, in better times, industrial action had forced employers to increase wages and improve conditions, now strikes had no impact. The people felt themselves threatened, powerless, and at the mercy of forces outside their control. They were ready to hear stories about hell-fire, punishment, damnation, sin, repentance, redemption, and salvation.

The last 'great awakening' in Northern Ireland took place in the period shortly after the partition of Ireland and the formation of the Northern Ireland state:

> Ulster has undergone many changes during the past four years. Its boundaries have been modified and its Government recast. . . . Four years ago, the North of Ireland was in a state of chaos. Fear and uncertainty filled the minds of the people. Politicians were at their wits' end. Murder and destruction, for the time being, seemed to be on the throne. No one could possibly describe the hopelessness of the situation, as things continued to travel from bad to worse . . . [but] man's extremity is always God's opportunity and in the day of trouble He never fails those who call upon Him.
>
> (Gamble 1976: 1–2)

God's solution was to send William P. Nicholson, an Ulsterman who had worked as an evangelist in America and Scotland (where he had been associated with Jock Troup). Nicholson conducted a series of meetings around the province and drew particularly large crowds of lower middle- and working-class Protestants in Belfast. Under his ministry, large numbers professed conversions, and there were identifiable increases in the membership of those Belfast churches most closely associated with the campaign (Barkley 1972).

Hammond, who accepts the reality of revivals but rejects the claim that they can be explained as reactions to changes in the social structure, objects to the uses of anomie or social stress as explanations, on the grounds that revivals do not occur in the most anomic periods of American history. Others have added that the identified social strains were not unique to the periods in question.

Although both of these are important points, they are not fatal to the possibility of an anomie explanation. Too many other variables are missing. First, what will be important in explaining a revival is not the level of anomie in a society as a whole (even supposing that such a thing could be measured), but the extent to which the people, whose behaviour is being explained, feel themselves to be adrift in a hostile world. Second, as those sociologists who have worked with notions such as social stress in the social movements field have argued, we cannot assume that the presence in the world of something which the academic observer depicts as stress means that people living in that world will uniformly react to their circumstances in the same way. Objective circumstances have to be socially constructed, and similar objective conditions may produce different intersubjective reactions. Social stress cannot be treated as an objective condition independent of the social definitions of the situation created by the actors involved.

Furthermore, as was suggested in the last chapter, it seems clear that a certain degree of stability in social relationships is a pre-condition for a collective response to anomie. Cross's history of nineteenth-century western New York state makes it clear that it was not the youngest frontier communities which were most prone to outbreaks of religous enthusiasm. 'The phenomenon of the Burned-over District belongs to a stage of economy either of full or of closely approaching agrarian maturity' (Cross 1982; 76). There are two important reasons for this. The first is that it is only when one has large numbers of people in objectively similar circum-stances that one is likely to have a collective response to those circumstances, irrespective of what that response is (although in this case, the response is revival). Thus the Scottish fishermen's revival affected only those people in the coastal communities who were dependent on fishing. Second, collective responses do not simply emerge mechanically from large numbers of people being confronted with the same objective circumstances. Collective action requires some degree of interpersonal communication, so that people can become aware that they share common problems and be recruited to a particular response. Hence conditions of extreme social disorganization are less likely to produce religious revivals than conditions of some disorganization afflicting relatively stable communities. Hence, as Cross argues, revivals tend to be characteristic of 'maturing' rather than 'immature' communities. Third, as was suggested in the last chapter, it may well be those people on the fringes of disorganization, who remember it or anticipate it, rather than the most dislocated, who see social change as a call to religious revitalization.

The different treatment offered to social disorganization or anomie theories here, and in the last chapter, calls for a brief comment. The penultimate section of the last chapter was less than enthusiastic about the postulation of something like anomie (of which America is said to have much more than Britain because of its higher rates of mobility) to explain the apparently greater popularity of the mainstream American churches. When the notion is used in a cross-societal comparison, operationalization is so difficult that it does not develop beyond being an element in social myths about mobile America and static Europe. When it is deployed in smaller comparative studies of more and less mobile Americans, the evidence does not support the thesis. However, the deployment of the argument in some cases of religious revival is more useful because the historical record can be used to demonstrate the coincidence between disruptive social change and an increase in enthusiastic religion. Longitudinal studies of real communities, as opposed to either same-time or retrospective comparisons of individuals, while imprecise in comparison with data from social surveys, can give us confidence that the changes in question actually occurred.

The problem with the above qualifications is that, while undoubtedly valid, they undermine the pretension to precision of those who deploy notions such as social stress. While the idea that social stress acts on communities of already basically religious people to cause religious revival seems intuitively plausible, it is almost impossible to utililize at anything but the small-scale local level. Only in the study of small communities can one identify the social processes which contribute to the construction of a shared response to social stress.

LATENT AND MANIFEST FUNCTIONS

In order to harmonize the above observations with the general sociological perspective of this book, and to lay the foundation for a simple but important point about secularization, a short theoretical excursion will try to clarify the mechanics of conversion in religious revivals.

There is a Marxist-influenced alternative to the anomie view of religious revivals which sees them as 'primitive rebellions', to take the title of Hobsbawm's book (1959). Its main thrust can be illustrated with the Scottish highlands, case. The conversion of the highland peasantry to evangelical Protestantism followed the disruptions of their social structure. The British government reacted to the 1715 and 1745 Jacobite risings by undermining the authority of the clan chiefs, banning many symbols of traditional culture, and imposing sufficient order so that the chiefs no longer needed standing armies to maintain their positions *vis-à-vis* rival clans. The pacification of the highlands and the incorporation of the chiefs into British political life, meant that the highland lords no longer needed the large numbers of lieutenants and peasants whom they had previously kept on the land as the source of their prestige and, in the frequent event of a feud, their power. At the same time the introduction of manufactures (mainly kelp-processing) meant that landless labourers were more profitable to the chiefs than subsistence farmers and the land, cleared of the uneconomic peasants, could produce increased rent income if it was used for sheep runs. As a consequence, many chiefs abandoned most notions of *noblesse oblige*, resettled their peasants on the inhospitable rugged coastline, and forced them into wage labour and fishing. Although their previous lives as subsistence pastoralists had been hard, the new conditions were, for most, considerably worse. In addition to a massive decline in their standards of living, the highland peasants had the psychological problems of adapting to a radical restructuring of social relationships, as traditional rights and obligations were replaced by contract, and as the chiefs became landlords (Youngson 1973).

The privations of the clearances were followed by religious revival. A contemporary and unsympathetic observer had no hesitation in linking the two. He said it was well known that 'the recent degradation and misery of the people have predisposed their minds to imbibe these pestiferous delusions to which they fly for consolation under their sufferings' (quoted in Bruce 1983c: 559). In his explanation of the revivals, Hunter draws upon parallels with the chiliastic movements of medieval Europe, the cargo-cults of

Melanesia, and the nineteenth-century Italian millennarian movements reported by Hobsbawm to depict the revival as a 'more or
less conscious attempt to come to terms with the realities of a social
and economic system dominated by landlordism rather than
clanship' (Hunter 1978: 102). Like Hobsbawm, Hunter sees the
apparently irrational religious behaviour as masking an underlying
rationality. The highland peasants were driven off their land by
rapacious landlords keen to exploit the economic potential of the
land by filling it with sheep. The social structure and value-system
of the peasants' old world had been destroyed. They had been
prevented from engaging in rational political protest by the limits
of their political thinking and by the power of the landlords. The
peasants therefore diverted their urge to rebel into an enthusiastic
religion which allowed them to see themselves as spiritually
superior to those by whom they were oppressed. Having lost the
right to the earth in this life, the meek were determined to inherit
it in the next.

Although intuitively plausible, both the anomie and primitive
rebellion models of revival are potentially flawed by the confusion
of intended and unintended consequences, or, to use Merton's
(1957: 19–84) terms, of latent and manifest functions. Although
apparently plausible at the level of the society, when unpacked in
the terms of the explanation of individual action, they produce
curious models of the motives of those who participated in the
revival.

If the real cause of the problems which people sought to solve
by getting saved was anomie or exploitation, then how did this
cause produce their action? If they had been aware that their
problems were secular in origin, surely they would have sought
secular solutions. If they were unaware that their problems had
secular causes, then how can we deploy those 'causes' in the
explanation of their action? Assuming for a moment that we could
identify unconscious motives, they may provide a satisfactory
explanation of individual irrational action. After all, the conscious
and the unconscious both inhabit the body that is doing the
acting. But, unless one is going to postulate a Jungian collective
unconscious, group or shared neuroticism seems implausible (as is
argued at greater length in Wallis and Bruce 1983).

Explaining collective social action by positing a 'cause' of which
the actors are unaware is so obviously suspect that analysts are

driven to hint at conscious desire and 'real' intent. Thus Hunter talks of a 'more or less conscious attempt' to come to terms with the new world, and says 'it was through a profoundly evangelical faith that crofters first developed a forward-looking critique' (Hunter 1978: 112). Again we have the suggestion that people participated in the religious revival in order to achieve the latent, rather than the manifest functions of the revival. That is, they were not really intent on getting right with God. They were actually engaged in primitive rebellion.

But if the crofters were really interested in developing a forward-looking critique of landlordism, why did they not do just that instead of wasting a lot of time and energy in an evangelical revival? And, if it occurred to them that they were really engaging in pseudo-rebellion, why did that knowledge not undermine their commitment to the religious activities into which they so enthusiastically threw themselves?

This is an example of the general problem of functionalist sociology as a method of explaining action. As suggested in the earlier discussion of secularization, it seems sensible to see social cohesion as being a consequence (or a function) of a primitive tribe's rain dance. But this is only to account for social cohesion; it does not explain the rain dance. An unanticipated and unintended consequence cannot be the cause of an action. The explanation of the rain dance remains what it was before the functionalist got to it: the rain dance is performed because the dancers (a) want it to rain and (b) think that the dance will make it rain.

In his discussion of functionalism, Elster (1982) makes the following sensible points. For a function to explain an event, we must have either an actor who desires that consequence (intention), or a homeostatic system in which natural selection operates to remove those cases which do not perform the appropriate functions (the survival of the fittest). While this latter model works well for biologists, it is completely unsatisfactory for sociology, and thus so is functionalism.[1]

To summarize; the functionalist and Marxist accounts of revivals, which postulate some sort of social stress as a cause of the revival, are both dogged by the same problem. While we can see how the religious revival had consequences which resolved some of the problems caused by social transformation, we cannot use

219

those consequences as an explanation of the occurrence of revival without showing how the desire for those consequences
manifested itself. We cannot use function as purpose, as sociological functionalists often inadvertently do, without showing
either evidence of that purpose or explaining why, in the absence
of evidence, we should believe that such a purpose was a cause of
the action in question.

The problem can be resolved if we refrain from deploying
anomie or some other social stress as a cause of revival and
consider the way in which people might see social stress as a
stimulus to renewed religious activity. Clearly, a pre-condition of
seeing the actions of greedy landlords as God's judgement and a
call to repentance is a belief in God. Where people already possess
the basis for a religious world-view, social and psychological
problems may be seen as amenable to religious solution. As Duthie
notes, the fishermen of Fraserburgh and Buckie were already
God-fearing men:

> For people whose religion was Calvinist, fundamentalist and
> commanded by the God of wrath, the recent history of the
> fishing communities lent itself to guilt-ridden unease. For some
> at least, the economic disaster of 1921 must have seemed divine
> punishment for the pleasurable worldliness of the war years.
>
> (Duthie 1983: 25)

Similarly, Cross says of the inhabitants of the Burned-over District:
'Most of the persons usually described by Baptist and Presbyterian
clergymen as irreligious, immoral and profane went to church
regularly and expected at some future time to experience conversion during a revival' (Cross 1982: 41).

Clearly, there are differences in the extent to which the various
people involved in religious revivals were recommitting themselves
to an existing faith. In the case of the Buckie revival, most of those
involved were already regular church-goers and people who
operated within a fundamentally religious world-view. The rest
were people who inhabited the same cognitive world but who did
not have a personal commitment to the religious ideology. Many
of those attracted to the field-preaching of Wesley and Whitefield
had only a tenuous connection with organized religion. But – and
this is the main point – there are very few religious revivals which
involved people adopting an entirely new world-view.

Mass conversion, as opposed to revival, is rare, and as it is not central to the argument of this study it need not be considered in detail. However, one or two points can be made about those religious revivals which do involve considerable divergence from the previous religious culture. In the highland revival case, the intrinsic appeal of the religion was augmented by the social and personal characteristics of the people who promoted it. When the old religious culture – a mixture of unreformed Christianity and paganism – was destroyed, the peasants had two choices. They could either accept the moderate Protestantism of the ministers of the established Church of Scotland or they could follow the enthusiastic evangelicalism promoted by lay evangelists, 'the Men'. The ministers of the Kirk had forfeited the trust of people by being, with one or two notable exceptions, time-serving, spineless, and uncritical supporters of the very landlords who were the cause of the peasants' sufferings. In contrast, 'the Men' who led the revival were ordinary peasants whose piety was respected and who were not tainted by a history of fawning to landowners and their agents. This suggests that a model for linking social stress and revival in a sensible manner can be derived from the badly neglected 'diffusion of innovation' research (Rogers 1962). A number of studies, initially of the impact of mass media on public opinion and, later, of the spread of new ideas and technical innovations, have suggested that the public tends to react most favourably to new information when it does not come directly from the mass media or some other distant source, but is mediated by 'community leaders' who have gradually acquired a reputation for being reliable sources and good guides.

To summarize the career of the highland revival, initially a number of pious lay evangelicals reacted to social stress by becoming committed believers and more aggressive evangelists. The rapid social transformation had destroyed previous community bonds, and the failure of the Kirk ministers to abandon their toadying to their patrons had left them largely discredited in the eyes of their people. The peasants found themselves in a position of having to choose between a religion which they found to be implausible, because of the behaviour of its spokesmen, and a new evangelicalism which was sponsored by people whom they trusted. They chose the latter. As an aside, it is interesting that nineteenth- and twentieth-century revivals were rarely led by professional clergymen. Jock Troup was a cooper turned evangelist. Evan Roberts, the leader of the 1904 Welsh revival, was a collier who dropped out of ministerial training because he found the Calvinistic Methodist ministers to be out of touch with the interests of the common people among whom he lived and worked.

Because both supporters and critics are liable to exaggerate the extent of the change that occurs in a religious revival, it is important to note that even in the case of the highland revival, where the new evangelicalism was significantly different from what had previously been the orthodoxy, there was still considerable continuity. Even those highlanders who moved furthest – from an only partly reformed Episcopalianism to evangelicalism – had still only shifted within a conservative and supernaturalist Christianity. The existence of a creator God, the importance of the Bible as God's word, the Trinity, the Virgin Birth; these things were accepted before and after the revival. Importantly, both 'before' and 'after' belief systems incorporated the idea that there was one truth which could be known.

This may seem like a tortuous route to arrive at a statement of the obvious, but the obvious is sometimes forgotten. The crux of the matter is this: how people react to anomie, social stress, social disorganization – call it what you will – is heavily influenced by their pre-existing beliefs. Rapid social change is not a *cause* of cultural change: it is an opportunity and an occasion for cultural change. Although it is not a universal and immutable law, it is generally the case that only religious people react to anomie or disorganization by engaging in collective religious action. To illustrate the point with a negative example, few occurrences in this century can have been as anomic or socially disorganizing as the First World War, and yet a large and detailed survey of British soldiers' attitudes to religion and the churches found no evidence of any major increase in interest in matters religious (Cairns 1919). The explanation is simple. Although many soldiers were privately religious, most were not, and there was no shared religious culture to furnish the cognitive or emotional resources for a shared religious reaction.

 If the above reasoning is generally correct, it follows that the decrease in the extent to which religious world-views are shared, and are important, will cause a gradual decline in the frequency, scale, and significance of religious revivals.

THE DECLINING SPIRAL

Although the career of enthusiastic religion in each of the settings under discussion followed a different time-scale, the trajectory has been similar. In the cycles of religious growth and decline which have characterized the last two centuries, each wave of growth has involved either fewer people, or made less impact, or both. The first and second great awakenings in America involved large numbers and had considerable impact, which can be seen not only in the growth of congregations but also in major social movements such as the temperance and anti-slavery agitations which followed them. The third great awakening was far less significant. If it is not already exaggerating to place it in the list, the fourth one – that attributed to Billy Graham in the 1950s – was even less important. The recent rise of the new Christian right has involved nothing that could even be called a revival. It is simply an assertion of the political power of American fundamentalists, a redressing of the balance in which people whose pietistic retreat from the world had previously denied them the influence which, by virtue of numbers, was always their due. There has been almost nothing by way of a net increase in the number of the 'saints' and, although claims to being 'born again' are now more commonly made, the changes in attitudes and behaviour previously associated with such claims have been considerably attenuated.

A large number of studies have demonstrated that the modern mass evangelism of people like Graham is consumed almost entirely by people who have already been pre-socialized into those beliefs (Ward 1980; Clelland *et al.* 1974; Bruce 1984a). In one sense, this is not new. For the reasons explained above, most revivals have had more to do with shifting people from nominal attachment and some acquaintance to deep personal commitment. It is not the case that present-day evangelists are less competent at doing that. Rather, the number of people in the penumbra of loose association to a faith, who could be shifted to a deeper commitment, has declined. It is not because their aim has become less accurate that modern mass evangelists are now casting more of their seed on stony ground. There is simply more stony ground.

Evidence can be presented for the claim that revivals have gradually declined in significance. The movements of Scottish dissent which led to the creation of the Seceder churches involved so many people that they grew to rival the established Church of Scotland in size. The highland revivals in the early nineteenth century had such an impact that almost the whole of the highlands came out of the Kirk to join the Free Church in 1843. Even in the urban lowlands where secularization was beginning to be evident, the impact of the Moody and Sankey meetings in the 1870s, although difficult to quantify, was considerable (Drummond and Bulloch 1978: 157–60). However, even then the new members brought to the churches through such missions did not compensate for those being lost.

In 1955 Billy Graham led a series of evangelistic crusades in Scotland. The programme was coordinated by the Church of Scotland and the other Protestant churches in a well-organized 'Tell Scotland' campaign, which involved extensive publicity before the meetings and considerable pursuit of prospects after the event. For those who could not personally attend the meetings, land-lines were arranged to relay the services to halls throughout Scotland and many ministers assisted in promoting the gospel (Allen 1955). In all, there were more than one million attendances at meetings (although how many of these were the same people night after night is not known). The Graham organization recorded 26,547 'inquirers'. Of the 19,835 inquirers at the Glasgow meetings, 79 per cent indicated that they were making a first-time commitment to Christ.

Just what did that mean for the life of the Christian Church in Scotland? We are fortunate that John Highet was already engaged in a survey of church attendance in Glasgow when the Graham meetings took place. The survey was continued for a year after, and we are thus able to assess the impact of Graham's work. The results showed that average attendance over three Sundays at seven non-Catholic denominations had risen by 10,575. Highet estimates the total non-Catholic church attendance for 1958 at around 580,000. Thus new attendance was some 1.8 per cent of the church-going population. A year later the number of new attenders had fallen by almost half of that gain to just 4,854 (Highet 1960). Thus the enormous effort that went into the campaign, which could not have been better advertised or promoted, and which was heartily supported by the Scottish press, produced an increase in attendance of less than 1 per cent, an increase in line with the growth of the adult population. Furthermore, the vast majority of the clergy who responded to questionnaires concluded that the campaign had made little or no difference to their congregations. More recent crusade campaigns have had even less impact.[2]

A similar tale could be told for Northern Ireland. The 1859 revival in Ulster revitalized the Presbyterian Church. W.P. Nicholson's 1922–3 crusades led to measurable increases in attendance in Belfast churches. More recent evangelistic endeavours, such as those strenuously engaged in by Ian Paisley in the formation of his Free Presbyterian Church of Ulster, have led only to denominational relocation and not to any measurable increase in the total numbers involved.

We cannot be sure what they were doing before Rowlands and Howell recruited them for Welsh Methodism, but we do know that well over 30,000 people had become Calvinistic Methodists and another 68,000 had joined the Baptists and Congregationalists by 1830, this from a total population of not much over half a million (Currie *et al.* 1977: 148). As in England, Welsh dissent grew most rapidly between 1740 and 1840. Between 1840 and 1906, the rate of growth decreased to the point where, while the churches were still growing, they were growing more slowly than the total population and this despite the rapid growth in membership during the 1859 revival. That revival apparently added some 90,000 new members to the three dissenting churches from a total population which was now around the million mark. There was another half-century gap before the third revival, which in the winter of 1904/5 added some 60,000 new members and, for the first time since 1859, caused church membership to increase relative to population growth (Williams 1952). But the period of net increase was short and did little to reverse the trend of decline relative to the total population, which was now about two million. By 1906 many of these new members had fallen away. Since then the churches have declined, not only relative to the growing population but also in absolute terms. There have been no subsequent revivals significant enough to be claimed by people other than Welsh evangelists. In 1961 the population of Wales was around three million. The membership of the three main denominations then numbered about 350,000: slightly more than a tenth of the population. A hundred years earlier, between a quarter and a fifth of the people of Wales had been church members.

In his analysis of the career of English dissent, Gilbert draws on his detailed studies of nonconformist church membership to argue for cycles of decline (Gilbert 1976, 1980). Martin and others have drawn on the institutionalization literature of social movements to argue that there is a common career pattern for religious organizations which can be explained in terms of internal processes of development. The radical dissenting body recruits rapidly but gradually loses its radical ethos as it develops a full-time professional ministry, and as its own membership becomes upwardly mobile. Part of the membership rebels and hives off to form a new radical sect. They combine with those people who would have been attracted to the old radical body in its early days. Thus as Methodism became respectable and settled down to be yet another largely middle-class denomination, the Brethren, the Salvation Army, the Churches of Christ, and others filled the gap in the market. This is clearly an accurate picture of the process but its significance for this argument lies in the numbers involved in each turn of the wheel.

> Between 1880 and 1911 the combined membership of . . . [the Methodist, Congregational and Baptist] denominations declined as a proportion of the adult English population from 6.6 per cent to 5.6 per cent. For the combined density index to have remained steady . . . would have required an additional net gain of more than 220,000 members. But the contemporary growth in England of the Salvation Army, the Plymouth Brethren and the Churches of Christ, combined with that of the smaller Victorian sects, would not have gone halfway towards closing such a gap.
>
> (Gilbert 1976: 44)

The conclusion of this discussion of religious revivals must be that such episodes have been of diminishing importance. This has been so much the case that it would be misleading to describe as 'awakenings' the growth of Paisley's Free Presbyterian Church, the increasing popularity of the language of born-again Christianity in

America in recent decades, or the rise of the charismatic and 'house church' movements. They have been movements of 're-location' or as changes in fashion.

As a culture becomes ever more secular, episodes of rapid social change and social dislocation are less and less likely to be seen as signs of God's displeasure, or as problems which might be solved through the acquisition of the correct religion. Though there may still be many individuals who see some sort of supernatural message in the quirks of their biographies, the decline of a *shared* religious culture reduces the likelihood of a community reacting to disruptive social changes by increased commitment to a common religion.

CONCLUSION

Even those sociologists who explain secularization as a result of industrialization, urbanization, and the increased rationality of the modern world, would have to recognize that Protestantism was importantly implicated in its own fate. Even if one concedes no more than that Protestantism played a part in the genesis and promotion of the rational, industrial, and urban world, one has the image of reformed Christianity as its own grave-digger. In adding to this irony the point that the fissiparousness of Protestantism hastened pluralism and hence secularization, I have not attempted to replace the more common explanations of secularization with the claim that the fragmentation of Protestantism was a sufficient cause of its own demise. Rather, I have tried to draw attention to an aspect of the process which has previously been neglected. When scholars have been interested in the content of the Reformation world-view, they have usually been concerned with the impact of what might be called substantive propositions. I am interested in the most abstract element of Protestantism: its epistemological position. Claimed reliance on the Bible as the sole source of authoritative knowledge, despite the best efforts of its promoters, has consistently failed to produce coherence, consistency, and uniformity. Instead, it has generated schism. The Holy Spirit's reported achievement at Pentecost of allowing people to hear the same message in different tongues has not been repeated; different tongues now bear conflicting and competing messages.

As Martin has said, the problem of Protestantism is that it is voluntaristic to a degree which makes it precarious (Martin 1978b:

9). Although Protestants have evolved a variety of organizational
devices to maintain cohesion (or continued with some of the pre-
Reformation Church's institutions and practices), such devices
have largely failed because they are not legitimated by any core
doctrine. It may, for example, be good to have an educated and
licensed ministry, but no genuinely reformed religion can
maintain that such an institution is essential for salvation. Despite
the best efforts of Protestants, fragmentation has not been
avoided.

Although the essence of reformed Protestantism may be
described sociologically as individualistic, the first wave of splits
were social, rather than idiosyncratic, and tended to follow the
fissures of ethnic, regional, and class differentiation. The
inevitable but unintended consequence was the rise of religious
pluralism and the expansion of the secular state. Those Protestants
who were not geographically insulated against modernization were
forced to choose between denominational accommodation to
pluralism or sectarian rejection. While the former course
produced a new variety of reformed Christianity, which was
attractive to Protestants who already had a strong grounding in
Christianity, it was organizationally precarious. Its attempts to win
the support of those outside the churches (and regain those who
were drifting in that direction) by trying to meet such people's
non-religious needs have largely failed in Europe (although they
have been slightly more successful in America). This should
occasion no surprise, given that modern societies are so well
provided with a variety of secular institutions that it is only in the
realm of religion, narrowly defined, that the churches possess
superior credentials.

The alternative to the denominational endorsement of
pluralism is sectarian rejection, with its attitudinal and behavioural corollaries of limited withdrawal from the world. To date,
the sectarian response has been more successful than
denominationalism in retaining the active support of church
adherents. Contemporary conservative Protestants are not entirely
world-rejecting, and their sub-cultures are not entirely separated
from the surrounding world, but they are sufficiently divorced
from its culture to be able to maintain their own deviant world-
view and to socialize their children in their distinctive beliefs and

values. The extent to which that strategy will continue to succeed depends on the degree to which modern societies continue to move towards cultural homogeneity.

Although this may sound paradoxical, the culture which most threatens conservative Protestantism is not some shared dominant ideology. An apocalyptic culture of the Anti-Christ would be a boon to sectarian Protestantism, as is recognized by those conservatives who attempt to construct multifarious threats into 'secular humanism' or 'militant communism'. What is most damaging is a liberal pluralistic hegemony which imposes nothing more specific than the refusal to endorse dogmatism. Particular elements of modern secular culture no doubt offend, but what corrodes is the constant denial of the possibility of there being one true faith. However much conservatives may try to construe 'secular humanism' as a coherent ideology which threatens their religion, it is the democratic attitude to religion expressed in that wonderful section on American forms which invites one to fill in 'the religion of your preference' which will do the most damage.

If modern societies continue to spread the liberal values of the centre to the peripheries, conservative Protestants will either face higher costs in the maintenance of their sub-cultures or be forced to fight back. Engagement with the world – even hostile engagement – requires some compromise and accommodation, and thus raises the possibility of another wave of liberalization. Any significant move by conservatives towards the centre will produce another wave of conservative revolt, and the creation of a new generation of purified sectarian social institutions. If the past is any guide to the future, the numbers involved in such a revolt will be considerably smaller than those who supported the last rejection of liberal Protestantism.

This then is a secularization story, although it involves no notion of evolution from ignorance to enlightenment, no expectation that decline will be even, and no assertion that small-scale localized revivals will not occur. Far from it. On the first point, Chapters 3 and 4 should have made it clear that toleration was rarely anyone's intention. It was a grudging reaction to the pluralism which in most cases resulted from conservative, rather than liberal, schisms. On the second, the impact of pluralism and other secularizing forces is bound to be uneven. Most people do not live in the abstract 'society' which we impute to them. They live in slices and chunks of it: their region, their class, their ethnic minority, their valley, their occupational group, and their family and friends. Major changes are filtered through these sub-economies, sub-societies, and sub-cultures. Not only will decline be uneven but it will be punctuated by periods of revival, both absolute and relative. If circumstances cause a community of believers to become even more committed to their faith and to engage more actively in evangelism, they may increase the number of the saints. There will certainly be relative revival because what is most precarious (and hence dies fastest) is liberal Protestantism, the least overtly religious form of modern Christianity. Because they will come to form a greater part of Protestantism, conservative varieties will seem to be increasing in popularity.

However, conservative Protestants will never again achieve cultural dominance because their success is self-limiting. So long as the essential fissiparousness of Protestantism remains, any position other than that of being under constant threat will allow internal divisons to re-emerge. Growth to any size which reduces the sense of being under pressure, which takes conservative Protestantism beyond the ghetto, and which brings access to wealth and power, will also produce a move towards accommodation. This view is generally that of Niebuhr when he argued that sects have a universal tendency to become denominations. Wilson (1982: 90–100) has correctly pointed out that Niebuhr's thesis only holds for certain types of sect. However, the mainstream of conservative Protestantism approximates mostly closely to the 'conversionist' type of sect discussed by Niebuhr. The relaxation of moral standards, the rise of a professional ministry, the diminution of what separates the saints from the world, and the increased relaxation of membership tests (which accompanies the rise in the proportion of the saints who are socialized in, rather than converted to, the faith), will produce another sectarian revolt and another turn of the wheel.

It also seems obvious that the rise of social differentiation in complex industrial class societies is irreversible. There will thus always be the two elements – Protestantism's essential fissiparousness and external social divisions – which interact to produce religious pluralism. Although a pluralistic culture, if sustained by an open structure, permits minorities the freedom to maintain their deviant world-views, it does not permit them to attain hegemony.

If it is not too foolish to attempt to reduce such a vast topic to a few sentences, the previous nine chapters can perhaps be distilled to the following essence. Since the advent of pluralism made the church type of religious organization impossible, believers have had the choice of the denomination or the sect. The denomination's lack of definitive differentiation from the surrounding culture makes it precarious. Its adherents are too easily absorbed by the society at large. Thus organized shared religion in modern industrial societies will come to be represented primarily by the sect, and the viability of the sect depends on the willingness of the encompassing society to permit sub-cultures to endure.

NOTES

CHAPTER 1: SECULARIZATION

1. For an extremely plausible vision of the long-term problems of a 'secular' society, see Wilson's Hobhouse Memorial lecture (1985).
2. Although such stories are doubtless exaggerated, there is good evidence that many are true in essence. See, for example, the reports of the consequences of W.P. Nicholson's crusade in Belfast in the 1920s (Gamble 1976).
3. For the reasons given by Runciman (1970: 59–70) any definition of 'religion' will cause almost as many problems as it solves. My own preference is for a substantive definition in terms of beliefs about the supernatural, but almost nothing in this book depends on the beliefs and actions in question being 'religious' rather than, say, political, ethical or moral. Indeed, one of the classic statements of the precariousness of diffuse belief systems concerns a socio-political movement (Demerath and Thiessen 1966), and the other is about a humanist association (Wallis 1980).
4. For example, Young (1970) entitles his essay 'The impact of Darwinism on conventional thought' when it is, not surprisingly, largely a discussion of the impact of Darwinism on intellectuals, church leaders, and the literati. We know very little or nothing about ordinary people's reactions to Darwinism.
5. The problems of accurately assessing degrees of religious commitment and orthodoxy for any period before the Victorian era are manifold (and remain considerable even for the present). There is certainly some evidence that the commitment of pre-industrial societies to Christianity has been exaggerated (Thomas 1971; Scarisbrick 1984; Reay 1985a). In the other corner there is the more traditional view of Laslett (1971) and Collinson (1982, 1983). I would tend to the Collinson view for two reasons. First, the detailed ecclesiastical court records which appear to show considerable indifference also ironically show the strength of religion in the very existence of such courts and the willingness of people to submit to them. Second, there is always a danger of assuming that the attentive

233

and thoroughly involved posture of our congregations is the religious mode *par excellence* and that anything else shows disrespect. This is rather ethnocentric. Jews in *shul,* for example, often wander around and break off from their prayers to chat to others about secular matters.

I would accept the argument of Abercrombie, Hill, and Turner (1980) that it was really only the dominant classes which were thoroughly incorporated within a 'dominant ideology'; the lower classes were largely kept in line by economic and political compulsion. However, that the extent of religious orthodoxy among the common people was not high enough reason for us to explain social order in terms of ideological incorporation is not reason enough for us to abandon the idea that the early modern world was Christian in a way that the 'post-industrial' one is not.

CHAPTER 2: THE FRAGMENTATION OF PROTESTANTISM

1. The view that the Bible was *inerrant* was only articulated later, around the turn of the century, and as a reaction to the 'higher critical' school of Biblical interpretation. But although reasoned argument that the Bible was the revealed word of God was new, the assumption that it was God's word and that it meant what it said, had, until the higher criticism, been the dominant, even 'taken-for-granted', position.

2. Given the point I make later that each of these sources is rarely accepted entirely exclusive of the others, the four components of the typology are clear closer to Weber's 'ideal type' (Weber 1964: 110–12) than to an 'average' type. But it is not important. The four sources are my distillation and compression of the answers that various self-identifying groups of Christians give to the epistemological question, and the epistemological issue has been chosen as the basis for identification because (a) it is very important to the actors, and (b) as the rest of the book will, I hope, demonstrate, it is useful for understanding the actions of different groups of Christians. Although I was not initially alert to the parallels, the four sources of authority have some correspondence with Weber's description of sources of legitimation. Culture/Reason could be Weber's rational authority; Bible could be his legal; Church could be his traditional; and Spirit his charismatic authority (Weber 1964: 324–62). However, what is more important than the actual mapping of my categories on to his is the common interest in the consequences of different sorts of authority for social action.

3. It is worth adding that the four sources do not all have the same 'magnetic pull' nor do they have the same presence in the history of the Christian Church. Culture/Reason, with its relativizing tendency, although present from the first as a logical possibility, has risen in popularity with modernity. For reasons explored in the vast sociological literature on bureaucratization, oligarchization, and the

routinization of charisma, Spirit is the weakest and most transient; Church the strongest and most enduring.

4. To translate these terms into the language of church, sect, denomination, and cult, church and sect are both uniquely legitimate (the church is respectable; the sect is deviant), while the denomination and the cult are pluralistically legitimate (the former is respectable; the latter is deviant). For further details see Wallis (1975: 35–43 and 1976: 11–18).

5. This is not to say that most leaders of schismatic Protestant movements are charismatic leaders in the Weberian sense; they are not. Rather, the respect that followers have for the courage, insight, piety, preaching and exegetical skills, and political leadership of the founders and leaders is often a restraint on the centrifugal force of the ready availability of legitimate authority. The standing of Ian Paisley in his own Free Presbyterian Church is a good example (Bruce 1986).

CHAPTER 3: DISSENT AND TOLERATION

1. The changes in the urban section of the Seceders and the Free Church are a good illustration of the Niebuhr thesis (1962) which points to the combined effects of the second generation being raised in, rather than having converted to, the faith, and 'Wesley's law' with its observation of the self-defeating nature of ascetic religion; the discipline learnt in the faith causes an increase in wealth and upward social mobility, which in turn increase the temptation to depart from the narrow asceticism.

2. On Hannah More and the Mendip schools, and other examples of evangelical interest in popular education see McLeish (1969) and Bradley (1976).

CHAPTER 4: ESTABLISHMENTS AND TOLERATION

1. The point cannot be too often made that what counts as appropriate demeanour during religious exercises is a *variable*. Too much weight should not be put on evidence that many members of the audience showed a detachment which we would think inappropriate.

2. For a recent analysis of the evidence which is closer to the Thomas view than that of Collinson, see Reay (1985a: 91–128).

3. At the risk of being tedious, the following point has so often been misunderstood that I will repeat it: I am not concerned with the *origins* of ideas but with the time and circumstances under which they become *popular*. Thus while far-sighted visionaries such as Barrow and Brown and other separatists are interesting to the church historian or the historian of ideas, they 'represented . . . a minute element in the religious life of their own day' (Dickens 1983: 426) and are thus not especially significant for my interests. On the separatists, see White (1971).

4. The relative unpopularity of religious tolerance can be gauged from the size of the various strands of dissent. The 'intolerant' Presbyterians and Congregationalists far outnumbered the 'tolerant' Baptists and Anabaptists. Good figures are not available until 1672, but the position fifty years earlier was probably not at all different. The 1,457 licences granted to individual ministers under Charles II's Declaration of Indulgence, which do not include the Quakers, were divided as follows – Presbyterians: 60 per cent; Congregationalists: 22 per cent; Independents: 3.4 per cent; Baptists: 6.6 per cent and Anabaptists: 7.3 per cent (Bebb 1980: 32).
5. There has been so much recent writing on the Civil War and the 'puritan revolution' that it is almost invidious to select only a few but this section draws heavily on Hill (1969, 1972, 1984, 1986a, 1986b) and Jones (1978). For a view from Scotland, see Mitchison (1983).
6. As an aside it is worth noting that the fear of rebellion which promoted the clampdown on dissent was not entirely without foundation. The belief of the radicals that the Commonwealth had come into being with God's blessing caused most of them fatalistically to accept the Restoration as also being part of divine providence. However, the millennarians saw it as proof of the imminence of the second coming and thought rebellion would hasten that event. The rising of Venner's Fifth Monarchy men in London in 1661 was small, but it confirmed the government's worst fears of the radical sects (Jones 1978: 139).
7. In the first decade of the eighteenth century, 1,219 temporary and 41 permanent places of dissenting worship were registered in England and Wales. By the fourth decade, numbers had fallen to 424 and 24 respectively (Bebb 1980: 39)
8. Field (1977) has demonstrated that the Methodist class profile was broader than is often assumed but his revisions do not threaten my point.

CHAPTER 5: THE RISE OF LIBERAL PROTESTANTISM

1. On perfectionism among American Methodists, see Jones (1974). For holiness in Britain, see Pollock (1964).
2. Evangelicals began to have doubts about the liberal direction of the SCM shortly after the turn of the century. The Cambridge evangelicals withdrew in 1910 and others followed (Pollock 1953; Barclay 1974; Johnson 1979). Starting with a national conference in 1919, they gradually constructed a national Fellowship of Christian Unions which exactly replicated the organizational structure of the old SCM. Everything which is said here about the SCM was originally formulated as one half of a contrast with the evangelical Inter-Varsity Fellowship, but for the purposes of this study the IVF details have been omitted. A more formal comparative presentation can be found in Bruce (1984a).

3. In addition to the published histories and biographies (Padwick 1930; Tatlow 1933; Braisted 1941; Fraser 1934; McCaughey 1958), my main source for information on the Student Movement was the SCM Archive in the Central library of the Selly Oak Colleges, Selly Oak, Birmingham, which contains Tatlow's diary. As I am rarely quoting directly from the records, I have not given detailed locations, but the material is stored in the order in which it came from the SCM offices. Letters and memoranda are filed chronologically under the department or task. Tatlow (1933) is a reasonably accurate history and contains highly detailed accounts of the debates within the Movement about relations with non-evangelicals, changes in the Basis of Faith, and the downgrading of the Missionary Department. Further details of the SCM and its conservative rival, the Inter-Varsity Fellowship, are given in Bruce (1980). I would like to record here my thanks to the Principal and Librarian of the Selly Oak Colleges for their assistance.
4. Too rigorous application of a membership test would, of course, have reduced contact with unbelievers and hence the possibility of evangelism. IVF solved the problem by having a very general formula for ordinary members of Christian Unions (along the lines of 'desiring to follow Jesus'), and applying the lengthy statement to committee members and invited speakers, whose 'known beliefs' had to be 'in accordance with the statement of faith'.
5. For a more sympathetic exposition of Barth and Bultmann, see Richardson (1961).

CHAPTER 6: THE DECLINE OF LIBERAL PROTESTANTISM

1. Kelley is discussed in more detail in the next chapter.
2. For recent figures on membership and attendance, see Brierley (1980, 1984, 1987), Brierley and Evans (1983), and Brierley and Macdonald (1985). The best source of long series of data is Currie et al. (1977) and Currie and Gilbert (1977).
3. One of the many problems of such statistics is that membership rolls are often not revised frequently. Part of the decline of the URC post-merger may be explained as a statistical artefact of major roll revision. The only hope is that the numbers involved are so large, and the time covered sufficiently great, for the effect of abrupt falls attendant on revision to be muted. Because the quality of the statistical data is so poor I have tried to avoid making claims to unwarranted accuracy; hence percentages have only been given to whole numbers and absolute numbers to the nearest hundred.
4. From a study of 681 mainstream United Presbyterian congregations in America, Hadaway (1980: 309) comes to the same conclusion about degrees of conservatism and growth.
5. This information comes from conversations with Andrew Walker, for whose assistance I am grateful, and from a large number of unstructured interviews with people attending the Dales Bible Week – a

major north of England house church movement event at the Harrogate show ground – in 1980 and 1981.

6. For two good first-hand accounts of such ministries and the hostility they aroused from more traditionally-minded members of the congregations, see Osborne (1981) and Christman (1978).

7. Another problem of resource management which dogged the SCM was its failure to control sub-units which it had initially established to strengthen its own organization. FCE Ltd, a company which Tatlow set up to administer the Swanwick conference centre for the Movement and to make a little profit on the side, became independent of the Movement. SCM in schools changed from being concerned with promoting the SCM to school pupils, so that they joined it when they went to university, to preparing general religious studies material for school classes. SCM Press, once the publishing arm of the SCM, became an ordinary publishing house whose only links with the movement was that the Movement owned most of the shares and took the profits. Each sub-unit developed away from serving the SCM to pursuing the logic of its own interests.

CHAPTER 7: THE CONSERVATIVE RESPONSE TO PLURALISM

1. This example and many others are discussed in detail in my sociological account of the new Christian right in America (Bruce 1988). Other aspects of American conservative Protestantism are discussed in my study of *Pray TV: the Sociology of Televangelism* (forthcoming).

CHAPTER 8: AMERICAN PROTESTANTISM

1. Planned legislation to permit more 'local' radio stations may change the British situation a little. Differences between British and American media structures are discussed at length in Bruce (forthcoming).

2. This case is just one of many in which fundamentalists and liberals are presently competing to define new boundaries of appropriate state intervention. Although the situation is flexible, there is no doubt that American sub-cultures have considerably more autonomy than their British counterparts.

3. The best guide to the voluminous literature on American nativism is Lipset and Raab (1978). For a Catholic view of nativism in America, see Kane (1955). On anti-Catholicism in Australia, see Campion (1982: ch. 3). On the New Zealand Protestant Protective Association, see Sinclair (1980: 230–50).

4. The BJU case and other recent church/state disputes are discussed in the various essays in Robbins and Robertson (1987).

5. The publications of Creation Science writers have been accepted rather uncritically by fundamentalists looking for publicly acceptable grounds for their beliefs. They concentrated more on showing

apparent inconsistencies in the work of evolutionists than on presenting their own alternative. The passage of various 'equal time acts' (which call for the teaching of evolution to be balanced with Creation Science) in state legislatures has proved a mixed blessing. Although the legislative victories were morale-building, they meant that the Creation Science alternative was subjected to critical public examination. Judge Overton, in his judgment on the constitutionality of the Arkansas Equal Time Bill, concluded that 'creation science' was not plausible independent of a fundamentalist reading of Genesis 1:12; hence it was a religion and not a science. For details of the Arkansas trial, see Gilkey (1985).

CHAPTER 9: THE SPIRAL OF DECLINE

1. For a detailed discussion of the problems of functionalist sociology, see Ryan (1970) and Filmer *et al* (1972).
2. In 1981 the Argentine-born evangelist Luis Palau staged a month-long series of evangelistic meetings in the Kelvin Hall in Glasgow. In terms of planning, the campaign was as well organized as Billy Graham's had been, and Palau was given considerable positive publicity, but the impact was negligible. I had intended to replicate Highet's study, and made some exploratory investigations, but concluded that the impact was so slight that there was no point.

BIBLIOGRAPHY

Abercrombie, N., Hill, S., and Turner, B.S. (1980) *The Dominant Ideology Thesis*, London: George Allen & Unwin.
Allen, T. (1955) *Crusade in Scotland ... Billy Graham*, London: Pickering and Inglis.
Ammerman, N. (1987) *Bible Believers*, New Brunswick, NJ: Rutgers University Press.
Anderson, A.B. (1977) 'A study in the sociology of religious persecution: the first Quakers', *Journal of Religious History* June: 247–62.
Anderson, A.L. (1978) *Divided We Stand: Institutional Religion as a Reflection of Pluralism and Integration in America*, Dubuque: Kendall/Hunt Publishing.
Ashton, R. (1985) *Reformation and Revolution, 1558-1660*, London, Paladin.
Ausubel, H. (1960) *In Hard Times: Reformers Among the Late Victorians*, London: Oxford University Press.
Barbour, G.F. (1924) *The Life of Alexander Whyte*, London: Hodder & Stoughton.
Barbour, J. and Quirk, T. (eds) (1986) *Essays on Puritans and Puritanism by Leon Howard*, Albuquerque: University of New Mexico Press.
Barclay, O.R. (1974) *Whatever Happened to the Jesus Lane Lot?*, Leicester: Inter-Varsity Press.
Barkley, J.M. (1972) *St Enoch's Congregation: an Account of Presbyterianism Through the Life of a Congregation*, Belfast: St Enoch's.
Barrett, D.B. (1982) *World Christian Encyclopedia: a Comparative Study of Churches and Religions in the Modern World, AD 1900–2000*, Nairobi: Oxford University Press.
Barrett, L.E. (1977) *The Rastafarians*, Kingston, Jamaica: Sangster's Book Store.
Beasley-Murray, P. and Wilkinson, A. (1981) *Turning the Tide: an Assessment of Baptist Church Growth in England*, London: Bible Society.
Bebb, E.D. (1980) *Nonconformity and Social and Economic Life, 1660–1800*, Philadelphia: Porcupine Press.

Bennett, G.V. (1969) 'Conflict in the Church', in G. Holmes (ed.)
Britain After the Glorious Revolution 1689–1714, London: Macmillan,
pp. 155–75

Berger, P.L. (1961) *The Noise of Solemn Assemblies: Christian Commitment
and the Religious Establishment in America*, New York: Doubleday.

Berger, P.L. (1963) 'A market model for the analysis of ecumenicity',
Social Research 30: 77–93.

Berger, P.L. (1969) *A Rumour of Angels: Modern Society and the Rediscovery
of the Supernatural*, New York: Doubleday.

Berger, P.L. (1973) *The Social Reality of Religion*, Harmondsworth:
Penguin.

Berger, P.L. (1979) *Facing up to Modernity: Excursions in Society, Politics
and Religion*, Harmondsworth: Penguin.

Berger, P.L. (1980) *The Heretical Imperative: Contemporary Possibilities of
Religious Affirmation*, London: Collins.

Berger, P.L. , Berger, B., and Kellner, H. (1974) *The Homeless Mind:
Modernization and Consciousness*, Harmondsworth: Penguin.

Berger, P.L. and Luckmann, T. (1973) *The Social Construction of Reality*,
Harmondsworth: Penguin.

Bibby, R. (1978) 'Why conservative churches really are growing: Kelley
revisited', *Journal for the Scientific Study of Religion* 17: 129–37.

Bibby, R. (1979) 'The state of collective religiosity in Canada: an
empirical analysis', *Canadian Review of Sociology and Anthropology* 16:
105–16.

Bibby, R. (1985) 'Religious encasement in Canada', *Social Compass* 32:
287–303.

Bibby, R. and Brinkerhoff, M. (1973) 'The circulation of the saints: a
study of people who join conservative churches', *Journal for the
Scientific Study of Religion* 112: 273–85.

Bibby, R. and Brinkerhoff, M. (1974) 'When proselytizing fails: an
organizational analysis', *Sociological Analysis* 35: 189–200.

Bibby, R. and Weaver, H.R. (1985) 'Cult consumption in Canada: a
further critique of Stark and Bainbridge', *Sociological Analysis* 46:
445–60.

Binns, L.E., (1928) *The Evangelical Movement in the English Church*,
London: Methuen.

Bishop, G.F., Tuchfarber, A.J., and Oldendick, B.W. (1986) 'Options on
fictitious issues: the pressure to answer survey questions', *Public
Opinion Quarterly* 50: 240–50.

Blaikie, N.W.H. (1972) 'What motivates church participation? Review,
replication and theoretical reorientation in New Zealand',
Sociological Review 20: 39–58.

Bolton, S.C. (1982) *Southern Anglicanism: The Church of England in
Colonial South Carolina*, Westport, Conn.: Greenwood Press.

Bouma, D. (1979) 'The real reason one conservative church grew',
Review of Religious Research 20: 127–37.

Bowden, J. (1970) *Who is a Christian?*, London: SCM Press.

Bowden, J. and Richmond, J. (eds) (1967) *A Reader in Contemporary*

Theology, London: SCM Press.

Bradley, I. (1976) *The Call to Seriousness: the Evangelical Impact on the Victorians*, London: Jonathan Cape.

Bradley, R. (1982) 'The failure of accommodation: religious conflicts between Presbyterians and Independents in the Westminster Assembly 1643–1646', *Journal of Religious History* 12: 23–47.

Braisted, R.W. (1941) *In This Generation: the Story of Robert P. Wilder*, New York: Friendship Press.

Brauer, J.C. (1985) 'Regionalism and religion in America', *Church History* 54: 366–78.

Brierley, P. (1980) *Prospect for the Eighties: From a Census of the Churches in 1979*, London: Bible Society.

Brierley, P. (1984) *UK Christian Handbook 1985/86 Edition*, London: Evangelical Alliance/MARC Europe/Bible Society.

Brierley, P. (1987) *UK Christian Handbook 1988/89 Edition*, London: Evangelical Alliance/MARC Europe/Bible Society.

Brierley, P. and Evans, B. (1983) *Prospects for Wales: Report of the 1982 Census of the Churches*, London: Bible Society/MARC Europe.

Brierley, P.and Macdonald, F. (1985) *Prospects for Scotland: From a Census of the Churches in 1984*, Edinburgh: National Bible Society for Scotland/MARC Europe.

Briggs, J. (1979) *Report of the Denominational Enquiry Group to the Baptist Union Council*, unpublished mimeo.

Bromley, D.G. and Shupe, A.D. (1979) ' "Just a few years seem like a lifetime": a role theory approach to participation in religious movements', *Research in Social Movements, Conflict and Change* 2: 159–85.

Brown, C. (1987) *The Social History of Religion in Scotland Since 1730*, London: Methuen.

Brown, G. and Mills, B. (1980) *The Brethren Today: a Factual Survey*, Exeter: The Paternoster Press.

Bruce, S. (1978) 'A witness to the faith: dilemmas of evangelism as reality and rhetoric', *Scottish Journal of Sociology* 2: 163–73.

Bruce, S. (1980) 'The Student Christian Movement and the Inter-Varsity Fellowship: a Sociological Study of Two Student Movements', upublished Ph.D. thesis, Stirling University, Scotland.

Bruce, S. (1983a) 'Identifying conservative Protestantism', *Sociological Analysis* 44: 65-70.

Bruce, S. (1983b) ' The persistence of religion: conservative Protestants in the United Kingdom', *Sociological Review* 31: 453–70.

Bruce, S. (1983c) 'Social change and collective behaviour: the revival in eighteenth-century Ross-shire', *British Journal of Sociology* 34: 554–72.

Bruce, S. (1984a) *Firm in the Faith: the Survival and Revival of Conservative Protestantism*, Aldershot: Gower.

Bruce, S. (1984b) 'A sociological account of liberal Protestantism', *Religious Studies* 20: 401–15.

Bruce, S. (1985a) *No Pope of Rome: Militant Protestants in Modern Scotland*, Edinburgh: Mainstream.

Bruce, S. (1985b) 'Authority and fission: the Protestants' divisions',
   British Journal of Sociology 36: 592–603.
Bruce, S. (1986) '*God Save Ulster!': the Religion and Politics of Paisleyism*,
   Oxford: Clarendon Press.
Bruce, S. (1988) *The Rise and Fall of the New Christian Right: Conservative
   Protestant Politics in America 1978–1988*, Oxford: ClarendonPress.
Bruce, S. (forthcoming) *Pray TV: the Sociology of Televangelism*, London:
   Routledge.
Budd, S. (1967) 'The Humanist societies: the consequences of a diffuse
   belief system', in B.R. Wilson (ed.) *Patterns of Sectarianism*, London:
   Heinemann, pp. 377–406.
Budd, S. (1977) *Varieties of Unbelief: Atheists and Agnostics in English
   Society: 1850-1960*, London: Heinemann.
Burleigh, J.H. (1973) *A Church History of Scotland*, Oxford: Oxford
   University Press.
Cairns, D.S. (1919) *The Army and Religion: an Enquiry and its Bearing
   upon the Religious Life of the Nation*, London: Macmillan.
Calley, M.J.C. (1965) *God's People: West Indian Pentecostal Sects in England*,
   London: Oxford University Press.
Campbell, A.B. (1979) *The Lanarkshire Miners; a Social History of their
   Trade Unions*, Edinburgh: John Donald.
Campion, E. (1982) *Rockchoppers: Growing up Catholic in Australia*,
   Victoria: Penguin.
Caplow, T. (1985) 'Contrasting trends in European and American
   religion', *Sociological Analysis* 46: 101–8.
Caplow, T., Bahr, H.M., and Chadwick, B.A. with Hoover, D.W., Martin,
   L.A., Tamney, J.B., and Williamson, M.H. (1983) *All Faithful People:
   Change and Continuity in Middletown's Religion*, Minneapolis:
   University of Minnesota Press.
Carroll, J.W. with Roozen, D.A. (1979) 'Continuity and change: the
   shape of religious life in the United States, 1950 to the present', in
   J.W. Carroll, D.W. Johnson, and M. Marty (eds) *Religion in America:
   1950 to the Present*, San Francisco: Harper & Row, pp. 1–36.
Cashmore, E. (1979) *Rastaman: the Rastafarian Movement in England*,
   London: George Allen & Unwin.
Catherwood, F. (1975) *A Better Way: the Case for a Christian Social Order*,
   London: Inter-Varsity Press.
Chadwick, O. (1970) *The Victorian Church: an Ecclesiastical History of
   England*, London: A. & C. Black.
Christie, I. (1982) *Wars and Revolutions: Britain 1760–1815*, London:
   Edward Arnold.
Christman, W.J. (1978) *The Christman File*, Edinburgh: St Andrew Press.
Church, R.W. (1970) *The Oxford Movement*, Chicago: Chicago University
   Press.
Clelland, D.A., Hood, T., Lipsey, C.M., and Wimberley, R. (1974) 'In
   the company of the converted: characteristics of a Billy Graham
   Crusade audience', *Sociological Analysis* 35 (1): 45–56.
Cohen, P.S. (1972) *Modern Social Theory*, London: Heinemann.

Collins, G.N.M. (1976) *The Heritage of Our Fathers. The Free Church of Scotland: Her Origin and Testimony*, Edinburgh: The Knox Press.

Collinson, P. (1982) *The Religion of Protestants: the Church in English Society 1559-1625*, Oxford: Clarendon Press.

Collinson, P. (1983) *Godly People: Essays on English Protestantism and Puritanism*, London: The Hambledon Press.

Cowan, I.B. (1976) *The Scottish Covenanters, 1660–1688*, London: Gollancz

Cross, W. (1982) *The Burned-Over District: the Social and Intellectual History of Enthusiastic Religion in Western New York, 1800–1850*, Ithaca, NY: Cornell University Press.

Currie, R. (1968) *Methodism Divided*, London: Faber & Faber.

Currie, R. and Gilbert, A.D. (1977) 'Religion', in A.H. Halsey (ed.) *Trends in British Society*, London: Macmillan, pp. 407–50.

Currie, R., Gilbert, A.D., and Horsley, L. (1977) *Churches and Churchgoers: Patterns of Church Growth and Decline in the British Isles Since 1700*, London: Oxford University Press.

Demerath, N. J. III and Thiessen, V. (1966) 'On spitting against the wind: organizational precariousness and American irreligion', *American Journal of Sociology* 71: 674–87.

Dickens, A.G. (1983) *The English Reformation*, London: Fontana.

Douglas, A.M. (1985) *Church and School in Scotland*, Edinburgh: St Andrew Press.

Doyle, R.T. and Kelly, S.M. (1979) 'Comparison of Ten Denominations, 1950–1975', in D.R. Hoge and D.A. Roozen (eds) *Understanding Church Growth and Decline: 1950–1975*, New York: Pilgrim Press, pp. 144–59.

Drummond, A. L. and Bulloch, J. (1973) *The Scottish Church 1688–1843: the Age of the Moderates*, Edinburgh: The Saint Andrew Press.

Drummond, A. L. and Bulloch, J. (1975) *The Church in Victorian Scotland 1843–1874*, Edinburgh: Andrew Press.

Drummond, A. L. and Bulloch, J. (1978) *The Church in Late Victorian Scotland 1874-1900*, Edinburgh: The Saint Andrew Press.

Duthie, J.L. (1983) 'The fishermen's religious revival', *History Today*, December 22–7.

Dynes, R.R. (1957) 'The consequences of sectarianism for social participation', *Social Compass* 35: 331–5.

Edwards, J. (1984) *On Revival*, Edinburgh: Banner of Truth Trust.

Eliade, M. (1971) *The Myth of the Eternal Return, or Cosmos and History*, Princeton, NJ: Princeton University Press.

Elster, J. (1982) 'Marxism, functionalism and game theory: the case for methodological individualism', *Theory and Society* 11: 453–82.

Erikson, R. and Goldthorpe, J.H. (1985) 'Are American rates of social mobility exceptionally high? New evidence on an old issue', *European Journal of Sociology* 1: 1–22.

Engeman, T.S. (1982) 'Religion and political reform: Wesleyan Methodism in nineteenth-century Britain', *Journal of Church and State* 24: 321–35.

Evangelical Alliance (1968) *Background to the Task*, London: Evangelical Alliance/Scripture Union.

Evans, E. (1982) *Revival Comes to Wales*, Bridgend: Evangelical Press of Wales.

Evans, E. (1985) *Daniel Rowland and the Great Evangelical Awakening in Wales*, Edinburgh: Banner of Truth Trust.

Ferguson, W. (1978) *Scotland 1689 to the Present*, Edinburgh: Oliver & Boyd.

Field, C.D. (1977) 'The social structure of English Methodism: eighteenth to twentieth centuries', *British Journal of Sociology* 28: 199–225.

Filmer, P., Phillipson, M., Silverman, D., and Walsh, P. (1972) *New Directions in Sociological Theory*, London: Collier-Macmillan.

Fletcher, R. (1971) *The Making of Sociology, vol. 1: Beginning and Foundations*, London: Michael Joseph.

Forster, P.G. (1972) 'Secularization in the English context: some conceptual and empirical problems', *Sociological Review* 20: 153–68.

Fraser, A. (1934) *Donald Fraser of Livingstonia*, London: Hodder & Stoughton.

Gairdner, W.H.G. (1910) *Edinburgh 1910: an Account and Interpretation of the World Missionary Conference*, Edinburgh: Oliphant, Anderson & Ferrier.

Gallup, G. Jr and Poling, D. (1980) *The Search for America's Faith*, Nashville: Abingdon.

Gallup, G.H. (1976) *The Gallup International Public Opinion Polls: Great Britain 1937–1975*, New York: Random House.

Gallup Organization (1976) *Religion in America 1976. Report No. 130*, New York: Gallup Organization.

Gallup Organization (1985) *Religion in America, 1935–85. Report No. 236*, New York: Gallup Organization.

Gamble, J.A. (1976) *From Civil War to Revival Victory: a Souvenir of the Remarkable Evangelistic Campaigns in Ulster from 1921 to December 1925, Conducted by Rev. W. P. Nicholson*, Belfast: Emerald Isle Books.

Gaustad, E.S. (1968) 'America's institutions of faith: a statistical postscript', in W.G. McLoughlin and R. Bellah (eds) *Religion in America*, New York: Beacon Press, pp. 111–33.

Gay, J. (1971) *The Geography of Religion in England*, London: Duckworth.

Giffin, R. (1962) 'Appalachian newcomers in Cincinnati', in T.R. Ford (ed.) *The Southern Appalachian Region: a Survey*, Lexington: University of Kentucky Press, pp. 79–84.

Gilbert, A.D. (1976) *Religion and Society in Industrial Society: Church and Chapel and Social Change 1740–1914*, London: Longman.

Gilbert, A.D. (1980) *The Making of Post-Christian Britain: a History of the Secularization of Modern Society*, London: Longman.

Gilkey, L. (1985) *Creationism on Trial: Evolution and God at Little Rock*, Minneapolis: Winston Press.

Gillies, J. (1981) *Historical Collections of Accounts of Revivals*, Edinburgh: Banner of Truth Trust.

Glasner, P. (1977) *The Sociology of Secularization*, London: Routledge & Kegan Paul.

Glock, C. and Stark, R. (1965) *American Piety*, Berkeley, Calif.: University of California Press.

Gordon-McCutchan, R.C. (1983) 'Great awakenings?', *Sociological Analysis* 44: 83–95.

Graham, H.G. (1937) *The Social Life of Scotland in the Eighteenth Century*, London: A. & C. Black.

Gray, J. (ed.) (1978) *W. R. The Man and His Work: a Brief Account of the Life and Work of William Robinson, M. A., B. Sc., D. D.*, Birmingham: Berean Press.

Hadaway, C.K. (1980) 'Conservatism and social strength in a liberal denomination', *Review of Religious Research* 21: 302–14.

Hadden, J.K. (1986) 'Religious broadcasting and the mobilization of the new Christian right', presidential address, Society for the Scientific Study of Religion, Savannnah, Georgia, 26 October.

Hadden, J.K. and Swann, C.E. (1981) *Prime Time Preachers: the Rising Power of Televangelism*, Reading, Mass.: Addison–Wesley.

Hale, F. (1981) 'The development of religious freedom in Norway', *Journal of Church and State*, 23: 47–68.

Halevy, E. (1938) *A History of the English People in 1815*, vol. 3, London: Penguin.

Hammond, J.L. (1983) 'The reality of revivals', *Sociological Analysis* 44: 111–15.

Hay, D. and Morisey, A. (1981) 'Secular society/religious meaning: a contemporary paradox', unpublished mimeo.

Hechter, M. (1975) *Internal colonialism: the Celtic Fringe in British National Development, 1536–1966*, London: Routledge & Kegan Paul.

Henderson, I. (1969) *Scotland: Kirk and People*, London: Lutterworth Press.

Henriques, U. (1961) *Religious Toleration in England, 1787–1833*, London: Routledge & Kegan Paul.

Herberg, W. (1960) *Protestant, Catholic, Jew: an Essay in American Religious Sociology*, New York: Doubleday Anchor.

Highet, J. (1960) *The Scottish Churches*, London: Skeffington.

Hill, C. (1969) *Reformation to Industrial Revolution*, Harmondsworth: Penguin.

Hill, C. (1972) *God's Englishman: Oliver Cromwell and the English Revolution*, Harmondwsorth: Penguin.

Hill, C. (1984) *The World Turned Upside Down: Radical Ideas During the English Revolution*, Harmondsworth: Penguin.

Hill, C. (1986a) *Puritanism and Revolution: Studies in Interpretation of the English Revolution of the 17th century*, Harmondworth: Penguin.

Hill, C. (1986b) *Society and Puritanism in Pre-Revolutionary England*, Harmondsworth: Penguin.

Hill, S. (1966) *Southern Churches in Crisis*, New York: Beacon Press.

Hobsbawm, E.J. (1959) *Primitive Rebels: Studies in Archaic Forms of Social Movement in the 19th and 20th Century*, Manchester: Manchester

University Press.

Hobsbawm, E.J. (1977) *Industry and Empire,* Harmondsworth: Penguin.

Hoge, D.R. (1979) 'A test of theories of denominational growth and decline', in D.R. Hoge and D.A. Roozen (eds) *Understanding Church Growth and Decline, 1950–1978,* New York: The Pilgrim Press, pp. 179–223.

Hoge, D.R. and Polk, D.T. (1980) 'A test of theories of Protestant church participation and commitment', *Review of Religious Research* 21: 315–29.

Hoge, D.R. and Roozen, D.A. (1979) 'Research on factors influencing church commitment', in D.R. Hoge and D.A. Roozen (eds) *Understanding Church Growth and Decline: 1950–1978,* New York: The Pilgrim Press, pp. 42–68.

Holt, J. B. (1940) 'Holiness religion: cultural shock and social reorganization', *American Sociological Review* 5: 740–7.

Hostetler, J.E. (1963) *Amish Society,* Baltimore, Maryland: Johns Hopkins Press.

Hunter, J.D. (1978) *The Making of a Crofting Community,* Edinburgh: John Donald.

Hunter, J.D. (1982) 'Operationalizing evangelicalism: a review, critique, and proposal', *Sociological Analysis* 42: 363–72.

Hunter, J.D. (1983) *American Evangelicalism: Conservative Religion and the Quandary of Modernity,* New Brunswick, NJ: Rutgers University Press.

Hunter, J.D. (1987) *Evangelicalism: the Coming Generation,* Chicago: University of Chicago Press.

Hunter, L.S. (1965) *Scandinavian Churches: a Picture of the Development and Life of the Churches of Denmark, Finland, Iceland, Norway and Sweden,* London: Faber & Faber.

Jackson, E. M. (1980) *Red Tape and the Gospel: a Study of the Ecumenical Missionary Struggle of William Paton (1886 –1943),* Birmingham: Phlogiston Publishing.

Johnson, D.J. (1979) *Contending For the Faith: a History of the Evangelical Movement in the Universities and Colleges,* Leicester: Inter-Varsity Press.

Johnson, P.E. (1978) *A Shopkeeper's Millennium: Society and Revival in Rochester, New York, 1815–37,* New York: Hill & Wang.

Jones, C.E. (1974) *Perfectionist Persuasion: the Holiness Movement and American Methodism, 1867–1936,* Metuchen: The Scarecrow Press.

Jones, J.R. (1978) *County and Court: England 1658–1714,* London: Edward Arnold.

Jordan, W.K. (1932) *The Development of Religious Toleration in England: From the Beginning of the English Reformation to the Death of Queen Elizabeth,* London: George Allen & Unwin.

Kane, J.C. (1955) *Catholic–Protestant Conflicts in America,* Chicago: Regney.

Kanter, R. (1968) 'Commitment and social organization: a study of commitment mechanisms in utopian communities', *American Sociological Review* 33: 499–517.

Kanter, R. (1972a) 'Commitment and the internal organization of millennial movements', *American Behavioural Scientist* 16: 219–43.

Kanter, R. (1972b) *Commitment and Community: Communes and Utopias in Sociological Perspective*, Cambridge, Mass.: Harvard University Press.

Kelley, D (1972) *Why the Conservative Churches Are Growing*, New York: Harper & Row.

Kelley, D, (1978) 'Why the conservative churches are still growing', *Journal for the Scientific Study of Religion* 17: 129–37.

Laslett, P. (1971) *The World We Have Lost*, London: Methuen.

Latourette, K. (1954) 'Ecumenical bearings on the missionary movement and the International Missionary Council', in R. Rouse and S. Neill (eds) *History of the Ecumenical Movement*, vol. 1, London: SPCK.

Lee, R. and Marty M.E. (eds) (1964) *Religion and Social Conflict*, New York: Oxford University Press.

Lenman, B. (1981) *Integration, Enlightenment and Industrialization: Scotland, 1746–1832*, London: Edward Arnold.

Lenski, G. (1963) *The Religious Factor: a Sociologist's Inquiry*, New York: Doubleday Anchor.

Lewis, L.S. and Brisset, D.B. (1986) 'Sex As God's Work', *Society* 23 (3): 67–75.

Lipset, S.M. (1968) *Revolution and Counter-Revolution: Change and Persistence in Social Structures*, London: Heinemann.

Lipset, S.M. and Raab, E. (1978) *The Politics of Unreason: Right-Wing Extremism in America, 1790–1977*, Chicago: University of Chicago Press.

Little, D. (1970) *Religion, Order and Law: a Study in Pre-Revolutionary England*, Oxford: Basil Blackwell.

Lyons, D. (1985) *The Steeple's Shadow: On the Myths and Realities of Secularization*, London: SPCK.

McCaughey, J.D. (1958) *Christian Obedience in the Universities*, London: SCM Press.

McGaw, D.B. (1979) 'Commitment and religious community: a comparison of a charismatic and mainline community', *Journal for the Scientific Study of Religion* 18: 146–63.

McGregor, J.F. and Reay, B. (1984) *Radical Religion in the English Revolution*, Oxford: Oxford University Press.

MacInnes, J. (1951) *The Evangelical Movement in the Highlands of Scotland 1688–1800*, Aberdeen: The University Press.

McKerrow, J. (1841) *History of the Secession Church*, Edinburgh and Glasgow: A. Fullerton & Co.

MacLaren, A. A. (1974) *Religion and Social Class: the Disruption Years in Aberdeen*, London: Routledge & Kegan Paul.

McLeish, J. (1969) *Evangelical Religion and Popular Education: a Modern Interpretation*, London: Methuen.

McLeod, H. (1981) *Religion and the People of Western Europe 1784–1970*, London: Oxford University Press.

McLoughlin, W.G. (1957) *Billy Graham: Revivalist in a Secular Age*, New York: The Ronald Press.

McLoughlin, W.G. (1959) *Modern Revivalism*, New York: The Ronald Press.

McLoughlin, W.G. and Bellah R. (eds) (1968) *Religion in America*, New York: Beacon Press.

McPherson, A. (1972) *History of the Free Presbyterian Church of Scotland (1893–1970)*, Inverness: Free Presbyterian Church of Scotland.

Manning, B. L. (1952) *The Protestant Dissenting Deputies*, Cambridge: Cambridge University Press.

Marsden, G.M. (1977) 'Fundamentalism as an American phenomenon: a comparison with English evangelicalism', *Church History* 46: 215–32.

Marsden, G.M.(1982) *Fundamentalism and American Culture: the Shaping of Twentieth-Century Evangelicalism, 1870–1925*, New York: Oxford University Press.

Marshall, G. (1982) *In Search of the Spirit of Capitalism: an Essay on Max Weber's Protestant Ethic Thesis*, London: Hutchinson University Library.

Martin, D. (1967) *A Sociology of English Religion*, London: Heinemann Educational Books.

Martin, D. (1969) *The Religious and the Secular: Studies in Secularization*, London: Routledge & Kegan Paul.

Martin, D. (1978a) *A General Theory of Secularization*, Oxford: Blackwell.

Martin, D. (1978b) *The Dilemmas of Contemporary Religion*, Oxford: Blackwell.

Martin, D.(1979) 'Revs and revolutions: church trends and theological fashions', *Encounter* January: 10–19.

Mathew, D. (1948) *Catholicism in England: the Portrait of a Minority, its Culture and Tradition*, London: Eyre & Spottiswoode.

Mechie, S. (1960) *The Church and Scottish Social Development, 1780–1870*, London: Oxford University Press.

Melton, J.G. (1978) *The Encyclopedia of American Religion*, Wilmington, NC: McGrath Publishing.

Merton, R.K. (1957) *Social Theory and Social Structure*, Glencoe, NY: The Free Press.

Merton, R.K. (1973) *The Sociology of Science: Theoretical and Empirical Investigations*, Chicago: University of Chicago Press.

Mitchison, R. (1983) *Lordship to Patronage: Scotland 1603–1745*, London: Edward Arnold.

Mol, H. (ed.) (1972) *Western Religion: a Country by Country Sociological Inquiry*, The Hague: Mouton.

Mol, H. (1976) *Identity and the Sacred: a Sketch for a New Social–Scientific Theory of Religion*, Oxford: Blackwell.

Nelson, H.M. and Whitt, M.P. (1972) 'Religion and the migrant in the city: a test of Holt's cultural shock thesis', *Social Forces* 50: 379–84.

Niebuhr, H.R. (1962) *The Social Sources of Denominationalism*, New York: Meridian Books.

Nugent, W.T.K. (1977) *From Centennial to World War: American Society, 1876–1917*. Indianapolis: Bobbs-Merrill.

Nyomarkay, J. (1967) *Charisma and Factionalism in the Nazi Party*, Minneapolis: University of Minnesota Press.

Osborne, A. (1981) *Focus on Ferguslie: a Report on the St Ninian's Team Ministry 1974–1980*, Edinburgh: Church of Scotland.
Padwick, C. (1930) *Temple Gairdner of Cairo*, London: SCM Press.
Parker, D. and Parker, H. (1982) *The Secret Sect*, Pendle Hill, NSW, Australia: The Authors.
Peshkin, A. (1985) *God's Choice: the Total World of a Fundamentalist Christian School*, Chicago: University of Chicago Press.
Peters, V. (1965) *All Things Common: the Hutterian Way of Life*, New York: Harper & Row.
Phillips, K.P. (1982) *Post-Conservative America*, New York: Random House.
Pinder, R. (1971) 'Religious change in the process of secularization', *Sociological Review* 19: 343–66.
Pollock, J. (1953) *A Cambridge Movement: a History of the Cambridge Inter-Collegiate Christian Union, 1877–1952*, London: John Murray.
Pollock, J. (1964) *The Keswick Story*, London: Hodder & Stoughton.
Preston, R. (1986) 'The collapse of the SCM', *Theology* 89: 431–9.
Princeton Religious Research Center (PRRC) (1980) *Religion in America, 1979–80*, Princeton, NJ: Princeton University Press.
Princeton Religious Research Center (PRRC) (1981) *Religion in America, 1981*, Princeton, NJ: Princeton University Press.
Powles, W.E. (1964) 'The southern Appalachian migrant: country boy turned blue-collarite', in A.B. Shostak and W. Gomberg (eds) *Blue-Collar World: Studies of the American Worker*, Englewood Cliffs, NJ: Prentice-Hall, pp. 270–81.
Quebedeaux, R. (1978) *The Worldly Evangelicals*, San Francisco: Harper & Row.
Ransom, S., Bryman, A., and Hinings, B. (1977) *Clergy, Ministers and Priests*, London: Routledge & Kegan Paul.
Reay, B. (1985a) *Popular Culture in Seventeenth-Century England*, New York: St Martin's Press.
Reay, B. (1985b) *Quakers and the English Revolution*, London: Temple Smith.
Reed, J.S. (1972) *The Enduring South: Subcultural Persistence in Mass Society*, Lexington, Ky: Lexington Books.
Richardson, A. (1961) *The Bible in the Age of Science*, London: SCM Press.
Robbins, T. and Robertson R. (eds) (1987) *Church–State Relations: Tensions and Transitions*, New Brunswick, NJ: Transaction Books.
Robertson, R. (1972) *The Sociological Interpretation of Religion*, Oxford: Blackwell.
Rogers, E.M. (1962) *Diffusion of Innovations*, Glencoe, NY: The Free Press.
Roozen, D.A. and Carroll, J.W. (1979) 'Recent trends in church membership and participation: an introduction', in D.R. Hoge and D.A. Roozen (eds) *Understanding Church Growth and Decline: 1950–78*, New York: The Pilgrim Press, pp. 22–41.
Rouse, R. (1967) 'Voluntary movements and the changing ecumenical climate', in R. Rouse and S. Neill, *A History of the Ecumenical*

Movement, Philadelphia: Westminster Press, pp. 310–57.

Roxborough, I. (1971) *The School Board of Glasgow 1873–1919*, London: University of London Press.

Runciman, W.G. (1970) *Sociology in its Place*, Cambridge: Cambridge University Press.

Russell, C.A. (1976) *Voices of American Fundamentalism: Seven Biographical Studies*, Philadelphia: Westminster Press.

Ryan, A. (1970) *The Philosophy of the Social Sciences*, London: Macmillan.

Scarisbrick, J.J. (1984) *The Reformation and the English People*, Oxford: Blackwell.

Seppanen, P. (1972) 'Finland', in H. Mol (ed.) *Western Religion: a Country by Country Sociological Inquiry*, The Hague: Mouton, pp. 143–73.

Sinclair, K. (1980) *A History of New Zealand*, London: Allen Lane.

Sjolinder, P. (1962) *Presbyterian Reunion in Scotland, 1870–1921*, Uppsala: Almquist and Wiksel.

Skeats, H.S. and Miall, C.S. (1891) *History of the Free Churches of England, 1688–1891*, London: Alexander & Shepheard.

Smelser, N. (1966) *The Theory of Collective Behaviour*, London: Routledge & Kegan Paul.

Smith, G.A. (1902) *The Life of Henry Drummond*, London: Hodder & Stoughton.

Smith, T.L. (1983) 'My rejection of a cyclical view of "great awakenings" in American religious history', *Sociological Analysis* 44: 97–101.

Snapp, H.F. (1973) 'Church and state relations in early eighteenth-century England', *Journal of Church and State* 15: 83–96.

Stark, R. (1964) 'Class, radicalism and religious involvement in Great Britain', *American Sociological Review* 29: 698–706.

Stark, R. and Bainbridge, W.S. (1985) *The Future of Religion Secularization, Revival and Cult Formation*, Berkeley, Calif.: University of California Press.

Storkey, A. (1983) *A Christian's Social Perspective*, Leicester: Inter-Varsity Press.

Stromberg, R.N. (1954) *Religious Liberalism in Eighteenth-Century England*, London: Oxford University Press.

Swatos, W.H. (1979) *Into Denominationalism: the Anglican Metamorphosis*, Ellington, Conn.: The Society for the Scientific Study of Religion.

Tatlow, T. (1933) *The Story of the Student Christian Movement of Great Britain and Ireland*, London: SCM Press.

Thomas, K. (1971) *Religion and the Decline of Magic*, London: Weidenfeld & Nicolson.

Thompson, D.M. (1980) *Let Sects and Parties Fall: a Short History of the Association of Churches of Christ in Great Britain and Ireland*, London: Berean Press.

Thorgaard, J. (1972) 'Denmark', in H. Mol (ed.) *Western Religion: a Country by Country Sociological Inquiry*, The Hague: Mouton, pp. 134–41.

Tocqueville, A. de (1969) *Democracy in America*, Garden City, Kan.:

Doubleday Anchor.

Turner, B.S. (1977) 'Class solidarity and system integration', *Sociological Analysis* 38: 345–58.

Turner, B.S. (1981) *For Weber, Essays on the Sociology of Fate*, London: Routledge & Kegan Paul.

Turner, N. (1972) *Sinews of Sectarian Warfare? State Aid in New South Wales 1836–1862*, Canberra: Australian National University Press.

Vidler, A. (1974) *The Church in an Age of Revolution*, Harmondsworth: Penguin.

Vincent, T. (1980) *The Shorter Catechism Explained From Scripture*, Edinburgh: Banner of Truth Trust.

Vogt, E.D. (1972) 'Norway', in H. Mol (ed.) *Western Religion: a Country by Country Sociological Inquiry*, The Hague: Mouton, pp. 381–401.

Vos, J.G. (1980) *The Scottish Covenanters: their Origins, History and Distinctive Doctrines*, Pittsburgh: Crown and Covenant Publications.

Wacker, G. (1985) 'The Holy Spirit and the spirit of the age in American Protestantism, 1880–1910', *The Journal of American History* 72: 45–62.

Walker, A. (1985) *Restoring the Kingdom: the Radical Christianity of the House Church Movement*, London: Hodder & Stoughton.

Wallis, R. (1975) *Sectarianism: Analyses of Religious and Non-Religious Sects*, London: Peter Owen.

Wallis, R. (1976) *The Road to Total Freedom: a Sociological Analysis of Scientology*, London: Heinemann.

Wallis, R. (1979) *Salvation and Protest: Studies of Social and Religious Movements*, London: Frances Pinter.

Wallis, R. (1980) 'Sociological reflections on the demise of the Irish Humanist Association', *Scottish Journal of Sociology* 4: 125–39.

Wallis, R. (1986) 'The Caplow–de Tocqueville account of contrasts in European and American religion: confounding considerations', *Sociological Analysis* 47: 50–2.

Wallis, R. (1987) 'Figuring out cult receptivity', *Journal for the Scientific Study of Religion* 25: 494–503.

Wallis, R. and Bruce, S. (1983) 'Accounting for action: defending the common-sense heresy', *Sociology* 17: 102–11.

Wallis, R. and Bruce, S. (1984) 'The Stark–Bainbridge theory of religion: a critique and counter-proposals', *Sociological Analysis* 45: 11–27.

Wallis, R. and Bruce, S. (1986) *Sociological Theory, Religion and Collective Action*, Belfast: The Queen's University of Belfast.

Walzer, M. (1965) *The Revolution of the Saints: a Study in the Origins of Radical Politics*, Cambridge, Mass.: Harvard University Press.

Ward, D.A. (1980) 'Toward a normative explanation of "old fashioned revivals"', *Qualitative Sociology* 3: 3–22.

Ward, W.R. (1972) *Religion and Society in England 1790–1850*, London: Batsford.

Warner, R.S. (1979) 'Theoretical barriers to the understanding of evangelical Christianity', *Sociological Analysis* 40: 1–9.

Watts, M.R. (1978) *The Dissenters, vol. 1: From the Reformation to the French Revolution*, Oxford: Clarendon Press.

Weber, M. (1964) *The Theory of Social and Economic Organization*, New York: Free Press.

Weisberger, B.A. (1958) *They Gathered at the River*, Boston: Little, Brown & Co.

Weller, J.E. (1965) *Yesterday's People: Life in Contemporary Appalachia*, Louisville, Ky: University of Kentucky Press.

White, B.R. (1971) *The English Separatist Tradition: From the Marian Fathers to the Pilgrim Fathers*, Oxford: Oxford University Press.

Williams, C. R. (1952) 'The Welsh Religious Revival, 1904–5', *British Journal of Sociology* 3: 242–59.

Wilson, B.R. (1959) 'An analysis of sect development', *American Sociological Review* 24 (1): 3–15.

Wilson, B.R. (1964) 'The paradox of the Exclusive Brethren', *New Society* 20 August: 9–11.

Wilson, B.R. (1966) *Religion in Secular Society: a Sociological Comment*, London: C. A. Watts & Co.

Wilson, B.R. (1967) 'Establishment, sectarianism and partisanship', *Sociological Review* 15: 213–20.

Wilson, B.R. (1968) 'Religion and the churches in contemporary America', in W.G. McLoughlin and R. Bellah (eds) *Religion in America*, New York: Beacon Press, pp. 73–110.

Wilson, B.R. (1970) *Religious Sects: a Sociological Study*, London: World University Library.

Wilson, B.R. (1976) *Contemporary Transformations of Religion*, London: Oxford University Press.

Wilson, B.R. (1982) *Religion in Sociological Perspective*, Oxford: Oxford University Press.

Wilson, B.R. (1985) 'Morality in the evolution of the modern social system', *British Journal of Sociology* 36: 315–32.

Wilson, J. (1971) 'The sociology of schism', in M. Hill (ed.) *Sociological Yearbook of Religion* 4: London: SCM Press.

Woodcock, G. and Avakumovic, I. (1968) *The Doukhobors*, Toronto: Oxford University Press.

Wuthnow, R. (1976) 'Recent patterns of secularization: a problem of generations?', *American Sociological Review* 41: 850–67.

Yearley, S. (1988) 'Settling accounts: action, accounts and sociological explanation', *British Journal of Sociology* 39: 578–99.

Young, R.M. (1970) 'The impact of Darwinism on conventional thought', in A. Symondson (ed.) *The Victorian Crisis of Faith*, London: SPCK.

Youngson, A.J. (1973) *After the Forty-Five: the Economic Impact on the Scottish Highlands*, Edinburgh: Edinburgh University Press.

Zald, M. and Ash R. (1966) 'Social movement organizations: growth, decay and change', *Social Forces* 44: 327–70.

INDEX